THE CHEESE PLATE

THE CHEESE PLATE

Max McCalman and David Gibbons

Clarkson Potter / Publishers
New York

This book is dedicated to Scarlett,
who has taught me so much, and who
continues to show graceful patience.

Grateful acknowledgment is made to reprint the recipe
on page 41, copyright © 2000 by Avice R. Wilson.

Published by Clarkson Potter / Publishers, New York,
New York. Member of the Crown Publishing Group.

Random House, Inc. New York, Toronto, London,
Sydney, Auckland
www.randomhouse.com

CLARKSON N. POTTER is a trademark and
POTTER and colophon are registered trademarks of
Random House, Inc.

Printed in China.

Design by Jill Armus

Library of Congress Cataloging-in-Publication Data
McCalman, Max.
   The cheese plate / by Max McCalman and David
Gibbons.
   Includes index.
   1. Cookery (Cheese) 2. Cheese. I. Gibbons, David,
1957– II. Title.
TX759.5C48 M39   2002
641.6'73—dc21
2001021451

ISBN: 978-0-609-60496-0

10   9   8   7

CONTENTS

FOREWORD

My interest in cheese began to percolate in the mid eighties when I went to work in France. Whenever I had a free evening, I'd dine out and partake of the cheese course. One of my colleagues would take us to his mother's country house on weekends, and she would prepare simple, delicious, fresh meals, with ingredients from her own larder and garden; there was even a pigeon pen and trout tank out back. She made all her own confits and preserves. And there was always a cheese course after the entrée. It was then that I truly began to appreciate the ritual of lingering over a selection of artisan cheeses at the end of the meal.

I realized dramatically that cheese is a precious living organism. In addition to being deliciously edible, it's a beautiful, natural artifact and a phenomenal conversation piece. My passion grew, not just for the incredible range of colors and textures, aromas and tastes, but for all the effort and care that goes into it. I love the way a perfectly ripe soft cheese oozes, the way the mottled rinds undulate, sometimes dusted with grayish mold or moistened with reddish bacterial rub.

I brought my new admiration for cheese back to the States and with it a determination to one day offer the best European-style cheese course in America. When we first opened Picholine Restaurant, it was a casual bistro. Frankly, we didn't have the means to put together a major cheese program. But I kept the dream alive. And as Picholine evolved toward more sophisticated dining, I decided it was time to fulfill it. In 1994, we began offering a selection of about a dozen cheeses. It quickly grew to fourteen or sixteen, then twenty. I was setting up the cart myself. Very soon, it began to impinge on my other duties. Max McCalman, recently hired as a maître d', showed interest so I put him in charge. It turned out he shared my inherent passion for cheese, and that's when things really took off. Within a year, we were able to offer fifty or sixty choices on any given day, and our cheese course was the talk of the town.

To say that Max took to cheese like a fish to water would be an understatement. Once he got going, there was no turning back. His passion for cheese is the number one reason he has become America's foremost *maître fromager*. But he also brought to the table an impressive capacity for study; sometimes we refer to him fondly as Mad Max. He goes about his cheese business like a mad scientist obsessed

with his experiments. Max's bone-dry sense of humor and his quirky way of expressing himself are particularly well suited to cheese. Because we're able to obtain the best cheeses and because Max's presentation is pointed and precise, I know our guests won't soon forget our cheese course. It's also why, from the time he took the cheese course and ran with it, I was convinced that he could write an excellent book on the subject.

If we created a bit of a monster with Max and the cheese course, the question soon became: How could we clone him? Everybody wanted a piece of Max—or at least his cheeses. I decided to launch a new cheese-oriented establishment, which would take our concept of creating the best cheese program in America to the next level. It would feature a restaurant where you could order regular meals with several cheese-based dishes as options; a café that offered a selection of up to 200 cheeses; and a retail operation where you could buy properly aged artisan cheeses, take them home, and create your own courses. We would acquire the world's best cheeses and ripen them in our own custom-designed caves. We would offer wine-and-cheese tasting flights based on the research Max did for this book.

As this book is being prepared for publication, the new establishment, called Artisanal, is being readied for opening. Both the book and restaurant were born of a dream I had nearly 20 years ago and were nurtured by the expertise Max has acquired. They share as their foundation our mutual passion for artisanal cheese. I am sure you, Max's readers, will gain as much satisfaction from this book as we have from the privilege of working with these great cheeses.

—TERRANCE BRENNAN,
New York City, 2001

A few of the many fine cheeses on display at Artisanal.

INTRODUCTION

WELCOME TO THE WORLD OF CHEESE

Ten years ago, I didn't know much more about cheese than your average man in the street. Because of chef Terrance Brennan's desire to create a European-style cheese program at Picholine Restaurant, though, I was thrust into the role of *maître fromager*—in addition to my duties as maître d'. At first, it seemed like a burden.

Once I started handling the cheese, my coworkers didn't seem to shake my hand as much anymore. . . . They would sniff around me for lingering cheesy aromas. . . . I found myself working long hours, 6 days a week, on my feet most of the time, researching, ordering, maintaining, and serving cheeses. I got cheese elbow. . . . These were the hazards of the profession. Yet they were a small price to pay for initiation into the endlessly fascinating world of cheese connoisseurship. I had no idea how fast it would come to rule my life. I discovered very quickly that it was bigger, more glorious, and more captivating than I could ever have imagined. Now cheese is my obsession—you could say my religion.

On the most fundamental level, cheese is an excellent source of nutrition and a tremendously satisfying food. Present-day civilization is descended from others that were sustained for thousands of years by cheese. Our ancestors taught themselves how to preserve the excess summer milk of their dairy animals, and it got them through many a cold, dark month when vegetation was sparse and the animals were scarce. They fermented their milk and their grape juice, and they were set for the winter. Wine, cheese, and bread . . . that's pretty much all you needed to survive. Today, cheese is a building block of the Mediterranean diet, a delicious source of protein, enjoyed as a quick snack or lunch or a leisurely *digestif* after a meal. In Old World cultures, it is consumed in moderation, with an appreciation bordering on reverence.

At a higher plane, cheese demands study and contemplation. In this respect, it goes hand in hand with many of the good things in life, especially fine wines and other delicacies. The more I learned about cheese, the more I realized how much there was to know, what a profound and worthy subject it was. I jumped on the cheese bandwagon, got excited, developed a rabid enthusiasm. Naturally, I wanted to share all of this, which is why I decided to write a book.

My career in the restaurant business and subsequent growth as a *maître fromager* coincided with the gastronomic revolution that swept America's shores over the final 2 decades of the twentieth century. Our country opened its arms to the world's gourmet

Liquid, luxurious, get-it-while-you-can: the Vacherin Haut-Rive has a short season.

Hazards of the job: cutting through hard, thick-rind cheeses is no easy trick, especially if you do it for a living. I have the elbow problems to prove it.

delights. Now we embrace all kinds of previously unavailable treats—fine cheeses among them. America may still be a nation of cheese neophytes, but we certainly have the resources and the desire to become a major player. Americans have always consumed a lot of cheese, most of it of the processed variety, yet the European-style cheese plate is a relatively new phenomenon on our side of the Atlantic. Fine artisanal cheeses have only recently become widely available. Now the cheese course is a real option, and we're prepared to branch out beyond the standard blues and Bries, Camemberts, and Gruyères.

I am excited to go to work every day because I consider it more than a job. I sincerely feel I'm on a mission. First, I'm out to dispel any negative notions about cheese, particularly the fear of fat. Yes, cheese contains fat. And yes, it is no exception to the rule that too much of a good thing can harm you. But cheese actually has less fat and more protein, vitamins, and minerals per weight than an egg. That goes for *any kind of cheese*—even the sumptuous French triple crèmes that have up to 75 percent butterfat. Those velvety smooth, super-rich cheeses are actually mostly water. (If you're watching your waistline, the idea should be to eat more cheese and less carbohydrates, especially later in the day.)

This book is not antidiet, nor is it pro bad cheese. It is about learning to find, judge, and appreciate the world's finest cheeses. So, with regard to health, I have one statement: real cheese is good food, plain and simple. It offers a full, healthy complement of proteins, fats, vitamins, and minerals; it provides all essential nutrients except vitamin C and fiber. Cheese is also a more environmentally friendly food than, say, a porterhouse steak. Clearly, it is a far more efficient use of pastureland than the raising of cattle for meat; over the years, a live cow gives a great deal of milk, which in turn yields thousands of cheeses. We can only eat a dead cow once.

One reason for cheese's negative image is there are so many bad exam-

CHEESE ELBOW

A PROFESSIONAL HAZARD OF THE MAÎTRE FROMAGER

ABOUT 3 YEARS AGO, I started to feel pain and stiffness all down my left (cutting) arm. I tried to go about my job and ignore it, but it didn't go away; it just got worse. I thought maybe it was a psychosomatic ailment related to stress in other areas of my life. I finally took the complaint to a doctor and was diagnosed with what is believed to be the first case of "cheese elbow" in America. I was advised to put a small brace on my elbow, similar to those worn by some tennis players. I wore it proudly, a badge of honor announcing my profession—*maître fromager*. In the following months, I used the brace for protection, did wrist curls to strengthen my arm, and was eventually able to cut cheese effectively without aggravating the condition.

ples of it on the market. I feel it's my responsibility as a cheese professional to uphold the highest possible standards among customers and suppliers alike, and this book is the ideal forum to do so.

Another aspect of my mission is that I want to diminish the alarm concerning raw milk. A significant segment of the population feels that real cheeses—the authentic, artisanal "table cheeses" that are the focus of this book—are a potential health hazard, particularly those made from "raw," or unpasteurized,

milk. As we'll discuss in Chapter 3, pasteurization kills bacteria, which are largely responsible for cheese aromas and flavors. In Europe over the past few decades, there have been several "cheese scares" involving outbreaks of food poisoning. In each instance, raw-milk cheeses were unjustly blamed, and pasteurized cheeses proved to be the culprits. Every time this happens, it reinforces U.S. regulations outlawing unpasteurized cheeses aged less than 60 days and lends credence to the argument that the same type of rules

The wonderful Orb Weaver, made by Marjorie Susman and Marian Pollock in Vermont's Champlain Valley, is a traditionally made farmhouse cheese—a fine specimen that proves that American handcrafted cheeses are better than ever.

should be imposed in Europe.

The standard bearers of quality have invariably been the raw-milk farmhouse-style cheeses. History has consistently proven that the authentic, old-fashioned artifact is better than its modern technology-enhanced imitation. Don't get me wrong, there are some commendable cheeses made with pasteurized milk, but more often than not, the process eliminates most of the desirable flavors, textures, and aromas.

Part of my mission as a purveyor is to join the chorus in favor of these real cheeses. In the United States, we're missing out on some of the greatest cheeses on the planet, particularly French ones—we can't get authentic, raw-milk Brie or Camembert, for example. The American Cheese Society (ACS) and other proponents of real cheeses are lobbying to change U.S. laws in this respect. Meanwhile, the Big Boys of the American commercial cheese industry, led by their lobby group, the National Cheese Institute, are proposing that the World Trade Organization make pasteurization a cheese standard worldwide, which threatens the very survival of real cheeses.

The approach I espouse is one of connoisseurship and appreciation without snobbery or elitism. At some level cheese is funny, ridiculous, even absurd. There are an awful lot of cheese jokes in the world. The word *cheesy* has always denoted something not quite up-to-par, less than completely neat and tidy, slightly unappealing. *Reductio ad absurdum*, cheese is nothing but spoiled milk. But put another way, it's the ancient, vener-ated method of preserving the precious, sustaining fluid of the mother animal. A noble food, indeed.

Yes, cheese is funny, and yes it can be smelly. Many of the best cheeses in the world smell like something you'd rather not have in your house; they taste strong and they spoil quickly. Cheese is an extreme food. Its more powerful examples can shock the palate. They make us turn up our noses, crinkle our eyebrows, clack our gums, pucker our cheeks, reach for a glass of . . . something—anything. Some of them launch a sneak attack: they tiptoe across our tongues, then explode at the back of our mouths with a tangy wallop. Others mount a full frontal assault, then melt sublimely away toward the back. In the end, the great ones *always* titillate our taste buds.

In Chapters 1 and 2, we provide some background—facts, definitions, history—which is always good conversational fodder. Chapter 3 tells how cheese is made—optional knowledge for the connoisseur, but we believe it's fascinating and enlightening. Chapter 4 offers practical advice on buying, storing, and serving cheeses, while Chapter 5 outlines the principles of tasting and appreciating cheeses. Chapter 6 explores the science and art of cheese pairings, mostly with wines, that other delectable product of controlled spoilage. Finally in Chapter 7 we offer some cheese plates as recipes to follow or guidelines to inspire, whichever way you choose to use them. Chapter 8 is a kind of extended appendix, listing some basic facts and figures about my selection of the world's finest table cheeses. Using all this theoretical ammunition and practical advice, readers should be able to go into any top restaurant or cheese shop and choose, with confidence, a selection of superb cheeses to delight, surprise, and stimulate even the most sophisticated palate.

The ultimate goal of this book is to give readers the tools they need to become cheese connoisseurs. There are no special requirements for being a caseophile. Whether or not you can recite the time and temperature at which Tuscan ewe's milk curdles to form a high-grade Pecorino will not make the cheese taste any better. But will this type of knowledge increase your appreciation of the final product? Quite possibly. There is a lot to know. Nevertheless, the entrée into the savvy cheese elite is really quite simple: start tasting cheeses and judge for yourself. All you need is an observant eye, a sense of taste and smell, and the desire to learn more. The best route to connoisseurship is to taste, taste, and taste some more.

As a *maître fromager,* I'm determined to open up my customers'— and readers'—palates to the wide range of amazing taste experiences possible with the world's finest table cheeses. I'd like you to experience the same thrill I do when I receive a shipment of these beautiful living artifacts. I want to share my admiration and awe at the vast store of knowledge and experience that goes into manufacturing them. From the milk of an animal grazing in a remote rocky pasture in northern Spain to a carefully arranged plate in a three-star restaurant in New York City . . . it's quite a journey, an astonishing chain of events that touches on history,

geography, animal husbandry, dairy farming, bacterial cultures, farm economics, and much more. The pride and care that go into making these precious little lumps of denatured protein and hydrolyzed fats are a constant source of wonderment for me. Each and every one of them is a marvelous artifact capable of tickling the tongue with eye-popping bursts of flavor—and also of telling a fascinating story to stir the intellect. Nothing has a right to be as delicious *and* nutritious as these world-class cheeses, but they are. And I'm lucky enough to be able to work with them every day.

In the larger scheme of things, you might say this cheese worship borders on lunacy. From my perspective, there's no question that cheese is one of the many wonders that adds up to the tremendous miracle of life on earth. So what's wrong with a little obsession? If you haven't caught the cheese bug like I have, bear with me for a few pages; I think you will. If you have, dig in and let's have some fun with spoiled milk.

—MAX McCALMAN
New York City, 2001

ONE | A TASTE OF HISTORY

THROUGHOUT HISTORY, cheese has been a staple food of the masses, their best—if not their only—source of protein. Experts on prehistory speculate that cheesemaking dates back more than 12,000 years to the first domestication of animals, although there isn't any hard evidence until somewhat later.

Archaeological surveys have established that the ancient Sumerian and Mesopotamian cultures of the Tigris-Euphrates basin raised cows and sheep and engaged in dairy production as early as 7000 B.C. Archaeologists discovered cheesemaking pots in Switzerland believed to have been from the sixth century B.C. The first historical reference to cheese is a Sumerian frieze from about 3000 B.C. Remnants of cheese were found in the tomb of a king of the Egyptian First Dynasty (c. 3000–2800 B.C.). So cheesemaking was definitely practiced in ancient Egypt and other parts of the Middle East and

The Dutch masterpiece Roomano has a rich, spicy flavor with overtones of caramel and butterscotch.

Europe at least 5,000 and possibly as many as 8,000 years ago.

By Greek and Roman times, cheese was an important commodity for trade. Homer mentioned cheese in his *Iliad*, which is believed to have been written at least 800 years before Christ. In the *Odyssey*, there is a description of the cyclops Polyphemus making cheese from goat's and ewe's milk in his cave. Cheese is also mentioned prominently in the works of Euripides (c. 480–406 B.C.), Aristophanes (c. 448–385 B.C.), and Aristotle (c. 384–322 B.C.), among other contemporaries. The famous ancient cookbook *De re conquinaria libri decum (Cuisine in Ten Books)*, attributed to Marcus Gavius Apicius, born around 25 B.C., mentions cheese as an important part of the Roman diet. Columella, the Roman food writer, outlined the basic steps of cheesemaking in his writings around A.D. 50.

The Romans left us the Latin word *caseus*, which is the root for our English "cheese," as well as for *Käse* in German, *queso* in Spanish, and *queijo* in Portuguese. *Caseus* is also the root for casein, the principal milk protein that is coagulated to make cheese. Ironically, it was a Greek word, *formos* (as in "form" or "mold," for the receptacle used to shape the cheese), that led to the Italian *formaggio* and the French *fromage*.

"The discovery of how to use rennin in cheese-making is one of the great steps forward in the history of supplying bulk food to mankind."
—AVICE R. WILSON, *Forgotten Harvest: The Story of Cheesemaking in Wiltshire*

BY ANY OTHER NAME . . .

. . . IN ANY OTHER LANGUAGE, CHEESE WOULD STILL TASTE AS SWEET

THE words for cheese in different languages:
DUTCH: kaas
FINNISH: juusto
FLEMISH: kees
FRENCH: fromage
GAELIC: cais
GERMAN: Käse
HINDI: paneer
ITALIAN: formaggio

HUNGARIAN: sajt
POLISH: sir
PORTUGUESE: queijo
RUSSIAN: ssyr
SCANDINAVIAN LANGUAGES: ost
SERBIAN, ARABIC: syr
SPANISH: queso
TURKISH: peyniri

It remains a mystery as to when and how the method of making aged cheese by using animal rennet—enzymes from the stomachs of suckling animals—was developed. (Before rennet, primitive cheeses with a short shelf life were made by simple acidification or souring of milk; more about this in Chapter 3.) One likely scenario is that ancient peoples carried milk in bags made from calf or kid innards and at some point noticed a quicker, more efficient curdling action that yielded longer-lasting, better-tasting cheeses. Renneting may have been practiced by the Etruscans 5 or 6 centuries before Christ and possibly by even earlier civilizations. In the first century B.C., Roman cheesemakers were following recipes for Parmesan-type cheeses that are still in use to this day. The Romans were adept at the use of rennet as well as the practice of salting cheese to preserve it; their most "modern" innovation, however, was the cooking of the curds, which allowed for production of harder, longer-lasting cheeses suitable for transport and trade.

As a main feature of the legionnaire's ration, cheese fueled the creation of the Roman Empire. Markets and trade routes were built up around the transportable, edible commodities such as wine, olive oil, spices, and cheese. The Jet Age was millennia away, but the Romans did get around. In conquered lands, they discovered local cheeses such as the blues of France's Massif Central and the mountain cheeses of the Alps, of which Roquefort and Beaufort, respectively, are surviving examples. They became the delicacies of a cosmopolitan culture. Their influence led to the widespread manufacture of modern-style aged cheese, believed to have begun in Switzerland around 60–50 B.C. and in Britain in A.D. 100–300.

Many of the great traditional cheeses of France, such as Cantal, Salers,

PANIR KHIKI

FROM THE STEPPES OF CENTRAL ASIA, A NOMADIC PEOPLE'S CHEESE

S OME of the world's first cheeses were made by nomads in the high plains or steppes of Central Asia and in the arid grasslands of Africa. Many of these traditional cheeses survive, including one called Panir Khiki. It was originated by the Bakhtiari tribe, which migrated annually from Isfahan, known as the city of mosques, in the summer to Shiraz in the winter. To make Panir Khiki, which means skin container, a goat or a lamb is slaughtered and its skin is removed whole. The skin is stuffed with fresh white cheese along with various herbs and seasonings, then sewed shut and left to mature in a cool place for 6 months. The residual enzymes from the animal's innards help ripen and flavor the cheese.

and the aforementioned Roquefort and Beaufort, existed in essentially their modern form when the conquering armies of Rome arrived, and they have enjoyed international acclaim ever since. (Rome's conquest of Gaul began in the second century B.C. and was completed by Julius Caesar in 58–50 B.C.) As the Roman Empire unraveled into the Dark Ages, monasteries became the sole oases of religious devotion, culture, and enlightenment. The monks upheld several pillars of civilization, including art, scholarship, fermented drinks (wine, beer, and spirits), and cheese. Once the monks had fulfilled their daily spiritual obligations, they found themselves with a little extra time for clearing pastureland, tending herds, and making cheeses. A number of artfully produced cheeses such as Chimay, Munster, and Maroilles are still referred to as "monk's cheeses," although they are no longer necessarily made in monasteries.

During the Age of Exploration and the Renaissance, cheeses' fame began to spread again across national borders and cultural and social boundaries. The Age of Enlightenment, arising out of the Renaissance, was a time of tremendous inventiveness and entrepreneurial spirit. Cheesemakers created new and exciting varieties to augment both the traditional cheeses passed down from Roman times and the monastic ones born in the Middle Ages. This was particularly true in France where the eighteenth and early nineteenth centuries witnessed the birth of cheeses such as Camembert and Brie along with many intriguing forms of goat cheese.

France today is widely recognized as first among cheesemaking nations. It is an incredible font of regional delicacies—anywhere from 350 to more than 700 depending on how you count. Britain, Italy, and Spain all vie for the runner-up spot.

FRANCE VERSUS BRITAIN

CHEESE AS AN EXPRESSION OF NATIONAL CHARACTER—VIVE LA DIFFÉRENCE!

CHEESE is just one of the ways in which these two great rival nations manifest their fundamentally different cultures. In Britain, cheese has always been food: the main ingredient of the ploughman's lunch—a quick, efficient, and lasting energy boost. In France, cheese is at once a fruit of the land and a marvel of human ingenuity: a work of art to contemplate and adore. British cheeses came from the labors of the farm, French ones from the intellectual rigor of the abbey, for the greater glory of God.

British cheeses satiate your hunger; the French ones satisfy your palate. The British give you lunch, the French dinner and dessert. The British cheeses are upright, firm, and stolid; the French cheeses recumbent, soft, and sensual.

STILTON AND CHEDDAR:
WHAT'S IN A NAME?

THE CRUCIAL IMPORTANCE OF PROTECTING NAMES AND UPHOLDING STANDARDS

ENGLAND'S two most famous cheeses exemplify one of the disasters that has beset farmhouse cheeses. Beginning in the 1850s, the word *cheddar* was used to describe a method of production rather than a particular cheese from a specific locale. Alas, the name was never protected by law; as a result, all kinds of bland industrial cheese have been sold under the rubric both in the United Kingdom and abroad, particularly America. Genuine farmhouse Cheddar is now very rare.

Stilton is protected, but it has suffered from a slackening of standards as manufacturers and wholesalers, in a quest for more sales and profits, have allowed less-than-premium cheeses to be sold under the name.

The modern history of cheese in Britain provides examples of the things that can go very wrong—and also very right— in the world of fine cheeses. Britain boasts the geography and dairy culture necessary to world-class cheesemaking. Its cheese tradition began well before the Roman conquest but came of age under Caesar. The hardworking dairy maid has been an enduring and beloved British icon since feudal times. By the early Middle Ages, the English countryside was dotted with farmhouses built for cheesemaking; in Renaissance times, there were perhaps a hundred British regional cheeses named after their places of origin. Most of the major types of local or regional cheeses were well established by the mid eighteenth century.

Several historical upheavals in the past 2 centuries nearly destroyed Britain's artisanal cheeses. The first was the Industrial Revolution, which was changing the face of Western civilization by the beginning of the nineteenth century. New methods of mass production and efficient transportation meant many artisans were supplanted by factories, including in the cheese industry.

Beginning in the mid–nineteenth century, the railroads were responsible for the spread of regional cheese throughout England. Ironically, it was also the railroads that contributed heavily to the near-demise of real British cheeses. Milk could now be delivered to London and other big-city markets in less than a day, meaning that farmers could dispense with the labor-intensive cheesemaking process and simply dispose of all their milk fresh for immediate consumption.

"Scientists who work in factories are dreaming up a whole set of rules to try to improve food safety. I'm not saying that anybody should be given a license to produce unhealthy food, but these types of regulations don't really apply to someone like Mrs. Kirkham. Her livelihood depends on making good cheese. There's no greater guarantee than that. She may not be able to recite the scientific formulas for starters and rennets but she can make far better cheese than most people who know all that stuff.

—RANDOLPH HODGSON, Neal's Yard Dairy

The first U.S. cheese factory was founded by Jesse Williams in Rome, New York, in 1851.

In the late nineteenth century, Britain experienced a large influx of cheap "colonial" imports from the United States and Canada, and its cheese factories began to fail. Nevertheless, the seeds had been sown for the modern phenomenon of mass-produced, "industrial" cheese, and the farmhouse cheeses were on their way to extinction. (At the turn of the twentieth century, for instance, there were 10,000 farms making Cheshire, England's, *ur*-cheese; today there are but three.)

The emergence of commodities markets, including the liquid milk market, permanently altered the way food staples were produced and distributed. In time, commodities producers and other industries formed trade groups of immense economic and political power. One such group was Britain's Milk Marketing Boards (MMBs), founded in 1933 to guarantee a market, organize and centralize sales and distribution, and promote industrialization. The MMB system had a huge negative impact on "real cheese" by encouraging multiple sourcing of milk and factory-scale manufacturing.

Britain's cheese scene was dealt another blow by World War II, which spelled more centralization, standardization, and of course rationing. By the time rationing ended in 1954, less than 10 percent of original farmhouse cheesemakers were still in operation. Those who survived faced a new challenge: the advent of supermarkets and practices such as precutting, prepacking, and shrink-wrapping. Real cheeses were being forced out of the marketplace by industrial ones. The real ones that did make it to the store were cut up and smothered in plastic.

In the 1970s, the MMBs promoted the myth that mass-produced block cheeses tasted just as good as traditional farmhouse ones. They also allowed many pasteurized-milk and block cheeses to be sold with the Farmhouse

A slice of heaven in the form of Montgomery's Cheddar.

> *"A slice of good cheese is never just a thing to eat. It is usually also a slice of local history: agricultural, political, or ecclesiastical. Knowledge of this enables us to distinguish the genuine from the imitation; it adds to our appetite for the cheese and to the relish with which we savour it."*
> —PATRICK RANCE, *The French Cheese Book*

English Cheese stamp. (The MMB system was finally judged a monopoly and abolished in 1994.)

Real British cheeses suffered another blow in the form of the *"Listeria* crisis" of the late 1980s. The crisis was brought on by several outbreaks of food poisoning that were blamed on unpasteurized cheeses—unjustly, it turned out. *Listeria* is a common bacteria, one strain of which can inhabit cheese. A few species of *Listeria* have been known to cause serious illnesses. In 1989, in the wake of the scare, the British minister of agriculture proposed to ban the sale of unpasteurized cheeses—the traditional farmhouse ones. In addition, all British supermarkets took the position that they would only stock pasteurized cheese. Facing extinction, many small independent cheesemakers caved in to this dictate, even though the evidence was clear that the risky cheeses were the soft ones, regardless of pasteurization.

Despite all the difficulties faced over the years, traditional farmhouse cheeses survive in Britain. Apart from a few brave farmers and cheesemakers, it is Patrick Rance who deserves much of the credit. In 1954 Rance and his wife, Janet, took over a small shop called Wells Stores in Streatley, Berkshire, and built it into a superb cheese emporium. He also wrote two of the best cheese books ever, *The Great British Cheese Book* and *The French Cheese Book,* the latter as a result of an exhaustive cheese tour of France. In the early 1980s, he launched a "campaign for the revival of traditional cheese," or Real Cheese Campaign, inspired by the 1971 Campaign for Real Ale. It stimulated demand and led to the rebirth of genuine farmhouse cheeses; fine cheese shops began opening around Britain and abroad. Patrick Rance was an instigator—a man with a passion for cheese that he conveyed gleefully and forcefully to others, making it his life's mission to save part of Britain's cultural heritage. An inspiration to us all, he died in 1999.

Another great cheese hero is the Frenchman Pierre Androuët. Pierre's father, Henri, was a Breton who moved to Paris and opened his own cheese shop in 1909. Henri, a legendary cheesemonger, is credited with naming the triple-crème Brillat-Savarin after the great gastronome. Pierre eventually took over the business, which still survives. Like Patrick Rance,

Androuët was more than just a merchant: his famous cheese encyclopedia, *Guide du Fromage,* was first published in 1971 and revised in 1977 and 1983. (The English edition was originally published in 1973; the book is currently out of print.) Androuët founded the *Guilde des Maîtres Fromagers* to promote relations between cheesemakers and cheesemongers. He also founded the *Confrérie des Chavaliers du Tastefromage de France* in 1954 and headed the *Confrérie des Compagnons de Saint-Uguzon,* a 700-year-old cheesemongers' guild. The mission of these organizations was, in Androuet's words, "to stimulate cheese lovers' interest in cheeses that are dying out."

Now, at the dawn of the new millennium, thanks to the far-reaching efforts of illustrious cheese proponents like Androuët and Rance, there is a new wave of cheese appreciation and connoisseurship. Importers and exporters are expanding their efforts to bring many more fine cheeses to the United States and to impose higher standards. Not only has the demand from the growing cheese-consuming public risen dramatically but so has the level of sophistication. You can't put just anything on the cheese plate and fool Americans anymore. This is an encouraging sign, and I'm convinced things will only continue to improve as long as lovers of real cheese continue to hold their torches high.

THE KIRKHAMS OF LANCASHIRE

ONE OF THE FEW SURVIVING MAKERS OF GENUINE BRITISH FARMSTEAD CHEESE

JOHN and Ruth Kirkham of Lancashire, in northwestern England, were among the few holdouts in the *Listeria* scare of the late 1980s. The Kirkhams remained steadfast raw-milk advocates; they even contemplated quitting altogether rather than resorting to pasteurization. The London wholesaler Neal's Yard Dairy began buying their cheeses and the Kirkhams were able to forge ahead; 5 years later, their Lancashire was named Supreme Champion at the British Cheese Awards. Demand soared and now Neal's Yard does a brisk business in Kirkhams' Lancashire, one of the few surviving examples of genuine British farmhouse cheese.

John Kirkham tends a herd of forty cows, milking them by hand twice a day. Ruth makes Lancashire cheese, 7 days a week. The Kirkhams are the epitome of the mom-and-pop family farm where the women make the cheese and tend the hearth while the men toil in the fields and herd the cattle. (Recently, the Kirkhams' son Graham joined the business.) The Kirkhams can derive great satisfaction and pride from the notion that they are keepers of a significant piece of their national heritage.

TWO | WHAT IS CHEESE?

BEFORE WE GET INTO BASICS such as components and manufacture, it's important to emphasize the distinction between artisanal cheeses—the ones we celebrate as the world's finest—and all the rest. Artisanal cheeses are handmade, primarily by small independent cheesemakers using traditional methods with no adaptations for efficiency. An artisan is a skilled worker or craftsperson, which perfectly describes the makers of real cheese. They painstakingly, lovingly oversee every aspect of cheesemaking, they maintain the highest standards, and their focus is squarely on quality rather than quantity.

Wabash Cannonball, a superb goat's milk cheese made by Judy Schad in Greenville, Indiana.

True artisanal cheeses are made with unpasteurized milk that originates from a single milk source, preferably the farmer's own herd. They are produced on a farm or in a small dairy, and they have naturally formed rinds (no plastic or wax). To the maximum extent possible, they are organic, which means no artificial treatments or ingredients are introduced at any stage of animal husbandry or cheesemaking.

What makes a cheese superior? Purity and integrity of raw materials, and individuality of character. Artisanal manufacturing alone is not an absolute guarantee of superiority; a great deal of extra attention is also required. Likewise, some factory-made cheeses are very good, even excellent; but they are the exceptions rather than the rule.

About a third of the cheeses I serve are factory made. They are consistent, satisfying, and guaranteed to offer few surprises—unpleasant or otherwise. Fine artisanal cheeses, which make up the majority of my inventory, are the ones that really talk to you. But they comprise merely the uppermost tip of a very large pyramid, the base of which is the vast tonnage of "industrial cheeses" churned out every year by the world's cheese factories. The best artisanal cheeses can be hard to find. They are not cost-effective to produce. Fine cheesemaking is a difficult art. In my tenure as a *maître fromager,* I've seen many master cheesemakers retire and then witnessed the inevitable drop-off in quality. Many artisanal cheeses fall into the category of endangered species; if we don't take extraordinary steps to preserve them, they may disappear.

PROCESSED CHEESE

MASS-MARKET "CHEESE FOOD" IS NOT REALLY CHEESE AND BARELY FOOD

P ROCESSED cheese or "cheese food" is an all-purpose term that covers any number of mass-market products. The basic "process" is that cheese is melted down and mixed with various preservatives, fats, flavorings, colorings, and water. It is then reconstituted in blocks, slices, or wedges, sometimes packed into tubs, often shrink-wrapped in plastic.

If you want good cheese, buy only freshly cut cheeses; don't buy anything that is prepackaged. If you must buy prepackaged, read the label and beware of chemical additives or preservatives as well as hydrogenated or partially hydrogenated fats or oils. And always remember that good cheese—real cheese—is made from milk, starter cultures, rennet or a plant coagulant, and occasionally a natural coloring or a mold culture. Nothing more.

THE GOLDEN RULES OF CHEESE

1. The best cheeses come from unpasteurized milk.
2. Real cheese is made in the traditional artisanal fashion.
3. No two cheeses are identical; even cheeses from a particular type or brand vary from day to day, week to week, month to month, and season to season.

FUNDAMENTALS

There are a few basic variables: Is the cheese made with cow's, sheep's, buffalo's, or goat's milk? From what breed? What type of vegetation do the animals consume? Is the milk raw or pasteurized? At what time of year was the cheese made? Is it pressed or nonpressed? Does it have a bloomy rind or a washed one, a clothbound rind or a waxed one? Is it from France, Britain, Italy, Spain, Portugal, Switzerland, the United States, or elsewhere? Who makes it?

All these factors produce a huge variety, not just in the types of cheeses, but even within a given type. Consider this simple matrix: a village with four separate pastures, three different cheese-producing seasons, and a cheese with three distinct stages of ripeness. With all other variables remaining constant—impossible in the real world, but let's assume it—by tweaking just these three (provenance, season, ripeness), you've instantly got thirty-six discrete expressions of a single type of cheese! Every wheel, button, or round has a personality. Even cheeses made at the same farm on different days can taste significantly different, depending on where the animals were grazing. Sometimes these differences are ever so subtle, but there is no question that they exist.

Because of all these variables, the world of cheese is a big one. In Spain alone, there are about thirty different breeds of sheep, and the cheese made from each one's milk tastes different. In addition, you have to consider what the animals are eating: the climate and terrain of the Extremadura, in west-central Spain, is very different from that of a nearby region such as La Mancha. For this reason, would take months to taste your way through the cheeses of Spain.

In this age of food scrutiny and diet consciousness, sometimes I feel it's helpful to justify cheese. I don't ever need an excuse to eat it, but there are those who could use some reassurance. I like to say that cheese is a more perfect food than the incredible, edible egg: a 3½-ounce chunk of hard cheese such as Cheddar or Emmental contains about twice as much protein as a chicken egg. A 4-ounce chunk of good, semihard farmhouse cheese supplies between a half and a third of the daily nutritional requirements of the average-sized adult human being. *Cheese provides delicious and efficient nourishment.*

Milk is between 80 and 87 percent water; its solid content ranges from approximately 12.5 percent in cows to about 19 percent in sheep. The solids are fat, proteins (primarily in the form of casein), a sugar called lactose, vitamins, minerals, and trace elements. Milk contains the vitamins A, B_1, B_2, B_6, B_{12}, D, E, and K; the minerals or salts of calcium, phosphorus, sodium, potassium, and magnesium; and trace elements, including zinc, iron, manganese, and copper. While all these vitamin and mineral components together account for less than 1 percent of the milk's total volume, nutritionally they are highly significant.

Milk also contains naturally occurring bacteria and enzymes and may contain "foreign matter" such as yeasts, molds, external bacteria, leaves, soil, and manure, all of which would be due to lax animal husbandry and milk-handling practices. It may also contain antibiotics given to the animals that can kill cheese-making microorganisms needed for flavor and aroma development.

Cheese has the same nutrients as the milk it came from except they are much more concentrated. There's less water in cheese and its nutrients are "predigested" due to the action of bacteria and enzymes during cheese-making. This means its proteins and fats have already begun to break down and thus are more easily absorbed into the human body; the carbohydrates,

PARMESAN

A SUPERIOR FOOD—AND ONE OF ITALY'S NATIONAL TREASURES

ONE pound of Parmigiano-Reggiano, Italy's superb aged hard cow's milk cheese, contains the nutritional equivalent of 2 gallons of milk. Due to the breakdown of proteins during aging, it is also easy to digest. Most animal protein we consume takes around 4 hours to digest; Parmesan takes just 45 minutes. This is why it is recommended for athletes, who need a quick replenishment of nutrients, as well as for infants, the elderly, and anyone who may have difficulty with digestion.

particularly sugar, have largely been eliminated by the cheesemaking process. Fine table cheeses contain no lactose because that milk sugar is drained away and/or metabolized during the manufacturing and aging processes, which makes such cheeses digestible for people who are lactose intolerant.

Another distinct advantage of cheese is that even the "rustic" or artisanal ones are labeled according to their fat content. The same cannot be said for a piece of steak or a chicken—or for any number of other gourmet foods. So while many of us will *always* face the challenge of controlling or curtailing our fat intake, at least with cheese we can keep track of it.

FAT

Don't be fooled into thinking you're getting less fat with a hard, grainy cheese like Parmesan than you are with a creamy, luxurious one such as Explorateur. The labels of rich "high-fat" cheeses such as the triple crèmes (Explorateur, Pierre-Robert, and so forth) proclaim 75 percent butterfat. So it would be reasonable to assume they have more fat than, say, a Parmigiano-Reggiano, which claims around 35 percent butterfat. The catch is that cheeses are labeled by percentage of fat in their *solid* materials. While much of the water in milk is extracted during cheesemaking, a significant amount is retained and determines the density of the cheese. The harder or denser a cheese, the less water it holds. A dense cheese with, say, 50 percent butterfat, could actually deliver more fat than a soft, runny one with 70 percent butterfat. This is because the softer one has a much higher water content and therefore *less fat per total weight.*

An example: Parmesan, which has about 35 percent butterfat and is about 30 percent water, delivers 25 grams of fat per 100 grams of cheese; Brie, which has 49 percent butterfat but is 57 percent water, yields about 21 grams of fat per 100 grams of cheese—less than the Parmesan.

Why is cheese labeled in this apparently misleading fashion? Because as it ages, it dehydrates—its moisture content decreases—whereas its fat content with respect to solids remains constant. If the fat percentage were given in relation to *total* weight rather than *dry* weight, that number on the label would have to be revised upward with age!

In general, whole-milk cheeses have about 45 to 50 percent fat content. French double-crème cheeses have from 60 to 75 percent while the triple crèmes have 75 percent or more. In France, the fat content is printed on labels or packaging as a percentage of *matière grasse*, often abbreviated to "m.g." In British and American parlance, the terms used are "butterfat content," "fat in dry matter" (FDM), or "fat on a dry basis" (FDB).

> *"Cheese is high in calories and in energy value; on the average, three ounces of cheese is equivalent to half a pound of meat. However, there is little risk of weight gain if you consume moderate amounts of cheese in the framework of a well-balanced diet."*
> —PIERRE ANDROUËT, *Guide du Fromage*

AROMAS AND FLAVORS

Each and every fine cheese has its own distinguishable aromas and flavors. Where do they all come from and what causes them to develop?

More than 700 chemical compounds are responsible for the flavors and aromas of wines; there are over 200 in cheese. Scientists have been quite successful at creating chemical profiles of cheese—that is, detecting and defining a given cheese's molecular components (proteins, fats, minerals, bacteria, enzymes and their various by-products). Yet the ability to predict which of these compounds are specifically responsible for each flavor is still a long way off. Ironically, the reasons for faults or taints have been pretty well delineated; for example, the milk might have been contaminated by a foreign microoganism that produced "off" flavors. But the causes of *desirable* flavors and aromas remain elusive.

What is clear is that the key contributing factors to flavor and aroma are volatile compounds—the ones that commingle readily with air and thus are conveyed most easily to our olfactory organs. The building blocks of these compounds come from plants eaten by the milk-producing animal. Some of these flavor-giving compounds are created by complex chemical reactions involving the breakdown of fats and proteins by enzymes during the ripening phase. Trace minerals from the soil that are transmitted through the animals' plant and water intake can also contribute flavor. Microflora— "friendly pests" such as molds and bacteria—can reach the cheese through the air in the cheesemaking room and create flavor-giving compounds. Other flavor-producing factors, such as the amount of acid or salt, are intentionally added and/or controlled during cheesemaking.

The generally accepted model to explain flavor and aroma is called the Component Balance Theory, espoused by Professor Frank Kosikowski, food scientist and founder of the American Cheese Society, and colleagues for many years. This commonsense approach assumes that not just one but a number of key components must be present in a particular cheese to create its unique flavor. Furthermore, these components must be in a certain balance or in certain proportions to one another to provide a characteristic

Monte Enebro, a rich farmhouse goat cheese from Spain, is a prime example of the flavor complexities that cheese can display.

flavor. The bottom line with regard to the science of cheese flavor and aroma? It is a complex and variegated field that begs much further investigation. While scientists have mapped the human genome, it will be a long time before they have thoroughly quantified the exact flavor mechanisms of cheese.

THREE | THE ART OF CHEESE MAKING

ANIMALS AND MILK

CHEESEMAKING IS COMPLEX and fascinating; as with any subject of this nature, it's best to start at the beginning— the very beginning. For cheese made from the milk of ruminant mammals, two determining factors are important: the breed of animal and the land on which it grazes. Cheese can be made from the milk of "exotic" animals, such as reindeer, yak, camels, and the water buffalo *(bufala)*, which is the source of Italy's highest-quality Mozzarella. For the purposes of this book, though, the animals that count are cows, sheep, and goats.

Queso de la Garrotxa, a goat's milk cheese from Catalonia, was an extinct type. Fortunately, it was revived! There is no other cheese quite like it.

It's often said that goat's milk is best for drinking, cow's milk makes the best butter, and sheep's milk the best cheese. The reason? Sheep's milk is rich and concentrated since ewes produce a relatively small amount of it. Cows, on the other hand, produce a much larger quantity of more diluted milk that is nevertheless very tasty. Goat's milk is the whitest and purest of all; it's easily digestible and has a mild, clean flavor.

"There's not very much mystery to good cheese in my amateur, subjective opinion. It relates primarily to two factors: what went into the milk and how fast the cheese was made. If the milk source was weak, if there isn't much flavor there, the cheese you make is going to be limited. If you make cheese very quickly and efficiently, the quality will suffer because you're killing off some of the enzymes you need." —DICK ROGERS, U.S. cheese importer

COWS

■ PRODUCTION: Cows have a relatively long lactation period, about 300 days, so with staggered breeding a herd can produce milk year-round. Being much bigger animals, cows produce more milk than sheep or goats, but they don't produce *proportionally* more milk. A 1,500-pound animal will produce up to 120 pounds of milk per day, less than 10 percent of its body weight. (Dairy professionals refer to milk production in units of dry weight; a pint of milk is about a pound, a quart is 2 pints or about 2 pounds.)

MILK: THE THIN AND THE THICK OF IT

CAMEL'S milk is at the low end of the spectrum, with around 12 percent solids, while reindeer's milk tops the charts, with only 67 percent water and a whopping 33 percent solids, including 17 percent fat and 11.5 percent protein. This no doubt helps Baby Rudolphs survive those harsh winters in northern climes. It also probably makes great cheese, not that I've ever tasted any, though I would be curious. . . .

"SHEEP'S MILK MAKES GREAT CHEESE"

As I go about my daily ritual of caring for my cheeses, I often find myself repeating a mantra: *"Sheep's milk makes great cheese, sheep's milk makes great cheese . . ."* If you doubt this, just take a taste.

■ CONTENT: Cow's milk is about 87 percent water and the rest solids.

■ COLOR: The vitamin A in cow's milk can come in the form of beta-carotene, an orange or yellowish substance naturally occurring in plants. (Carrots have a high level of it, which accounts for their color.) In general, raw, unprocessed, unpasteurized cow's milk is off-white or ivory-colored to slightly yellow, but it turns somewhat darker in the summer months when the animals ingest more beta-carotene out in the pastures. This holds true of the standard milk producers—Holsteins, Brown Swiss, Simmental, Jerseys, and Guernseys. The exception is the Ayrshire breed, which produces pure white milk.

SHEEP

Sheep are hearty animals that can survive—even thrive—in much sparser conditions than cows. This is why regions with windswept, rocky pasturelands—parts of Spain, Portugal, southern France, Italy, Greece, Romania, Macedonia, and Bulgaria, for example—tend to produce more cheese from sheep's milk than from cow's milk.

■ PRODUCTION: Sheep have a shorter lactation period than cows, between 150 and 240 days. Their gestation period is 5 months; the lambs are weaned when they are 1 month old, and ewes continue to produce milk for up to 8 months. Ewes can only produce up to 3 percent of their body weight or, for a 150-pound animal, 4½ pounds of milk per day. But since their milk is thicker, the nutritional yield is nearly equal.

■ CONTENT: Sheep naturally produce a smaller quantity of richer, more concentrated milk over a shorter period of time than cows. Since cheesemaking is a process of concentrating milk—that is, extracting its water and retaining its solids—ewe's milk is already one step closer to the goal (cheese). It can be expected to contain about twice as much fat as cow's milk, an equal amount of sugar (lactose), and 75 to 100 percent more protein (casein). With a relatively high solid content (close to 20%), ewe's milk

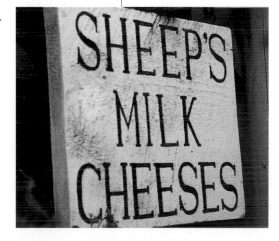

FACTORS ESSENTIAL TO GOOD CHEESEMAKING MILK

- Healthy, unstressed animals
- Proper feed
- Pure milk
- Sanitary milking, handling, and storage conditions
- Quick, efficient cooling

averages around 9 percent fat, about 4.5 percent sugar, and between 4.5 and 6 percent protein.

- COLOR: Ewe's milk is pure and white.

GOATS

Goats are even hardier than sheep, and they are the ultimate omnivores, able to consume and digest all kinds of food that might be considered unacceptable to others. There is, however, a popular misconception that goats are *strictly* a bunch of wiry, ornery scavengers that thrive only in sparse, rocky terrain with little available fodder. Actually, the goats that produce many of the world's most celebrated cheeses, for example the chèvres of France's Loire Valley, graze in lush green pastures and are mellow, well-fed farm animals.

Another popular misconception is that goats and their milk have a pronounced "goaty" smell. Actually, the pungent odor is an aphrodisiac to the female goats that comes from scent glands behind the ears of the male goats. (By the way, they're properly known as "does" and "bucks" not "nanny goats" and "billy goats.")

- PRODUCTION: Goats produce a relatively large amount of low- to medium-fat milk. They breed in the fall, give birth from January until mid-March, and, like cows, lactate for about 10 months. They usually go out to pasture beginning in the early spring; consequently, the best goat's milk cheeses are the ones made from spring and summer milk. Swiss goats weighing around 150 pounds commonly produce 15 pounds of milk daily.
- COLOR: Goat's milk, like that of Ayrshire cows, has no carotene and is therefore pure chalky white.
- CONTENT: As compared to cow's milk, goat's milk has a slightly higher fat content and about the same amounts of proteins and sugar. When properly handled and cooled, goat's milk is slightly less acid than cow's milk with a somewhat sweet taste and no odor.

Fresh goat's milk is superior for cheesemaking, but even some of the strict

French Appellation d'Origine Contrôlée (AOC) regulations, which protect the names of top regional cheeses, allow the use of frozen milk or imported curds. This can yield dull, characterless cheeses, sometimes with off flavors.

Even within a species, breeds can produce milk with significant differences that affect cheesemaking. Jersey cow's milk, for example, has a higher solid content than Holstein milk; likewise, Nubian goats produce milk with higher solids than their cousins, the Swiss, which are the biggest milk producers.

The animals' breeding and lactating cycles also have a significant effect on cheesemaking. Early milk is relatively high in fat and protein, but as the volume of production peaks around midcycle, the milk becomes more diluted. Then as the volume tails off toward the end of the cycle, it becomes more concentrated. "Aftermath," a traditional designation of English farmhouse cheeses such as Cheddar and Wiltshire, indicated cheeses that were made from the richest milk very late in the cycle. On the other hand, very early milk (from the first week after the birth of the calf, kid, or lamb), called colostrum or beestings, doesn't work well for cheese. It is yellowish and contains much immunoglobulin, which supports the newborn's fragile immune system.

Evening milk is generally higher in fat than morning milk; furthermore, as a given milking progresses, the fat content of the milk also goes up. This is why animals are usually subject to two complete milkings per day. Modern methods that ensure a longer milking season also play a role. Through artificial insemination and staggered breeding, some of the world's finer goat's milk cheeses, for example, are now available year-round. But winter cheese

HOW MUCH MILK DOES IT TAKE TO MAKE CHEESE?

A LOT. As a rule of thumb, 1 pound of cheese requires about 10 pounds of cow's or goat's milk or about 6 pounds of sheep's milk, which is considerably richer. A few examples:

■ It takes some 1,000 pounds of milk to make a superior 100-pound alpine cheese such as the Beaufort Haut-Montagne of France's Haute-Savoie region. Each cow produces between 40 and 120 pounds of milk per day (roughly 5 to 15 gallons), which means it takes a day's production from a herd of between 8 and 25 cows to make a large wheel.
■ Every 2-pound Roquefort requires about 12 pounds of milk from the Lacaune breed of sheep.
■ It takes nearly 11 pounds of cow's milk to make a pound of Reblochon, the French alpine cheese made from the second milkings.

Queso de la Serena, one of Spain's best cheeses at peak ripeness.

tastes different because the animals are consuming dry fodder, not the fresh plants and green grasses of spring and summer.

Animal husbandry is the bedrock upon which cheesemaking is founded: Happy mammals make happy cheese. These points cannot be overemphasized. I still have vivid impressions from my visit to Blythedale Farm in Corinth, Vermont, where Karen Galayda and Tom Gilbert make Jersey Blue and a few other superior cheeses. Not only is their dairy spotless, but their Jersey cows are some of the most beautiful beasts I have ever seen. No wonder their cheese is superb.

> *"Every region has its own special magic which chemistry and technology have thus far been unable to duplicate. The character, subtlety and perfection of a cheese attest to centuries of refinement in individual cheese-making methods within limited geographical areas sometimes no larger than a few fields. Vegetations, climate, rainfall, subsoil, and breed all contribute to the production of a cheese which is unique and inimitable."*
> —PIERRE ANDROUËT, *Guide du Fromage*

Cows need water, shade, and shelter from the wind. If they're exposed or mistreated, they're not happy. Stressed or irritated cows yield milk that ripens into cheese with defects in flavor or texture. Sheep and goats are a little heartier and inclined to roam farther afield, but they too require some TLC. The traditional "organic" approach to farming, when practiced correctly, maintains healthy animals and produces better-tasting, more distinctive cheeses.

TERROIR: THE LAND

Among wine connoisseurs, you hear a lot about the concept of *terroir*. In France, it's like a religious creed. In America, our blind faith in our own ingenuity once led us to believe we could produce superior wines from almost any site through technology. But you can't make good wine unless you've got good grapes, a good climate, and, most important, good soil. The same is true of cheese. Climate, weather, soil conditions, the presence or absence of certain minerals—unique combinations of key elements—create a distinctive character in each growing site that is transmitted to the cheese. This is why it's virtually impossible to imitate a fine cheese outside its place of origin.

Mixed natural pastures yield better milk—there's less dilution, more concentration of flavors. The alpine pastures in famous cheesemaking regions such as Haute-Savoie, France, harbor anywhere from thirty to fifty different species of plants, including grasses, clovers, alpine wildflowers, and herbs, all edible for cows. These pastures have more plant variety, better-defined seasons, more extremes of temperature and light exposure. They are about as far from the controlled, manicured growing environment of a single-strain grass meadow as you can get. Forget about efficiency; you need variety.

In wine, *terroir* can account for two very different expressions of a given grape variety from nearby vineyards. Likewise, a cheese from one side of a pasture can emerge with a slightly bitter taste while one from the other side, made by exactly the same recipe, will yield a pleasantly tart one. More broadly, a particular soil type will often shine through: if the land is chalky or salty or sulphurous, you'll taste that. Coastal lands, with high salt and mineral contents in their soil, yield cheeses with a tangy mineral flavor. The water the animals drink also affects how a cheese tastes. Pure alpine water contributes to the high quality of mountain cheeses.

In addition to *terroir,* the milk and cheese will reflect the seasonal quality of the herd animals' fodder. During the winter in northerly climates, the animals are housed mostly indoors and eat hay, cereals such as oats and barley, and other silage. The highest cheesemaking standards—as reflected in France's AOC and Italy's Denominazione di Origine Controllata (DOC) laws, for example—require that the animals eat only fresh grasses and flowers in spring and summer and hay from local pastures in winter. Cheeses made in winter have a whiter paste while the summer ones are yellowish from flowers and grass, which contain carotene (except for goats and Ayrshire cows, which have no carotene in their milks). In his *Guide du Fromage,* Pierre Androuët, always wonderfully precise, explains that the best milk is produced at three times of year: during the first sprouting of grasses in early spring, during the flowering of the meadows, and during the second growth of grasses—

YESTERDAY'S CHEESE, TODAY'S CHEESE

EVERYTHING AFFECTS THE FINAL PRODUCT—EVEN THE WEATHER

CYNTHIA MAJOR is a world-class cheesemaker who, with each shipment of her Vermont Shepherd cheese, encloses a note about its characteristics: what the ewes were eating, their temperament, the weather. You'll hear about a glorious dry sunny day when the sheep were grazing in a field with lots of clover or tarragon. And there is absolutely nothing frivolous about this. If you pay close attention and really get to know a cheese, you will begin to notice the distinctions:

■ *Major Farm Batch 56:* Made 8/25/97. There were thunderstorms day and night. The ewes were grazing across the street from Cindy and David's house. Batch 56 was one of the largest of the season: 14 wheels from 680 lbs. of milk.

■ *Major Farm Batch 57:* Made 8/27/97. A foggy, mild day. The ewes were grazing on really lush grass after yesterday's rain. We made 9 wheels from 449 lbs. of milk.

in late summer and early fall, just after they've been mowed for hay.

The history of the land also plays a role. In viticulture, old vines produce better grapes and subsequently better wines. Likewise, old permanent pastures yield better cheeses. There has yet to be a detailed scientific explanation for this, but it's probably due to the better concentration of minerals and the variety and complexity of plants. Viticulturists theorize that older vines, having deeper roots, get better and more varied nutrients from the soil. Farmers have for many years observed that their grazing animals *prefer* old pastures to newly seeded or recently plowed areas. This is no sentimental view; left to their own devices, animals seek variety. Cows, sheep, and especially goats like to munch clovers (red, white, and green), alfalfa, fenugreek, wildflowers, and many other kinds of "weeds" along with their grass. The resulting cheeses have more profound and distinctive flavors. By the same token, milk can become tainted with off flavors if the animals graze on such strong-flavored plants as wild garlic, mint, kale, or chicory.

A final word on pastureland management and animal husbandry: it should be organic or as close to it as possible. Chemical fertilizers, pesticides, or herbicides applied to the plants and ingested by the animals can affect the texture and flavor of a cheese. Milking machines, a technological marvel,

"*Watching cows munching their way through the grasses of an English pasture, one can see why our British cheeses have a reputation for their sweet, creamy, rich and complex scents and flavours. The characteristic sea spray freshness of Cheshire can only be obtained from the rich salt deposits lying just below the surface of the pastures while the distinct herby, slightly metallic blue taste of Stilton must surely be influenced by the mineral rich seams of coal and iron running through the rolling fields of Nottinghamshire, Leicestershire and Derbyshire. These are the great territorials of Britain.*"
—JULIE HARBUTT, *Guide to the Finest Cheeses of Britain and Ireland*

can cause mastitis by pulling too hard on the cow's udder. Overuse of antibiotics may allow harmful microorganisms to develop resistant strains that find their way into cheeses. It is now widely acknowledged that chemicals in our food can have long-term cumulative effects on our bodies, not to mention the loss of character in the foods themselves. Farmers of many different ilks are switching back to traditional methods such as crop rotation, use of organic fertilizers, integrated pest management, and biological pest control. There is really no substitute for doing it the old-fashioned way.

"From the earliest of times it has been recognized that a contented cow gave the best milk for cheesemaking."—AVICE R. WILSON, *Forgotten Harvest: The Story of Cheesemaking in Wiltshire*

ALPAGE

MIGRATING HERDS AND THE MIRACLE OF MOUNTAIN CHEESES

IN FRANCE, Italy, Switzerland, and other European countries, humans and beasts have adapted to seasonal extremes with the miraculous migratory trek called *transhumance,* wherein herds and herders gradually move from sheltered winter refuges in the valleys to the lush high-mountain pastures in summer. In spring, when the snows at lower altitudes have melted and given way to green pastures, the animals are let out of their barns and begin to eat their way up the mountainsides, reaching altitudes of nearly 10,000 feet by mid-August to graze in pastures above the tree-line. By the end of September, when temperatures begin to drop and the occasional snowstorm descends, the herds have eaten their way back down to the valleys; the pastures they ate in the early spring are green again, renewed in the animals' absence.

The mountain pastures are dotted with chalets, where herders, often hired hands known as *bergers* in French, make cheeses. These *alpage* cheeses represent the elite, coming from happy bovine gourmets who have partaken of the fresh air, sunshine, pure mountain water, and natural plant delicacies all summer long. The bergers, meanwhile, have worked long and hard—3 or 4 months straight of 16- to 18-hour days—tending the herds, manufacturing and caring for the cheeses. Everything is done by hand. The first milking begins at three or four o'clock in the morning; there is cheesemaking, cheese-turning, and all manner of other chores to complete before the evening milking. We need only taste such cheeses alongside their factory-made imitators to realize that all this effort is thoroughly justified.

COLLECTION, SELECTION, AND PREPARATION OF MILK

One of the first cheesemaking decisions is what type of milk to use: morning milk, evening milk, or a combination? Skimmed, partially skimmed, or with extra cream added? Some cheeses are enriched by adding cream, skimmed from the morning milk, to the previous evening's milk. The French triple-crème cheeses, such as Explorateur and Pierre-Robert, are made this way and wind up with 75 percent fat; other cheeses, such as Parmigiano-Reggiano and Simmental Swiss, are made from skimmed or partially skimmed milk and have between 30 and 45 percent fat in dry material.

Multiple sourcing of milk—that is, obtaining it from different farms outside the immediate vicinity—is not compatible with artisanal cheesemaking. In the classic family farm model, the cheesemakers are also *eleveurs,* the French term for farmers who raise and care for animals. (The verb *elever,* by the way, also applies to the raising of children or grape vines or anything else that takes plenty of time and trouble.) The source of the milk is circumscribed: it is the farm's own herd grazing in known pastures. In cases where the farm is too small to sustain a cheesemaking operation

David Major and his wife, Cynthia, are responsible for Vermont Shepherd. Here he is leading his flock.

of its own, the next best thing is a cooperative where only local farmers contribute milk to the town dairy. Once the operation becomes large enough to start collecting milk in refrigerated tank trucks from a wider radius, the specter of tainting and contamination arises. (Are the sources reliable and has the milk been properly handled in transit?) At some point, the operation reaches factory scale and pasteurization becomes necessary. This is the big trade-off. Pasteurization may be insurance against potentially tainted milk, yet it also spells loss of character. If the small producer takes care, employing every basic means to ensure milk purity and dairy hygiene, *that* is the best guarantee; there is no need to pasteurize.

THE BASIC STEPS OF CHEESEMAKING

1. Selection and preparation of milk Type and quality of milk; method of transport and/or storage.

2. Souring or acidification of milk (formation of curds) Type and amount of starter; rate of acidity development.

3. Renneting (coagulation of curds) Type and amount of coagulant; acidity at which it functions.

4. Stirring, cutting (consolidation and concentration of curds) Method(s), timing, and extent of curd manipulation; at what acidity and firmness is it done; desired size of curds.

5. Cooking or scalding of curds* Method, timing, and extent of heat; effect on curd development, drainage and acidity.

6. Drainage (separation of curds from whey) Method and timing; amount of whey exuded from curds.

7. Molding Method, timing, and mold configuration.

8. Pressing Method, duration, and amount of pressure exerted.

9. Salting Method of application; type and amount of salt; duration of salting.

10. Formation of rinds Method, timing, storage conditions; special applications (e.g., washing, rubbing, spraying of mold).

11. Ripening or aging Conditions; special treatments; duration.

GENERAL CONSIDERATIONS: Temperature control, timing, and duration of treatments—at all stages of cheesemaking; the amount of fat in the milk; the acidity of the curds as they develop and are manipulated; and the degree of extraction and concentration (amount of moisture to be left in cheese).

*NOTE: Not all curds for cheeses are cooked or scalded. For some cheeses, the curds are inoculated with a mold or bacteria to produce special effects such as holes or blueing.

PASTEURIZATION

The French deserve credit for making some of the best cheeses in the world. They also deserve credit, in the person of the great Louis Pasteur, for inventing pasteurization. Between 1856 and 1875, Pasteur conducted research on fermentation. He focused on wines and beers, but his findings also applied to dairy products. Among his many discoveries was that certain types of bacteria can be anaerobic—that is, they can function without air. The significance of this for cheesemaking is these bacteria can thrive in the airless environment that is the interior of a ripening cheese. Pasteur also discovered that heat could cripple or kill bacteria. As early as 1857, he experimented with heating milk to destroy its bacteria and thus prevent quick spoilage.

Standard pasteurization involves heating milk to a temperature of about 158 to 162 degrees F for approximately 15 seconds, then cooling it quickly to between 45 and 55 degrees F. A gentler form of pasteurization, often called simply heat treatment, raises the milk's temperature to between 135 and 155 degrees F for approximately 30 minutes. Nowadays, cheesemakers and dairy technicians refer to the two major types of heat treatment as Low Temperature Long Hold (LTLH), which is up to 149 degrees F for up to 40 minutes, and High Temperature Short Hold (HTSH), which is up to 167 degrees F for up to 40 seconds. Certain enzymes and bacteria will survive LTLH, which makes it preferable for cheesemaking.

"As bacterial life ceases in cheeses at three months, pasteurization is a wasteful, expensive and inefficient substitute for clean milk."—PATRICK RANCE, *The Great British Cheese Book*

Pasteurization kills 99 percent of the bacteria in milk. Unfortunately, from the point of view of fine cheeses, it destroys not only the bad bacteria but also the good. (Heat treatment, while somewhat of a compromise, also kills a large portion of the "bennies.") It obliterates the enzymes that are responsible for imparting flavors and aromas. Cheeses made from pasteurized milk not only have less nutrition and less character than traditional farmhouse ones; they can also develop "cooked" flavors and a rubbery and/or pasty consistency. Try a genuine farmhouse Cheddar (Keen's or Montgomery's) alongside a factory version; you'll taste the difference.

Furthermore, by aspiring to an antiseptic existence I believe we actually risk weakening our species. In cheese, bacteria form a protective shield against potentially dangerous contaminants. This means that cheeses made from pasteurized milk may actually be *less safe* than those made from "raw" (unpasteurized) milk. Raw milk is generally *not* dangerous if it is kept clean. If the milk is dirty, the cheese simply does not come out right. Any type of unwelcome microorganisms in the milk will cause it to curdle incorrectly, to develop off flavors and even to bloat or break up. Cheese made from contaminated milk is easy to recognize: it doesn't look or smell right and, if you eat it, it certainly doesn't taste right!

Pathogenic bacteria—the ones that can make us ill—are a different matter. In the unlikely event that any pathogens were to creep into an artisanal cheese via its milk, all of the renneting, heating, salting, drying, and curing would kill those pathogens within 2 months. Cheeses that are aged under 2 months are protected from invasive pathogens by their rinds, which usually consist of a layer of natural molds (more on this below), and by careful storage and handling. With their higher populations of good bacteria, cheeses made from raw milk are protected from dangerous pathogenic bacteria.

Nevertheless, pasteurization is on the rise. Over the years, the perceived superiority of French cheeses has driven worldwide demand for them sky high. Small producers—the farmers who milk one herd and make the finest cheeses—can no longer meet this demand. So the cheeses are made increas-

"Raw milk cheeses are worth saving. They are a distinct value-added product niche. Because they provide a high return on investment, they are able to sustain agriculture in a form that is rapidly disappearing—the small farm." —PAUL S. KINDSTEDT, Professor, University of Vermont

> *"It is no surprise to find that those arguing for universal pasteurisation are the large producers or milk product manufacturers for whom the pasteurisation of milk is a necessity. Those arguing in favour of raw milk are the small producers, using milk from their own herd to sell or turn into milk products. Both views are legitimate within their own, very different modes of production. What is illegitimate is when one view seeks to impose itself upon the other without taking these differences into account."*
> —DOMINIC COYTE, Neal's Yard Dairy

ingly in large dairies and factories. Milk is collected from multiple sources and transported in refrigerated stainless steel containers. Such large cheese-making companies can't afford to take any chances. They don't have the inherent controls that smaller operations have so they are forced to resort to pasteurization—and their cheeses risk losing individual character.

Can great cheeses be made from pasteurized milk? Yes, but they are exceptions. Colston-Bassett Stilton is one example. It takes a highly skilled cheese-maker to fashion pasteurized milk into superior cheese.

SOURING OF MILK

The simplest possible explanation of cheesemaking is that it is the process of extracting the solids from milk and preserving them in some sort of palatable—preferably delicious—form. You'll recall that milk is roughly 85 percent water and the rest pretty evenly divided among protein (mostly casein), fat, and sugar (lactose), with smaller amounts of vitamins and minerals rounding out the mix.

Cheese in its most basic form is nothing more than curds—the coagulated solids of the milk—in whey, the milk's liquid component. To reach this state of separation, the milk first needs to begin souring. In cheesemaking, once the proper quality and mixture of milk is attained and the temperature is regulated, souring begins. This souring, called acidification or lactic fermentation, occurs when strains of *Streptococci, Lactobacilli,* and related bacteria feed off the milk sugar (lactose), leaving lactic acid in its place and releasing some carbon dioxide. These microorganisms are called, somewhat paradoxically, lactic acid bacteria. (How many animals do we know that are named after the main by-product of their feeding process?)

> *"Cultures are like women: they don't function to their fullest until they're warmed up and nurtured."*—AVICE WILSON

Fresh milk, which is naturally somewhat sweet, will eventually sour naturally. But the majority of cheesemakers, in their eagerness to create cheese, will hasten fermentation by adding a starter culture—a small sample of healthy lactic acid bacteria, including *Streptococcus lactis* (amazingly, from the same family of bugs that causes infections such as strep throat), lactobacilli such as *Lactobacillus lactis,* and possibly some species of the *Leuconostoc* genus. The type and quantity of bacteria used in a starter culture depend on how acidic the cheese needs to be as well as other desired effects during the ripening phase. The best cultures are the mixed-strain active ones.

Traditional cheesemakers prepared their own starter cultures simply by storing a portion of the previous day's milk or whey overnight in cheesemaking conditions, a method that helps preserve the unique local character of the bacteria and thus the cheese. Nowadays, starters often consist of a commercially produced culture grown in a lab, factory, or dairy. Such cultures come in concentrated form—that is, freeze-dried to a powder or fresh-frozen. Designed for quick, efficient acidification, they are simply tossed into the vats of warm milk, a procedure called Direct Vat Inoculation (DVI). The cheesemaker then waits for the milk to set. To produce superior cheeses, however, it is necessary to use fresh liquid cultures, which contain a wider variety of bacteria strains, the flavor-makers as well as the quick acid-producers.

The best cheesemakers today will buy commercial cultures and nurture them for several days, combining them with a small amount of their cheesemaking milk and allowing them to develop the desired complexity before introducing them into the vat. Unfortunately, too many cheesemakers shy away from taking this extra step, and therefore their cheeses fall short of their potential.

> *"The question, 'Where do the bacteria of cheese come from?' can be answered in several ways. They come in small numbers from the healthy udder, from post-contamination of the milk or cheese anywhere along the collection and processing route, or through purposely culturing cheese milk."* —FRANK KOSIKOWSKI and VIKRAM MISTRY, *Cheese and Fermented Milk Foods*

Like most types of spoilage, the souring of milk depends heavily on temperature. Following a strictly traditional farmhouse or artisanal method, the cheesemaker can dispense with a starter and instead simply monitor the temperature of the milk, waiting for ambient bacteria to acidify it. Different types of bacteria thrive at different temperatures. Lactic acid bacteria—like many similar organisms—cannot function below a certain temperature. If the milk is frozen or very cold, the bacteria are essentially comatose. (This is why refrigeration can be used to buy time for fresh milk before natural spoilage sets in.) Likewise, if the temperature goes too high, the bacteria die. Acidification of milk generally takes place between 70 and 115 degrees F. As the temperature rises within that range, bacterial action becomes faster and more widespread. Most milk for cheese is soured in the narrower range of 80 to 90 degrees F.

Ideally, fresh milk is delivered to the dairy for cheesemaking straight from the animal at or near body temperature; if it has been refrigerated, however, it needs to be reheated. How much the temperature is allowed to rise over the entire course of cheesemaking will determine a lot about the eventual character of the cheese. At this early stage, however, the temperature level primarily affects the beginning and ending of the fundamental chemical reaction—lactic fermentation.

Simple lactic acid formation will yield the most primitive type of cheese. One can imagine the products of an age long before more sophisticated

A SIMPLE CHEESE

A RECIPE YOU CAN MAKE AT HOME THAT USES NYLON STOCKINGS

THIS recipe is based on a farmhouse soft cheese from Wiltshire, England, originally made from raw cream that soured naturally. As raw cream is practically impossible to obtain in the United States, regular sour cream is used. A sour cream with a strong acid flavor is preferable.

Take a pair of knee-high nylon socks. Place one inside the other, then put them in a 1-quart plastic container and stretch the elastic edge over the top, forming a well. Spoon in 1 pint of sour cream and tie a knot just above the cream line. Wrap the elastic end of the stocking round the neck of a quart bottle that is full. Place the bottle on the shelf of a refrigerator, allowing the stocking full of cream to hang down in front of the shelf. Below the stocking, place a small plastic container to catch the draining whey. (This is delicious to drink, or can be used in cooking.) Allow to drain 3 or 4 days. When the cheese is fully drained, the top of the stocking starts to dry out.

Cut the stocking and turn the cheese into a small bowl, discarding the stocking. (Herbs may be added to taste.) Cover the bowl with plastic wrap. The keeping quality of this cheese is very similar to any other soft cheese.

For those who are calorie conscious, a mixture of one-third yogurt and two-thirds sour cream is also very tasty, but do not use more than 1 pint per stocking. Either way, the recipe makes about 12 ounces of cheese.

cheesemaking methods evolved. The milk was allowed to sour naturally and the resulting curds were drained in a cloth or sieve. Modern-day buttermilk, yogurt, and fresh tub cheeses such as German *Quark* are the result of such simple acidification and curdling. Take it just one or two steps further—to pressing and molding—and you have a basic cheese. Rustic or primitive cheeses of this nature probably had a relatively bland flavor at first and lasted a week or two, depending on how hot the weather was. Today's cheese connoisseur might not be impressed, but I imagine they would have tasted pretty good to a hungry Viking.

COAGULATION: SEPARATION OF CURDS FROM WHEY

After acidification, the next step in cheesemaking is the addition of rennet, which encourages the second important chemical reaction after souring—coagulation of the curds.

Rennet is a substance extracted from the lining of the fourth stomach (called the abomasum or vell) of young ruminant mammals. Rennet consists primarily of the enzyme rennin, which is designed to begin breaking down mother's milk so the young animal can digest it. (In scientific texts, rennin is frequently referred to by its other chemical name, chymosin, so as not to confuse it with renin, an enzyme produced by the kidneys.) The nursling from which the rennet is extracted must be young enough not to have consumed anything but its mother's milk; otherwise, it will have developed other enzymes that could potentially spoil the cheese.

In traditional cheesemaking, well into the nineteenth century, strips of the fourth stomach were prepared and then soaked in the cheese milk to initiate coagulation. Later, extraction processes were developed to allow the

---

ENZYMES

ENZYMES are complex organic compounds that act as catalysts in many chemical reactions crucial to sustaining life on this planet, including the decomposition of dead and decaying organisms and—within the bodies of live animals—digestion. There are roughly forty enzymes in milk and they come from one of three sources: the milk itself as it comes out of the udder (these are considered "naturally occurring enzymes"); microorganisms in the milk, such as bacteria, either living, dormant, or dead; and external or contaminating microorganisms that were allowed to enter the milk. Enzymes can be proteolytic (they break down proteins) or lipolytic (they break down fats).

enzyme to be added without the actual stomach lining. There are two other types of rennet: vegetable-based ones, which are extracted from plants such as thistles, nettles, figs, and safflowers; and microbial ones, which are made from fungi or yeasts. Rennet made from the cardoon thistle *(Cynara cardunculus)* is the best plant coagulant and has always been the basis for Portuguese Serra-type cheeses. In cultures that don't believe in slaughtering animals, either they've used vegetarian rennets or they've extracted stomach juices using a large needle, presumably causing only momentary discomfort to the sacred young cows.

Acidification due to lactic fermentation and coagulation due to the action of the enzymes in rennet are separate but related processes that work hand in hand. Cheese can be made utilizing just one or the other, but there is usually a combination of the two. Once lactic acid forms, it begins to coagulate the milk; the rennet enzymes accelerate that effect. Without the more complete coagulation brought on by rennet, the curdling process can take much longer, especially in cooler environments where chemical reactions are slower, and there is a danger of excessive acid buildup or incomplete curdling.

Molecules of the milk protein casein exist in a colloidal state, meaning they are suspended—not dissolved—in the liquid and thus can be precipitated out by rennin. Casein molecules are essentially long chains of amino acids in helix form—that is, the chains are twisted or braided around one another. The main action of the enzyme rennin is to attack these protein chains and break their chemical bonds at key junctures. The chains are then reconfigured into a lattice-type structure, often referred to as a "protein matrix" or "network," that is not unlike the interior of a sponge. The other milk solids—fat globules, vitamins, minerals, trace elements, lactic acid— become trapped inside this network as integral parts of the coagulating curds. The looser the lattice work, the higher the moisture and fat content of the curds, and the softer the resulting cheese.

As coagulation proceeds, the protein network contracts, solidifies, and naturally expels whey. It's as if the "sponge" is being gently squeezed by an invisible hand. The further this contraction is allowed to go, the more liquid is separated and the denser the curds become. At the same time, segments of the chains are released in the form of flavor-giving amino acids and other related compounds. Coagulation is just the beginning stage of this protein breakdown (proteolysis), which continues gradually throughout aging and ripening.

Besides casein, the other proteins in milk, called "whey proteins," remain dissolved in the whey to be drained away and/or extracted during cheesemaking. With its significant protein content, the whey is quite nutritious, has relatively little fat, and can make some interesting, useful white cheeses such as Ricotta and Brocciu (from Sardinia). Otherwise, it can be fed to the hogs, which makes them very happy. Whey can also be spread on farm

Epoisses de Bourgogne, a cow's milk cheese. The superior raw-milk version is not available in the United States.

fields as organic fertilizer, dried into a powder for bakery products, or carbonated into soft drinks.

While certain enzymes begin breaking down the proteins, others go to work on the fats. This is another gradual process, called lipolysis, that continues throughout the cheese's maturation period.

Lactic acid coagulation is slower than rennet coagulation and it yields softer, less cohesive, more granular curds with higher water content (think cottage cheese). Rennet coagulation is faster and results in firmer, thicker, more malleable curds (e.g., dense cheeses such as Cheddar or Swiss). The softer lactic acid curds tend to drain naturally under their own weight; the firmer rennet-induced curds generally need help with draining by extractive processes such as cutting and pressing. Lactic acid coagulation depends on milk temperature and on the amount of bacteria present. Rennet coagulation also depends on temperature, how much rennet is added to the milk, plus acidity. The more rennet added, the faster the cheese coagulates, and the firmer the curds become. In typical cheese recipes, there are between 15 and 30 milliliters of rennet extract added per 100 liters of milk (about 1 to 2 tablespoons per 26 gallons). The temperature during rennet coagulation is usually between 75 and 115 degrees F, most often in the range of 85 to 95, but there are exceptions. Like any chemical reaction, coagulation speeds up at higher temperatures. At about 68 to 80 degrees F, the curds are softer and jellylike; at around 85 to 95 degrees F, they become firmer, even rubbery, and don't yield their whey as easily.

As the milk coagulates or clots, it begins to take on the appearance of a uniform gel or puddinglike mass often referred to as "coagulum." This stage is often called setting. It is important that the milk be allowed to set properly and retain all the components necessary for cheese. At first, the coagulum must be treated gingerly—just one of many instances where subtle cheesemaking skills come into play. When mixing in the rennet, for example, cheesemakers must use extreme caution not to overstir the curdling milk lest they rupture its delicate network of proteins before it has had a chance to gel. (In that case, the cheese could lose firmness and texture; in addition, many of those precious milk components would be sloughed off with the whey.)

At the souring and renneting stages there are several possible types of additions that can affect the final product. Even before starter is added to

Testing the consistency of the curds.

HOW IT'S MADE:
WABASH CANNONBALL

THIS is a chèvre-style goat's milk cheese made by Judy Schad at Capriole, Inc., in Indiana. Cannonballs are produced only from the milk of Capriole's own goats. On the first day of cheesemaking, 1 to 2 days' worth of milk is slowly heated to 145 degrees F. The milk is held at this temperature for at least 30 minutes and then cooled down to about 70 to 72 degrees F, depending on the time of year and ambient temperature. Tiny amounts of starter culture are added to the warm milk, which ripens for several hours. Then ½ teaspoon of calf rennet is added for each 40 gallons of milk. The following day, when the whey reaches the proper acidity, it is hand-ladled into cheesecloth-lined baskets where it drains for 5 to 6 hours. Salt is added to the curd and the cheese-filled cloths are hung overnight. On the third day, the curd is taken down, weighed, shaped into *boulets* (balls) by hand, then placed in a cool, dry room with good air flow for 20 to 24 hours. On the fourth day, the surface of the cheese is coated with vegetable ash. The cheeses are removed to the cave and held there at 52 degrees F and high humidity for a total of about 6 days. The cave is regularly seeded with *Penicillium* mold spores. White spots of mold develop in about 3 days and a healthy bloom in about 6. The cheeses are then loosely wrapped in paper, stored, and shipped in poplar crates, which allow them to breathe.

the milk, some propionic acid bacteria can be added; they will cause a secondary fermentation during the ripening phase that produces flavor-giving substances such as acetic acid and releases carbon dioxide, creating the interior "air holes" that are the signature of many mountain or Swiss-type cheeses. Spores of a blueing mold—*Penicillium roquefortii* for Roquefort or *Penicillium glaucum* in the case of Gorgonzola—can be added. Annatto, a natural food coloring that turns the cheese's paste a darker, more orange shade, can be added. Herbs or spices can be added for flavor.

From the onset of coagulation, it can take between 10 minutes and several hours for curds to fully develop. If the milk has been allowed to sit overnight or for any significant length of time, it has already begun to acidify and the curds will develop more quickly, particularly at higher temperatures. Hard Swiss mountain cheeses such as Emmental or Gruyère develop sufficient curds in 25 to 30 minutes, and they are then scalded for 45 to 50 minutes. For farmhouse Livarot, a semisoft deliciously pungent cheese from

HOW IT'S MADE:
ROQUEFORT

THIS is one of France's finest and certainly among the world's most distinguished and ancient cheeses. Its manufacture is a labor-intensive, time-consuming, and fascinating saga.

The milk is renneted at between 82 and 88 degrees F. *Penicillium roquefortii* spores are mixed in either before the rennet is added or to the curds before they are placed in the molds. The curds develop in about 1½ to 2 hours; they are cut, then stirred and drained on a grid. The drained curds are ladled into molds, then moved to a draining room at 63 to 68 degrees F for 4 to 6 days with four to seven turnings per day.

The cheeses are then removed from their molds; they weigh about 3 kilos, or 6½ pounds, and are ready to be transported to the caves for ripening (blueing). They are initially stored at 50 degrees F for between 6 and 11 days, with one turning and salting at the beginning and another at the halfway point. Next they are scraped and smoothed, then pierced with needles to allow carbon dioxide to escape and more air to enter.

Typical conditions in the caves, where they now go to ripen for a minimum of 3 months and as many as 6, are 46 to 48 degrees F and 96 to 98 percent humidity. Blueing can begin as soon as 10 days and takes about 3 to 6 weeks total. The entire process is carefully monitored by expert *affineurs* (ripeners) or *trieurs* (graders). Once they're judged ready, the cheeses are wrapped in a light foil before packing and shipping.

How do the *affineurs* of Roquefort collect the *Penicillium* molds from the caves of Combalou, as they must according to AOC laws? (No other mold will do.) They use the traditional method of placing large loaves of rye bread in the caves for a couple of months to gradually attract the mold. When the bread is thoroughly mold-ridden, its crust is removed and its interior is dried for 8 days at 95 degrees F. Then it is broken up and sifted to yield the mold spores that will be stirred into the curds during cheesemaking.

pH

ACIDITY is measured by pH, which is the concentration of hydrogen ions in a solution. On the pH scale, which ranges from 0 to 14, the lower the number, the higher the solution's acidity; the higher the number, the more alkaline or base the solution is. Water, being neutral, is at the center of the scale and is assigned a value of 7.0. Anything between 7 and 14 is considered alkaline; between 0 and 7 acidic. Acidic substances taste sour; alkaline ones bitter. Milk is slightly acidic at pH 6.6 while vinegar and lemon juice are quite acidic at 2.9 and 2.3, respectively. Toothpaste is fairly alkaline at 9.9 and household ammonia solution is even more so at 11.9. Lactic acid coagulation begins when the pH level of milk reaches about 5.2; the milk fully coagulates at about 4.6. Simple lactic cheeses have relatively high acidity in their curds, with a pH of around 4.7 to 5.0, while Feta and other similar Near Eastern briny white cheeses are even more acidic, with a pH of around 4.0. Milder soft cheeses such as Brie have a curd pH in the range of 4.9 to 7.0. For Cheddar and other hard-pressed varieties, the pH in the curds reaches approximately 5.25.

Normandy, the milk is allowed to sit at room temperature for 16 to 24 hours; curd coagulation after renneting takes 75 to 100 minutes. For Parmesan, the milk ripens for 5 to 20 minutes after starter is added and curds form within 20 to 30 minutes after renneting; then it is cooked and pressed extensively to yield its hard, dense texture.

ACIDITY

Aside from temperature, the other critical factor to be monitored throughout the souring, renneting, and curd-consolidation stages is the pH, or acidity level. Controlling acid development in the curds is one of the cheesemaker's most important skills. If it is not carefully regulated, it leads to nothing more than spoiled milk—not cheese. As mentioned, the curds harden and become more granular as they acidify. Acid affects the eventual taste of the cheese with its tangy, sharp, biting flavors. Different microorganisms function best at different acid levels. Acidification encourages the growth of beneficial bacteria (e.g., the *Lactobacillus* family) and suppresses the potentially hazardous ones (coliforms and *Clostridia*). Although it involves a slower, more gentle form of coagulation, the acidifying stage of curdling must not be allowed to proceed too far. The rennet needs to go into effect within a certain pH range in order for the curds to coagulate into a plastic, malleable form that can then be molded and/or pressed. Otherwise, the cheesemaker is liable to wind up with an amorphous tub of cottage-cheese-like curds. Timing is everything!

A given cheese's acidity peaks when the maximum amount of lactose has been converted into lactic acid, usually around the time of salting. After that, as ripening and maturation begin, milk components are slowly but surely broken down, releasing a number of more alkaline substances, including ammonia, and the pH heads back up to a more balanced or neutral level.

In a factory environment, the pH level is tested by modern scientific methods. Artisanal cheesemakers, however, often gauge this key factor strictly by feel—the equivalent of a navigator's dead reckoning at sea. They'll note the curds' consistency merely by sensing their resistance while stirring or scooping up a small dollop with a finger. From these simple cues they form crucial judgments about acidity.

CONCENTRATING OR CONSOLIDATING THE CURDS

Once the curds achieve the desired texture and acidity, according to whatever recipe is being followed, it is time to start turning them into cheese by employing one or more techniques of consolidating and concentrating them, including heating, stirring, draining, cutting, molding, and pressing.

The first major step after coagulation is usually cutting. A certain amount of natural drainage already occurs as the curds harden and contract during coagulation. Cutting the curds into smaller pieces increases the surface area of their amassing protein network and allows them to expel more liquid. The rule of thumb is the smaller the curds, the harder the cheese. Larger curds hold more water and yield a softer cheese; smaller curds yield a cheese with denser texture. Although they may be subject to some stirring or breakage, the curds for softer cheeses such as Camembert, Brie, or the farmhouse-

MOISTURE IN CHEESE

MILK is 80 to 88 percent water. How much of this has to be removed to make cheese? It depends on the desired density of the cheese. Approximate water contents are as follows: hard cheeses, such as Parmesan, Cheddar, and Emmental, are 30 to 35 percent water; semi-hard cheeses, such as Morbier, are 40 to 50 percent water; soft cheeses, such as Camembert, Brie, and Brin d' Amour, are 50 to 60 percent water; tub cheeses, such as cottage cheese, are 70 to 80 percent water.

style chèvres are cut very sparingly, if at all. They are often scooped or ladled by hand into perforated molds—a time-consuming process—where they drain under their own weight and take on shape. The curds for harder cheeses such as Cheddar or Emmental are cut small—even to the size of grains of rice—and then further manipulated by stirring, heating, and pressing.

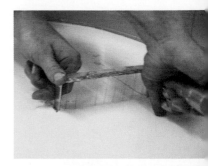

Curds are cut using a knife or swordlike tool or, more likely, a device like a large hair comb or rake called a harp. It has a long metal handle and stiff tines or blades that can be pushed and pulled through the mass of curds. The harp, or "Swiss harp," is just one of a variety of specialized cheese tools—scoops, trowels, cutters, paddles, and so forth. There are almost as many tools as there are types of cheeses, and they often go by colorful names in local dialects.

Cutting the curds.

The size of curds after cutting is defined in each cheese recipe either by their precise numerical dimensions (e.g., "1 centimeter cubed") or, more quaintly, by comparison with some other well-known food item, for example, "cut to the size of walnuts" (fairly large), hazelnuts (still quite large), peas or beans (medium), rice or wheat grains (small).

The decision about when to cut the curds is a difficult one that tests the cheesemaker's experience and judgment. The coagulation process has to have gone far enough so that the curds are indeed cuttable but not so far that they are rock-solid and immovable. If the curds are cut too early or too late, it can have a disastrous effect on the eventual texture of a cheese. It's important that the cutting blades or wires be sharp enough to slice cleanly rather than crush or tear the curds, which could result in loss of valuable fats from the curd mass. These are the types of details no cheesemaker can afford to overlook.

COOKING OR SCALDING

In conjunction with cutting, the curds for harder cheeses are cooked or scalded, another process that strongly affects the eventual texture and density of the cheese. When you hear of "cooked cheese," this has nothing to do with melting it, with making pizza or fondue. It refers to a heating process that is popularly referred to as "cooking the curds in their whey." The vat full of curds and whey is heated until it reaches a specified temperature for a certain period of time, the effect of which is to further contract the molecular network of proteins, shrinking the curds and causing them to expel yet more whey.

The hotter and longer the cooking, the smaller the curds and the firmer the cheese. Given two comparable cheeses made by similar methods, the cheese whose curds have been raised to a higher temperature will have a firmer paste. (Some cheeses have herbs, spices, or wines added at this stage as well.) For traditional hard cheeses, the entire coagulating mass of curds in whey is typically fired in a copper cauldron to a temperature of up to 130 degrees F.

Scalding is a somewhat gentler step whereby the vat itself or a steam jacket surrounding the vat is heated to a predetermined level so that the higher temperature only affects the outer surfaces of the curds, yielding a semihard or medium-hard cheese. To make Swiss or Parmesan-type cheeses, the cut curds are first cooked while being stirred, then they are further cut and scalded, eventually resulting in a harder interior. (The curds for some cheeses, notably the Italian *pasta filata* family, which includes Mozzarella, Caciocavallo,

Val Bagner's firm paste is created by cooking the curds.

and Provolone, are given a bath in very hot water, which has several effects: diluting their acidity, washing away excess whey, and heating them to firm them up.) Cooking the curds also affects the microbes in the cheese; at temperatures of 104 degrees F and above, bacterial activity is seriously inhibited.

SALTING

Salt is an extremely important ingredient in cheesemaking. It functions as a seasoning, a preservative, and as a means of drawing out water. Salting signals the end of the draining of whey and the beginning of curing or aging. Salt is an antibacterial agent; with few exceptions, bacteria become inactive or die in the presence of significant amounts of it. Coliform bacteria, for example, can thrive in a 3 to 4 percent salt solution, but they cease to function when the salt content reaches 12 percent or more.

Cheeses are treated with from .25 to 7 percent of their weight in salt. Blue cheeses and brine cheeses such as Feta are at the higher end of that spectrum. Salt plays an important role in rind development; some cheeses hold up to 20 percent salt in their rinds. This staves off most surface bacteria except the highly desirable *Brevibacterium linens,* which grows happily in the moist, salty environment of a brine-washed rind. Salt in the rind prevents any of the cheese's enzymes from beginning to digest it, which

HOW IT'S MADE:
PARMIGIANO-REGGIANO

PARMIGIANO-REGGIANO, made from partially skimmed milk, is a cooked, molded cheese that undergoes a lengthy brine bath and extensive aging. These processes give it a tough rind and yield its characteristically grainy texture and full flavor.

To make Parmesan, evening milk rests overnight, then is partially skimmed and combined with whole morning milk. Starter, in the form of the previous day's fermenting whey, is added and the temperature is regulated at around 90 degrees F. Rennet is stirred in and the curds form quickly. Using a long-handled whisk, the cheesemaker cuts the curds into pieces the size of wheat grains, then cooks them briefly to a tem-

perature of 130 degrees F. The curds amass at the bottom of their copper kettles and are then carefully scooped out with wooden paddles into cheesecloth. Whey drains off and the curds are placed in wooden molds for further drainage. The cheeses are stamped all over their as-yet soft rinds with the distinctive dot-lettered "Parmigiano-Reggiano" logo. They are turned repeatedly for several days to keep their top and bottom surfaces flat. Next they receive a brine bath for 3 weeks, which begins hardening the rinds. The cheeses are briefly sun-dried, then placed on wooden shelves in aging rooms where they receive regular brushings and turnings for at least 14 and sometimes as many as 48 months.

Traditional farmhouse-style Lancashire, made by the Kirkhams in northwest England, is a splendid example of a milled cheese.

CHEDDARING

SLABS OF CURD ARE CUT, STACKED, AND RESTACKED

T H E so-called textured cheeses, which consist mostly of English medium- to hard-bodied pressed ones such as Cheddar, Cheshire, Double Gloucester, and Lancashire, undergo what is called curd manipulation, the most famous form of which is cheddaring, essentially an alternate form of pressing. After the initial acidification and renneting of the milk, the curds are allowed to coagulate into a large mass, which is then cut into medium-sized slabs that are stacked, left to drain, then restacked and left again. Eventually, when the slabs reach the desired uniform consistency, they are ground ("milled") into small pieces by passing them through a "mill" or grinder. Then they are salted, placed in cloth-lined molds, and pressed for at least 12 hours to yield a cheese with a smooth, thick, rich texture. The desired curd texture of Cheddar is often compared to the striations of meat in a properly cooked chicken breast. It is dense yet subtly layered and tender at the same time—neither underdone (sinewy) nor overdone (dry).

would render it rough or uneven. Dry salt also serves to dehydrate the rind, making it harder and crustier than the rest of the cheese and thus protecting its interior from excess moisture and undesirable molds.

Salt can be applied to cheese in four ways: in the form of a brine bath, usually for hard and semihard cheeses; as an external sprinkling, for soft cheeses; as a rubbing, washing, or brushing, for semisoft cheeses; or as a combination of the preceding. Brine gives a uniform coating of salt; cheeses can be submerged in it for as little as half an hour or as much as 2 weeks. Salt rubbings or brine washings often occur on a regular basis during the drying, ripening, or aging phases of cheesemaking. With a few cheeses, the salt is actually sprinkled into the curds before molding or pressing, rather than being applied to the surface. St. Paulin, a semihard French monastery cheese, receives a bath in 22 percent salt solution for 15 to 18 hours. Sainte-Maure goat cheese from the Loire Valley is rubbed with 1 to 2 percent of its weight in salt. After being milled, the curds for Cheddar are sprinkled with 2 percent of their weight in salt, then carefully mixed.

MOLDING AND/OR PRESSING

Pressing is another way of consolidating the curd mass, giving it a shape or form and forcing it to give up additional whey.

After stirring, cooking, or cutting (or any combination of these), the curds are taken from the vat or tub where they were formed and placed in molds. This transfer process itself involves a certain amount of drainage and some passive pressure. First, the curds might be pushed to one end or side of the vat and a valve opened to let the whey drain out. In some cases, the curds will be scooped out, leaving most of the whey behind. Large blocks of curd can sit in a vat for a while and be subject to the pressure of their own weight.

With larger cheeses, the curds are often hoisted out of the vat in a big bundle of cheesecloth. The cloth bundle acts as a sieve, allowing the whey to cascade back into the vat. Soft cheeses are usually either pressed very lightly or not pressed at all; their curds avoid manipulation and are simply poured or pumped into a mold where they can begin ripening. The molds are often perforated—they resemble baskets, colanders, or sieves—which allows for further drainage of whey. Some cheeses, such as Afuega'l Pitu, Berkswell, Pavé D'Auge, and Perail, still bear the imprints of the basket molds or the cheesecloth on their rinds when you buy them, a fitting reminder that they are handmade artifacts. Most of the whey drains away in the initial separation process—from cut curds in a vat to cheese forming in a mold—but drainage can continue, little by little, for up to several days as the cheese consolidates and/or is pressed in its mold. Among the "untextured" or smooth-bodied cheeses made in this fashion—that is, without further curd manipulation—are Taleggio, Fontina, Asiago, Munster, and Pecorino. Once

The molds—in this case, plain old, industrial plastic buckets—in which the cheese is formed.

The most traditional form of pressing—by hand. Mechanical pressing of Vermont Shepherd.

they take on their form, they are ready to be sprayed, washed, brushed, and/or salted as part of the rind-formation and ripening process.

A number of hard cheeses pass through an intermediate stage of drainage in baskets or colanders before being placed into molds for pressing. Often their molds are lined with cheesecloth or a similar material, which helps to smooth and harden the outer edges of the forming cheese and thus to create a uniform rind with no cracks or fissures where unwanted molds could intrude.

Pressing must be gentle at first so as not to expel fats from the curds' protein matrix, which would yield a cheese that is greasy or oozes butterfat. The aim is to produce a consistent texture that integrates all the key milk components into the body of the cheese. Some cheeses are pressed mechanically or hydraulically. Others are stacked in their molds and simply allowed to contract under their own weight. Sometimes the molds are stacked in interlocking fashion and weighted, another variation of pressing.

As the cheeses rest in the dairy, draining and hardening into their final shapes, they need to be turned so their edges don't collapse or bulge, and so that any residual moisture or fat leeching out doesn't pool at the bottom of the cheese. Turning remains an important step throughout the draining and the ripening phases to maintain regular shape and interior consistency.

MOLDS

There are quite a few molds that, like various bacteria, are most definitely cheese-friendly. Molds are aerobic organisms, which is why cheeses destined to become blue are usually lanced or pricked—to allow air to feed the mold inside the cheese. Probably the most famous species of cheese mold is *P. roquefortii,* native to the caves of Combalou around the village of Roquefort and responsible for the blueing of the renowned cheese of the same name. Another famous mold is *P. candidum,* which is responsible for the "bloomy rinds" of many soft cheeses, mostly of French origin. The first bloomy-rind cheese was Camembert, which was popularized by Madame Harel in Normandy in the late 1700s (although it had been made for nearly a century before). It originally had a bluish surface from natural bacteria and mold; *P. candidum,* which is bright white, was first applied to the rinds in 1910.

Molds are actually fungi, members of the same group as mushrooms. They live a parasitical existence, growing off living organisms or dead decaying ones and reproducing by means of spores. Molds have no chlorophyll, which is why most of them aren't green like other plants. The parts of molds or fungi that we see—the mushrooms growing off the forest floor or the grayish, bluish streaks in cheeses—are the mycelia, which are the flowers or vegetative parts of the organism.

Some moldy cheeses are still made the old-fashioned way—that is, strictly from ambient molds. But in most cases today, cheeses are inoculated with the molds, which are then encouraged to grow in the controlled environments of the ripening caves. With some aging cheeses, mold is not part of the recipe. If their rinds crack, however, molds whose spores naturally circulate in the air can easily establish a happy home inside. Preventing unwanted interior molds is a constant challenge for farmhouse Cheddar makers and ripeners. On the other hand, many sophisticated cheese connoisseurs consider this a highly desirable feature. At Neal's Yard Dairy, London, and other superior British cheesemongers, some fine Cheddars and Cheshires with blue mold are actually sold at a premium. Not only can these molds taste delicious, they are also considered marks of superiority: only the finest, richest cheeses will attract them.

RINDS

Whether or not rinds are encouraged by such procedures as washing, brushing, rubbing, salting, coating with ash or herbs, or spraying, they protect cheeses, enveloping them in a layer of paste that's become hard and dried or in slimy, fuzzy, or crusty coatings of benign mold. (The word *crust*—*croute* in French—is often used to describe the rind.) Here are the categories:

Fresh Cheese (No Rind)

These are often amorphous tub cheeses, in which case there is no such thing as a rind. The most famous of these in the States is cottage cheese, which is nothing more than curds "dressed" in cream. Some fresh white "farmer's cheeses," which come in blocks, don't keep long enough to develop a rind. A brine-soaked or pickled cheese like Feta has no rind but is protected from spoiling or drying as long as it bathes in its salty solution.

Natural Rind

The surface and outer edges of these cheeses harden naturally from contact with air. This category includes the blue cheeses, which generally develop a hardened, yellowed exterior that protects the softer, more delicate interior. Some blues are wrapped in light foil or another protective coating; traditional Cabrales, for example, was wrapped in sycamore leaves.

Goat's milk cheeses are another category that can be said to have natural rinds; traditional farmhouse goat cheeses are first dried, then left to cure for a relatively brief period in a cellar where they attract bluish or grayish molds.

The natural-rind category also encompasses a subcategory of many hard and semihard cheeses, including British farmhouse ones such as Cheddar, Cheshire, Single and Double Gloucester, and Llangloffan; hard alpine cheeses such as Emmental, Beaufort, and Comté; semihard sheep's milk

Various molds are responsible for the remarkable tastes and textures of the "blues": here, counterclockwise from the foreground, Bleu de Gex, Gamonedo, Stilton, Roquefort, Mont Briac, and in the center, Shropshire.

cheeses such as Pecorino, Roncal, and Berkswell; and semisoft Italian cheeses such as Montasio and Asiago, not to mention the venerable Parmigiano-Reggiano. Although it occurs primarily by natural hardening from contact with air, rind formation in these cheeses is often helped along with some type of relatively noninvasive treatment such as trimming, smoothing, scraping, or encasing in a "bandage" of cheesecloth. Then the cheeses may be buttered, oiled, rubbed, or polished as necessary. British farmhouse cheeses are wrapped in cloth, which in turn may grow a layer of mold that forms the exterior of the rind. This mold layer allows moisture and gases to escape but prevents air from getting in and promoting interior mold. The rinds, in other words, are semipermeable. If gases were trapped, they could cause bloating or form unwanted interior holes. Likewise, excess moisture needs to escape during maturation in order to concentrate the cheese's flavor and bring its texture to the desired firmness.

Bloomy Rind (or Surface Mold)

This type of rind is characterized by a soft, white, fuzzy coating of mold, usually a species of *Penicillium* such as *P. candidum, P. camemberti,* or *P.*

HOW IT'S MADE:

CAMEMBERT

ONE of France's most famous cheeses, Camembert is a fine example of a soft, bloomy-rind cheese. In French, "bloomy rind" is *croute-fleurie*, for which the literal translation is "flowering crust." Camembert comes from Normandy, in the northwest, a province known for its abundance of butter and cream as well as its fine cheeses, including Pont L'Evêque, Livarot, Mimolette, and Pavé D'Auge. Here is a typical recipe.

Cows, preferably of the Normande breed, are milked morning and evening. The next morning, the milk is skimmed and heated to about 30 degrees C (86 degrees F). Starter is added, if necessary. The milk is renneted and curds begin to form in 15 to 18 minutes. Full coagulation takes up to 2 hours. The surface of the curd is skimmed

to clear off any impurities, then it is sliced in layers and ladled into perforated molds, which are laid on straw or cane mats for drainage. The fresh cheeses are turned several times over about a 12-hour period; then they are removed from their molds, salted, and dried at 18 degrees C (64 degrees F) and 70 to 80 percent humidity for up to 2 days. Next they are sprayed with a solution of *P. candidum* spores on top and left to mature for up to 12 days at 12 degrees C (54 degrees F). They develop their rinds, which consist of a dusting of soft white mold, and collapse to about half their original height as they shrink from evaporation. Finally, the cheeses are wrapped in paper and packed in wooden boxes, then shipped to wholesalers or retailers where they should ripen for another 2 weeks before sale.

glaucum. The "bloom" is often introduced by spraying a solution containing the mold spores onto the cheese and allowing it to grow under humid conditions in a ripening cave. A number of prominent French soft or semisoft cheeses employ this method, including Brie, Camembert, and the triple-crème cheeses such as Explorateur, Brillat-Savarin, and Pierre-Robert. The semihard *tomme* cheeses of France's Savoie region often grow a furry whitish "cat's hair" mold naturally. It is brushed off after about 8 days, and the remaining crust starts to turn gray and harden into a good protective rind.

Washed Rind

The exterior of the cheese is washed—with water, brine, wine, beer, marc, or a combination thereof—to stimulate the growth of *B. linens,* among other bacteria and molds. (*Marc,* by the way, is a strong spirit made from grape skins after they're pressed for wine; it is the French version of Italian *grappa.*) Some of the world's greatest cheeses owe their existence to these beautiful little *B. linens* bugs. They lend the rinds their distinctive orangish, pinkish, or reddish tints, and their ripening effects penetrate the surface of the cheese, softening and mellowing it from the outside in, adding complexity and depth of flavor. A frequent by-product of this *B. linens* ripening is a very strong, borderline putrid odor. These are the stinky cheeses! Being an aerobic bacterium, *B. linens* needs oxygen to thrive, which is why it dwells on the surface of a cheese. It also needs humidity, which explains why these cheeses are often bathed or given moist rubdowns during their maturation period. Surface-ripened cheeses like this are generally smaller. They require a higher surface-to-volume ratio than large cheeses such as Cheddar or Swiss; otherwise, the ripening effects of the bacteria would never reach the center of the cheese. Among them are Chimay, Epoisses, Livarot, Munster, and Taleggio.

Other Coatings

Handmade goat cheeses often receive a protective dusting of charcoal or ash and are called *cendré* in French. Commercial goat cheeses often have *P. candidum* or blue mold added to their exterior. Some cheeses are coated with herbs or encased in leaves or bark, others are wax coated. In terms of rind categories, some cheeses are hybrids. Traditional Brie, for example, always has a matte white coating of *P. candidum,* but it may also develop some pinkish growth of *B. linens* as it fully ripens. Gruyère gets a regular light-brine rubbing during its aging period, which helps it develop a thin reddish-brown coat of *B. linens.* Yet it does not by any means belong in a category with the classic pungent, washed-rind Munster, Epoisses, or Livarot-type cheeses.

Cynthia Major patting down the rind.

RIPENING, AGING, OR CURING

The curds have been cut, stirred, molded, salted, and/or pressed; they are no longer merely gelatinous blobs of soured milk. Now, to become delectable morsels of real cheese, they must undergo a gradual period of maturation also known as ripening, aging, or curing.

What gives cheese its ability to improve with age? Drying, acidification, and development of a protective coating—the rind—all represent aging potential. Under random conditions, cheese will eventually rot. But under ideal conditions—steady, regulated temperature and humidity, adjusted according to the desired effects; the introduction of certain beneficial bacteria or molds; and careful hygiene—cheesemakers can achieve "controlled spoilage."

The ripening of cheese involves many biochemical reactions. As these reactions proceed, the body of the cheese imperceptibly softens and its various

The many faces of cheese rinds.

components meld into a uniformly delicious consistency. It is the most fascinating and least understood phase of cheesemaking. After 3 months of proper curing, most of the bacteria remaining from the milk have been destroyed by the acids in the cheese. At this point, enzymes have taken over, breaking down fats and proteins and releasing various volatile compounds essential to creating aroma, flavor, and texture. Among those compounds are aromatic esters, amino acids, fatty acids, aldehydes, ketones, alcohols, even ammonia.

It takes a relatively small amount of aroma and flavor components in specific and as-yet unknown combinations to give a cheese its character. As a general rule, a large portion of the milk's fat and about two-thirds of its protein survive to the end of maturation. In cheesemaking, macromanagement is important for control over the general character and nutritional value of the final product. Micromanagement is equally critical, because it is those relatively tiny amounts of compounds undergoing chemical transformations that determine a cheese's unique distinguishing characteristics.

High acidity levels inhibit proteolysis. As mentioned, cheesemakers control acidity during the earlier stages of cheesemaking by regulating the amount of lactic acid fermentation. Later, at the beginning of the ripening phase, they can also introduce a basic or alkaline substance to the surface of a cheese to help neutralize it. Ash or charcoal, for example, are often rubbed on fresh, tangy goat cheeses. Another way of neutralizing a cheese is to encourage the growth of surface molds, which consume lactic acid and also produce alkaline by-products such as ammonia.

Proteolysis causes the release of peptides, which are chains of amino acids that have been separated from the complex helix-shaped protein molecules. They float free and can be perceived as flavors or aromas. It is the terminal amino acid in each peptide chain that gives it its typical flavor. Different amino acids are associated with different flavors. Some are sweet, some bitter; others are "brothlike" and so forth. An immature cheese may exhibit a bitter flavor because it contains a significant amount of peptide chains that end in a bitter amino acid. It can mellow with age when enzymes attack some of those chains, cutting off their bitter terminal acid and leaving in its place a sweet-tasting one.

In meat and fish, the flavor is in the fat, and this is at least partly true with respect to cheeses. You'll notice that totally fat-free cheeses are usually bland. The butterfats from the milk—which, like its proteins, undergo transmutation or conversion—contribute vastly to a cheese's flavors, aromas, and body. How does this occur? Some of the flavor-giving compounds that come from the animal's fodder are fat soluble; on a molecular level, this means they become bound within the fat globules of the milk. As the cheese ripens, enzymes break into the globules and release these compounds, which are then integrated into the body of the cheese.

In addition to having less flavor, cheeses with less butterfat—skim-milk or nonfat ones—are more susceptible to microorganisms that can cause spoilage. In that sense, the fats that have been converted to fatty acids act as preservatives. The aging process also renders the fats in cheese more digestible and less likely to coat our arteries.

The best cheeses have a balanced proportion of well-integrated fat—that is, the fats blend smoothly into the consistency of the cheese rather than ooze out and lend the cheese a greasy impression.

Fat breakdown or lipolysis releases free fatty acids, ketones, and alcohols—all potentially flavor-producing. Like the amino acids, each has its own characteristic flavor; for example, caproic, caprylic, and capric acids, most often found in goat's milk, are peppery tasting, hence the pleasant, mild bite of a good goat cheese.

Maturing cheeses are subject to dehydration; as they cure and inch toward perfection, they are literally evaporating, losing anywhere from 5 to 20 percent of their weight. A Stilton, for example, can lose about 15 percent of its weight in 2 months of aging as it takes on a beautifully ripe, rounded, and delightfully moldy flavor. A typical French farmhouse-style goat cheese such as Crottin de Chavignol might weigh 150 grams (a little over 5 ounces) before maturation; after up to 4 days of drying and 4 weeks of ripening, it will have lost nearly half its weight, shrinking down to around 80 grams (just under 3 ounces). Dehydration concentrates a cheese's flavor. The same is true of a fine aged steak; it steadily dries up, accentuating its natural flavors and bringing them to the fore.

Enzymes are certainly the most important contributors to the ripening of cheese, but there are other significant factors, including the molds that make blue cheeses blue and the propionic bacteria that give other cheeses their "eyes" (air holes). Among the different species of cheesemaking bacteria, there is an ebb and flow of populations as the cheese matures. A certain type of cheese might harbor a larger population of a particular species and thus

THE CHEMICAL REACTIONS CRUCIAL TO CHEESEMAKING

1. GLYCOLYSIS: Sugars are converted to acids; for example, in lactic fermentation where lactose (milk sugar) becomes lactic acid.
2. PROTEOLYSIS: Enzymes break down proteins. It happens in our stomachs as part of digestion and in nearly any acid solution, which is why marinating a piece of fish in lemon juice tenderizes or "cooks" it.
3. LIPOLYSIS: Enzymes break down fats. As in proteolysis, some of the resulting compounds yield flavors and aromas.

feature its effects; for example, cheeses with a preponderance of *Lactobacilli* will develop a rich, milky flavor and texture (Cheddar is a good example of this). Then there are the various types of molds that cause rind development and exterior blueing. The brine or *morge* (a solution of wine, cheese scraps, and sometimes whey) that is applied to washed-rind cheeses contains, literally, *hundreds* of species of bacteria that work their magic, ripening cheeses from the outside in while forming a protective layer. Part of the cheesemaker's subtle art is to achieve balance. If the pendulum tips too far in any direction, if the aging ceases and spoilage takes over, the pleasingly funky aromas and flavors of a cheese can suddenly turn to defects. This is the miracle of cheese aging.

Along the continuum of maturation—from soured milk to ripe cheese—there are different stages and gradations. In a dairy or farmhouse, maturation is often a two-stage process: the cheeses typically undergo a relatively brief sojourn (from 2 to 8 days) in a drying room, then spend a longer period in a ripening area or cave. Generally, the thicker and larger a cheese, the longer curing or aging it will require. The smaller the cheese, the more sensitive it is to fluctuating or unfavorable ripening conditions because of its higher surface-to-volume ratio.

Conditions in the ripening area or cave must be kept constant, with relatively moderate temperatures and high humidity. The cave must be sanitary, with no flies or extraneous germs, yeasts, and so on. It must be well ventilated to provide a fresh supply of oxygen for beneficial bacteria and molds and to clear away the gases—mostly ammonia and carbon dioxide—that are the by-products of cheese ripening. Bacteria and other microorganisms generally prefer a moist habitat, warm but not too hot; the higher the temperature within their range of tolerance, the faster they will multiply and the faster their chemical reactions will proceed. Bacteria usually thrive in a neutral environment, molds in an acidic one. Salt removes moisture and hinders bacterial development. All these factors come into play in determining optimum ripening conditions in a cave.

The gradual maturation process can last anywhere from a couple of weeks for the fresh goat cheeses to 6 years for Dutch Roomano. Cheese ripening—*affinage* in French, the language of cheese—is an art and a science that demands careful attention. Control of temperature and humidity is sometimes difficult to accomplish. The cheesemaker needs to keep a careful eye on changing weather conditions, especially in traditional farmhouse cheesemaking where there is much less reliance on machinery. If the weather is especially warm and humid (low pressure), for example, he or she must make sure the cheeses receive sufficient ventilation; if it's cool and dry (high pressure), the cheeses are well enough protected. Often, the only adjustments available to a cheesemaker in a rustic setting would be to open and close the windows of the cheese attic.

Nowadays, artisanal cheesemakers can employ modern technology for precise temperature and humidity control; it may be as simple as hooking a laptop computer up to a small refrigeration system. Nevertheless, the skills and techniques of fine cheesemaking have changed little over the years. The cheeses must still be carefully tended by turning them, salting, rubbing, washing, or bathing them and by tweaking the controls as varying conditions dictate.

WRAPPING AND PACKAGING

Soft-ripened cheeses such as Brie, Coulommiers, and Camembert, along with their washed-rind cousins such as Munster, Livarot, and Epoisses, whose pastes have a tendency to melt and go runny at room temperature, are usually wrapped in greaseproof paper then enclosed in a wood-chip or cardboard box to hold their shape. Large pressed, cooked cheeses such as Cheddar, Parmesan, and the Swiss mountain cheeses are protected by their rinds and can be packed in large crates, barrels, or cartons for shipping. Some of these are oiled or greased to provide an extra layer of protection on the outside of the rind. The major challenge with these cheeses is their size and weight; a wheel may measure anywhere from 18 to 36 inches across and weigh between 30 to 230 pounds. This is not an easy item to move around.

"MITEY" AND "MAGGOTY" CHEESES

SOME TO BE AVOIDED, SOME (SURPRISINGLY) TO BE PURSUED

T HERE are two small pests that can infest cheeses and, depending on who you talk to, either ruin them or improve them. Cheese flies (*Piophila casei,* aka "skippers") burrow into small cracks and lay their eggs, which in turn hatch maggots that feast on the cheese's interior and eventually turn into very small flies. The cheese mite (*Tyroglyphus siro)* is an insect that looks like a tiny spider. Maggots are more likely to invade a rough-surfaced cheese such as Stilton, Roquefort, or Cabrales, while mites go after hard-textured cheeses such as Cheddar. Individual mites are invisible to the naked eye, but a congregation of them looks like a brownish powderlike dust. One way to tell if dust on a cheese is mites is to make a small, neat pile of some of it and then check on it a couple of hours later. If it's moved, particularly into regimented lines, it's definitely the little bugs on the march. Otherwise, it's either dust or dead mites. In certain circles, maggots and/or mites are considered badges of honor, both for the noble old cheeses that attract them and for the people who are willing to eat them. Some connoisseurs of "mitey" cheese swear it tastes like curry; if you're curious, try the brownish rind of a Stilton.

Blue cheeses are wrapped in aluminum foil, sometimes with an outer layer of tissue paper. Goat cheeses are wrapped in paper and, particularly in the case of the fresh ones, carefully packed in small shipping crates or cartons because they can be so easily dented or squashed. The key to packaging fine cheeses is that they must be protected but not smothered.

AFFINAGE

Traditional cheesemaking artisans were just as likely to deliver their cheeses to a middleman—a cheese ripener—as they were to do the ripening themselves. Without great raw materials (pasture, animals, milk) you cannot make great cheese; without proper ripening, great cheese will never achieve its optimal state. So the cheese ripener is paramount. As usual, the French have a classy word for it—*affineur*—which to me echoes "refinement" and implies a sense of sophistication, mystery, and deep knowledge that comes only with experience. Like the *negociants* who bottled, packaged, aged, and marketed the fine wines of small producers, the *affineurs* would select the best cheeses from the mom-and-pop farms and small cooperative dairies, oversee the aging of those cheeses, and eventually bring them to market. Their talents extended from selection and grading of cheeses to ripening and marketing them.

What are the secrets of the *affineur*? These expert cheese selectors rely on an experienced eye, a sensitive nose, and discerning taste buds. Triers or graders, who rate cheeses and select only the best representatives of a type, taste them by drawing plugs out of a large drum or wheel with a small core-sampling tool called a cheese iron. (This is impossible with smaller cheeses.) The graders visually examine the development of the rind; they tap or thump a cheese to gauge its consistency (this is called "listening to a cheese"). Even before taking a taste, these visual and auditory clues can tell volumes about a cheese's stage of ripeness. Traditional *affineurs* still operate in the world of fine cheeses, mostly in France. They represent the all-important link between the cheesemaker and you, the consumer. In addition, the best gourmet shops and restaurants are all involved in *affinage* to some degree.

Stenciling the cheese to identify the maker and batch.

FOUR

PRACTICAL MATTERS:
BUYING,
STORING, AND SERVING
CHEESES

KNOW YOUR SOURCES

THE CLOSER YOU ARE to your source, literally and figuratively, the better product you will be able to obtain; anybody in the food business knows this well. In a physical sense, if you can't be close to the source of the cheese, you need to be completely aware and utterly confident of the shipping and handling. Due to the logistics of

The cave at Artisanal, with individual compartments offering specific temperature and humidity controls.

importation, it's not possible to buy foreign cheeses directly from their makers. With my American cheeses, however, I deal directly with the farm-house producers, which is exciting. As a consumer, you can "stay close to the source" by learning as much as possible about your cheeses and their producers. Just ask your merchants; if they don't have the information handy, they ought to be able to obtain it for you.

How do I select cheeses? Occasionally, I'll have to pursue them. But for the most part, since word got around in the mid nineties that Picholine was serious about its program, the cheeses have been finding me. In addition to those producers from whom I order directly, I deal with approximately seven importer-distributors virtually on a daily basis; their numbers are keyed in to my cell phone's speed-dial function. They're always on the lookout for new discoveries while remaining determined to uphold traditional standards—an approach we all share.

DICK ROGERS,
HANDS-ON IMPORTER

AN IMPORTER WHO CARES IS A CHEESE LOVER'S BEST FRIEND

DICK ROGERS is one of those people I rely on to deliver the best artisanal cheeses. For many years, Dick worked on Wall Street. When the company he ran was sold in the late eighties, he found himself looking for a job. His father-in-law owned some cheese-import licenses; Dick had a passion for food and wine tasting, which he had pursued extensively. So he decided to put these interests to work in a commercial enterprise.

One of Dick's first contacts in Italy was Giovanni Rocca who was among the most celebrated negociants in the Parmigiano-Reggiano business. Signor Rocca used to select cheeses for Rogers International, but he sold his name and business to a large dairy company. So Dick, a cheese neophyte not so long ago, is now closely involved in the selection process, weeding out the superior artisanal cheeses from among the predominance of "merely good" ones. To push the cheeses to a higher level takes extra trouble that isn't worthwhile for most producers. Instead, they look for efficiencies—replacing the local breed of red cows with special hybrid milk producers, keeping them in barns year-round, aging the cheeses just 2 years instead of 3 or more.

Dick recognized what was happening with Parmigiano-Reggiano. In the early nineties, he began establishing direct links with top-quality farm producers. He went to the hills, took pictures, visited the small *latterie* and the farms, broke open wheels of cheese and tasted them. He worked with local businesspeople to bring the farmers up to speed on the logistics of exporting their cheeses. With this type of hands-on work as the foundation, Dick created the Appennino trademark for his Italian artisanal cheeses and the Picos de España trademark for his Spanish ones, each named after a mountain range where key cheeses were produced. Look for them.

One of the big boards
at Picholine.

CHEESE SERVICE
IN RESTAURANTS

Some people first encounter fine cheeses at a gourmet shop, others discover them at a restaurant. While the quality and availability of fine cheeses at retail is increasing, there has been almost no traditional European-style cheese service in American restaurants until quite recently.

From the restaurant's point of view, cheese demands a great deal of extra time and expense with a relatively low profit margin. However, it also delivers tremendous value by generating public relations, customer traffic, and beverage sales. One risk that restaurateurs run is that diners may take extra time lingering over their cheeses at the end of a meal, thus delaying the all-important turnover of the table. On the other hand, that same diner might decide to purchase a beverage mate for the cheese . . . and that's where a restaurant can earn profits.

When we first started to develop the cheese program at Picholine, we expected that the waiters would have time to serve the cheese. But they were already consumed with their regular responsibilities, so it became part of my job as maître d'. Cheese got so big so fast that I had to concentrate on it almost exclusively. It continued to grow, and I enlisted a number of colleagues to help out; an assistant *fromager* was designated from the waitstaff.

You may wonder what a *maître fromager* really does—how it consumes all the waking hours of a reasonably intelligent, highly motivated individual with more than 2 decades of experience in the food-service industry (me).

My professional duties start early in the day and end late at night. First thing in the morning, I am on the phone with my cheese contacts—importers, distributors, cheesemakers, anyone else who might have information about the cheeses I need. I go into the restaurant around midday, reading about cheeses as I ride the subway, talking to cheese people on my cell phone as I walk.

Every day, as part of the process of preparing the cheese board, I take inventory of the cave. I keep track of each individual chunk, noting which ones are ripe and ready and which others need a little more time. The cave at Picholine harbors between 70 and 100 different cheese types at a given time—and I wish I could fit more. If that number falls to around fifty, say after a busy weekend, I know it's definitely time to get on the phone and reorder.

Our biggest receiving day is generally Tuesday—when we take several consolidated deliveries from distributors—but cheeses may arrive from producers or other sources on any weekday. My first duty on receiving is to break down the packages, open them up, and inspect the cheeses. If the Pouligny-Saint-Pierres arrive a little young with great potential, I'll get right back on the phone to order another case. If the cheeses are defective, overripe, or damaged beyond repair, I'll let my supplier know and arrange for a replacement shipment.

After lunch service, I set up the boards for the evening rush. We currently prepare two essentially duplicate boards with about fifty-five cheeses on each. On a busy evening, it's highly likely that at some point we'll have two or even three simultaneous requests for cheese service. When the place is in full swing, I'm often on call for 6 hours of unbroken cheese service, 6:30 p.m. until 12:30 a.m., pushing the cart, bending, cutting, serving, and delivering my "cheese spiel."

Whether I'm involved with cheese maintenance and prep or maître d' duties (I still fill in as necessary), when the call comes for cheese service I spring into action. The dishes have been cleared. We hand out a small cheese menu, and the diners wait with an air of anticipation and excitement. Then comes the arrival of the board, truly an impressive sight, especially for someone who's never seen—or even imagined—such a kaleidoscope of cultured milk. I've got to read my customers pretty quickly. If they want engaging repartee, I'll give it to them. Sometimes they'd rather continue their conversation and let me work in the background, selecting an assortment of cheeses without their input. Since there are so many cheeses on our big board, there is no way I can go through the entire lineup for each table. I'll always ask my customers whether they have any preferences or would rather just have me make some selections. I usually initiate the conversation by asking for parameters: Does anybody have favorite cheeses or types? Are there any they want to rule out? Normally, I'll give a three- or four-sentence summary of each cheese, highlighting the dominant flavors and key facts, then open up the floor to questions. I also try to place a particular cheese within a progression. Oftentimes, diners will choose by the look of the cheeses. Some people will ask me to create an eclectic plate with a few cheeses they've never had or even heard of. This is a good sign: my cheese eaters are curious and adventurous.

One of the most requested cheeses is Stilton. Although I feel a strong urge to offer an alternative—something I'm almost certain the diner has never tried and will enjoy immensely—it's also important to provide positive reinforcement, to encourage someone who's recognized a marker in the arcane world of fine cheeses. Most likely, the person who asks for Stilton has tried a good example of it at some point. They are headed in the right direction but they may not yet have reached the promised land. Perhaps they haven't tried Colston-Bassett, the crème de la crème. It's like the wine drinkers who order the proverbial "glass of Chardonnay." I want to honor their request and certainly I can serve them a good glass of Chardonnay. At the same time, I'd like to help expand their horizons. There's a whole world of white wines out there that are far more exciting. Ditto with cheeses.

The perennial favorite Stilton, a pasteurized-milk blue, is also known as "The King of English Cheeses."

Sometimes I'll take the diner's cue; for instance, if they ask for a good fresh goat cheese or a spicy blue. On the other hand, if someone asks for Brie, I politely inform them that I don't carry it. As a raw-milk cheese aged under 60 days, the real thing is actually illegal in the United States and the imitation ones aren't really up to snuff. "While we don't carry Brie," I might say, "I can offer you a cheese from the same region, which is the triple-crème Pierre-Robert." Or I may be able to offer another equally satisfying soft ripened cow's milk cheese.

After a meal, it's typical that one out of four diners at a table will order the cheese plate. When the board is wheeled up to the table, I can almost guarantee raised eyebrows. Sometimes I see looks of mild regret from the others. In any case, once the choices are made and the plate(s) served, there's always heightened curiosity. Fellow diners invariably witness the look of supreme satisfaction on the cheese eater's face, maybe a few "oohs" and "aahs." Then the sharing begins. Very often, we'll receive requests for another cheese plate—or at least an additional serving of a cheese.

I'll always try to solicit feedback. If I recommend a cheese, I want to know whether it worked. Everyone's palate is different; a young Roquefort may taste strong and salty to one person and somewhat bland to another. (I also try to remember my regulars' preferences.)

Whenever appropriate, I'll add anecdotes. It's always easier for someone to remember the details—a cheese's name, provenance, and specifications—when there's a story. Fortunately, many cheeses do have stories to tell. I like to tell people about Valençay, the goat's milk cheese from the village of the same name in the Loire Valley. It was originally made in a pyramid shape and was a favorite of Napoleon. When the emperor had a tough time of it in Egypt, the top of the pyramid was lopped off in deference to him. Other anecdotes include: the Great Cheddar Heist, where 274 prime cheeses were lifted from the Montgomery family farm in the dead of night; the fact that beginning in feudal times a number of cheeses were used as currency to settle debts and pay tithes; or the one about how *boules* of Mimolette were once used as cannonballs when the French navy ran out of the iron kind. (I don't know where I heard it, but it sure is a good story.)

What you should expect from your *maître fromager* is a board offering a fine selection of ripe cheeses, with variety across a fairly broad spectrum; friendly, informative, nonintrusive service with a personal touch—and hopefully some humor—when and where appropriate; well-maintained cheeses at or near peak ripeness served at room temperature with suitable accompaniments. The server should be able to offer accurate and relevant information about each cheese and to recommend a proper sequence of cheeses as well as matching beverages.

As for portions, the typical restaurant serving is between 1¼ and 1¾ ounces per cheese on a plate of anywhere from three to ten or more cheeses. The price for a plate of cheeses should be in the same range as what you'd pay at a retail shop for a pound of good cheese. This represents a fairly high markup, but it's not really such a stiff price to pay once you account for the accompaniments, selection, ripening, and expertise, not to mention the nutritional value and gustatory pleasure.

THE RUNAWAY CHARIOT

ON THE DANGERS OF SERVING MANY CHEESES IN GRAND STYLE

IN A busy dining room, things can get pretty hectic. One evening—a day when I received a large delivery—I was hurrying to finish up the last-minute touches on the cheese board when the first order came in. Although it was still early in the evening, it was high season at nearby Lincoln Center and the restaurant was full. I immediately rolled the board onto the floor. The *gueridon* (French for food-service trolley) was fully loaded with its 40-pound marble slab, on top of which was arranged another 30 pounds of cheese, not to mention all the accoutrements (cakes, dates, quince paste) along with silver service, china, and serviettes. As I was rounding a corner, one of the trolley's legs snapped and it collapsed. Most of the china smashed on the floor. Fortunately, I was able to grab the marble slab full of cheeses in midair. A hush descended on the entire dining room as I stood there balancing the cheese board. Two waiters rushed to my aid. The casualties were limited to one Roquefort, a hunk of Brin D'Amour, and a piece of Roncal. It could have been a lot worse.

YOUR FRIENDLY CHEESEMONGER:
WHAT TO EXPECT, WHAT TO DEMAND

If you want to experience the world's finest cheeses, it's absolutely essential that you find a retailer who takes good care of his cheeses and provides good service. Cheese should always be cut to order and you should be allowed to taste before you buy. Don't be bashful! If a taste isn't offered, ask for one. If it's refused, leave. (The only instance where tasting is impossible is with a small- to medium-sized cheese that is meant to be sold whole—Berthaut's Epoisses, for example.)

Many grocers think selling cheese is no different from selling books, CDs, or videos: buy it and put it on the shelf. That makes for a very unhappy cheese. Thoroughbred cheeses need a lot of attention. I started out merely serving the cheeses, but it became apparent very quickly that there was so much more to it. It bothers me to see good milk wasted on production of "cheese food" or bad cheesemaking. Likewise, I hate to see fine cheeses mishandled, ignored, suffocated, clumsily merchandised, poorly cut, haphazardly served, or badly stored to the point where they misrepresent themselves to the public.

A good retailer, like a maître fromager, realizes that a cheese is a living thing and treats it accordingly. Good retailers handle their cheeses with tender loving care, just as we do in our caves at the restaurants, and aim to sell them at their absolute peak. If the cheeses aren't perfectly ripe, the cheesemonger should either not sell them yet *or* let the customer know and offer advice on how to bring them to peak ripeness. You shouldn't have to concern yourself much about storing cheeses if you have a conscientious cheesemonger. You can buy what you need and not worry about committing the cardinal sin of wasting fine cheese.

The cheese shop should offer a wide range of cheeses as well as a staff that knows its stock. That said, I prefer a shop that carries 50 to 100 superb cheeses, caring for them well, to one that carries 500 cheeses and treats them indifferently.

"A cheesemonger worthy of the name will offer only cheeses that may be eaten within the next 48 hours. For no cheese, I repeat, no cheese will benefit from being kept too long at home."—PIERRE ANDROUËT, *Guide du Fromage*

HOW MUCH TO BUY

If you are unsure of how much cheese to buy, I recommend buying less. "What?!?" you might say, "Max, you're contradicting your mission statement!" No. A little bit of real cheese goes a long way.

How much to buy is largely a matter of common sense and a function of how you are going to serve your cheeses. For a tasting of five to ten cheeses, I recommend between 1 and 1½ ounces of each per person. With a more extensive lineup, the ration should be no more than ¾ ounce. (With a full ounce each of sixteen cheeses, each taster would consume a pound of cheese, which is too much.)

Clearly, very few people are going to take the trouble to weigh out small pieces of cheese on a kitchen scale. And it's very difficult to approximate the weight of a slice by size since cheeses have significant differences in densities. So here's a practical strategy: First, determine approximately how much of each cheese to buy per person; multiply that weight by the number of people being served, and buy that total weight. Then simply divide the cheese up into even slices or chunks once you're ready to serve it. If it is inconvenient for you to buy cheeses frequently, remember that the harder cheeses will have longer shelf lives.

NEAL'S YARD DAIRY

CHEESE PURVEYOR PAR EXTRAORDINAIRE TO LONDON AND THE WORLD

NEAL'S Yard is the brainchild of Nick Saunders, a visionary entrepreneur who was among those spearheading redevelopment of the old Covent Garden market and surrounding warehouses after they had fallen into disrepair in the early 1970s. Saunders bought twelve buildings in and around a small street called Neal's Yard and built them into thriving businesses, one of which was the dairy, founded in 1979. Although its milk came from outside sources, it represented a revival of sorts. Full-fledged dairies with their own pastures and herds had survived within the perimeters of London until World War II.

Neal's Yard soon evolved into a full-service cheese purveyor. The company stocks an impressive array of the best artisanal British cheeses and is well established as among the most significant cheese operations in Britain, if not the entire world. Staff members pay regular visits to farms and dairies throughout Britain and Ireland to select the best cheeses when young or maturing, which are ripened in the company's cellars.

Neal's Yard Dairy now exports cheeses to top retail shops and restaurants in the United States Members of its staff call on these businesses regularly to ensure its cheeses are well stocked and properly cared for. The cheeses I receive from Neal's Yard are almost always ripe and ready, which saves me the trouble (but also deprives me of the pleasure) of bringing them along myself.

ASSESSING A CHEESE

Before you lay down your hard-earned dollars for a hunk of gourmet cheese, you need to able to judge whether it's worthy of purchase. If you're buying from a top-notch, trustworthy cheesemonger, that selection process should have already have been performed for you. Nevertheless, take the time to examine the cheeses and their labels, wrappers, boxes, or rind markings for the following information:

■ Name, origin, and producer

■ Type of producer (e.g., is it farmhouse, local dairy or coop, factory or industrial?)

■ Status of cheese: is it protected or defined by laws or regulations, are there any official seals or symbols either on the label, wrapper, or box or stamped onto the cheese itself?

■ Type of milk

■ Fat content (expressed as "fat in dry matter")

Take a careful look at the cheese's outward appearance, note as many details as possible, and compare it with examples from your experience or the standards in Chapter 8. No cheese should appear brittle, bruised, or bumped; it should not have any cracks or major indentations; and it shouldn't be bulging or bloated from lack of air exchange. Soft-ripened, bloomy-rind, or washed-rind cheeses should not be hardened or dried up.

Max working the counter at Artisanal.

Some of my best cheeses arrive with travel fatigue. Maybe they've been held up by the FDA and languished in a warehouse for an extra week or two where, all wrapped up and too hot, they start to sweat, causing their paper wrappers to stick. Taleggio is one of the worst sufferers, with its wrapper almost always plastered to its rind, which can be very difficult to detach without seriously damaging the cheese (see "How to detach a stuck wrapper," page 77).

Sometimes cheeses are stored too cold. They're not dead, they're not ruined, but they're not 100 percent happy. All my cheeses have to be well adjusted and healthy before I even consider putting them on display. If you spy cheeses in a shop whose wrappers haven't been properly unstuck or that aren't being allowed to breathe, think twice before buying.

Sometimes a cheese that looks pretty bad on the outside is actually at its

TASTINGS
  5–10 cheeses: ¾ to 1 ounce
  15–20 cheeses: ½ to ¾ ounce
APPETIZER PLATES
  3–5 cheeses: 1 to 1½ ounces
MAIN COURSES
  3–5 cheeses: 1½ ounces
  5–10 cheeses: 1 to 1½ ounces
AFTER-DINNER PLATES
  3–5 cheeses: 1¼ to 1¾ ounces
  5–10 cheeses: 1 to 1½ ounce
  more than 10 cheeses: ½ to 1 ounce
  NOTE: All weights are per person per cheese, so simply multiply by the number of people you expect to serve. For denser cheeses, reduce the portions by as much as ½ ounce. Better to err on the side of caution and serve smaller pieces.

METRIC Conversion

100 grams = 3.5 ounces

150 grams = 5.3 ounces

250 grams = 8.8 ounces

500 grams = 17.6 ounces (or 1 pound, 1.6 ounces)

1 kilo = 2.2 pounds

To convert grams to ounces, divide by 28.35

To convert kilos to pounds, multiply by 2.2 (or divide by .454)

peak. Some of the moldy growths such as mucor, also known as *poil du chat* ("cat's fur" in French) because of its characteristic furry appearance, can appear alarming. Yet they are likely making an important contribution to the ripening of the cheese.

Too often, someone between the dairy and the consumer does something to the cheese that the cheesemaker would never have considered. Fine cheeses have glue splashed on them and labels slapped on top. Soft young cheeses are thrown in freezers or left unturned for 3 weeks (another sure route to suffocation). One of the biggest problems is the use of thick plastics for wrapping. The French are generally quite accomplished at packing their smaller, more delicate cheeses in crates so they are cushioned and can breathe. Yet these painstakingly prepared crates are often shrink-wrapped. Cheese coffins, *mes amis!* Many U.S. producers wrap their cheeses in semi-permeable paper or plastic, which allows for breathing; then they defeat the purpose by packing them in Styrofoam cooler-type boxes and taping them shut! More cheese coffins, full of dead cheeses.

RIPENESS

Exactly how and why cheeses ripen remains somewhat of a mystery. From the consumer's viewpoint, suffice it to say that cheese is a living, breathing foodstuff, rife with bacteria and enzymes, continually developing. As a cheese guy, my goal is to serve cheeses at their peak, what the French call *à point*. Therefore, judging the ripeness of cheeses is a crucial part of my job. You can apply some of the same criteria and techniques.

The concept of *à point,* implying a particular point of perfect ripeness, probably indicates more exactitude than is possible. Every real cheese is in a constant state of change, and a given cheese may pass through as many as six or seven stages of ripeness (see sidebar on page 80). With many cheeses, there is a definite peak where one would *prefer* to eat them, but they can be good to eat at several or more of their stages.

The softer, fresher, more moist cheeses are fleeting; they have narrow windows, usually a period of about a week, when they are just begging to be eaten. They should be supple and creamy (to borrow a phrase from Pierre Androuët), but not runny, which can mean they retained too much water, were subject to excessive lactic fermentation, and may be too sharp. Soft and semisoft mold-ripened cheeses ferment from the outside in. The question is: are they as soft in the middle as they are around their outside edges? If so, they are probably ripe. Harder, drier, longer-aged cheeses are sturdier and have broader windows. They undergo a more gradual ripening process; they retain less moisture and thus don't spoil as easily. Goat cheeses go through a remarkable series of transformations, with an ocean of difference between a soft, young goat cheese and a hard, sharp, flinty mature one.

Certain cheeses can be completely transformed in a relatively short period of time. (Likewise, they can go bad overnight if they're ignored.) A blue cheese can turn much bluer in a matter of minutes when its molds are suddenly exposed to air after a sojourn in the cave. A ripening soft or semisoft

HOW TO DETACH A STUCK WRAPPER

WITHOUT DAMAGING, RUINING, OR INSULTING THE TREASURE WITHIN

SHOULD you wind up with a cheese whose wrapper is stuck on, first set it down "face up" and gently try to pull the paper off. If this doesn't work, turn the cheese over and pry off a small portion of the wrapper—enough to cut through the rind directly without pushing the paper down into the cheese. Cut out a wedge of cheese, going through both top and bottom rind but not the bottom of the wrapper. Then lift up the cut portion free of the paper, leaving the loosened wrapper on the cutting surface, still attached to the main body of the cheese but exposed and ready to be peeled off. If this fails, simply take the sharp edges of the knife and carefully scrape away the wrapper or label, trying to avoid, as much as possible, wounding the rind underneath.

cheese can melt to a smooth, spoonable consistency after less than an hour at room temperature.

Timing is everything. Relatively fresh cheeses such as the Pouligny can have windows of no more than 3 to 5 days; washed-rind cheeses may have windows of less than a week; an Epoisses that arrives nearly ripe may only have a couple of days. Also to be taken into account vis-à-vis ripeness is the crucial matter of personal preference. I may take my Epoisses 24 hours closer to the compost heap than you do. Fine. No problem. Neither of us, however, wants one that's putrid.

Many of the world's finest cheeses—Munster and Pecorino, for example—are sold and consumed at a young, unripe stage, particularly in and around their zones of production. Some are sold in what amounts to two different versions: young and aged. Dutch farmhouse Gouda (Boeren Kaas) is a good example of this. Others have several or more age gradations. Various Italian cheeses are sold *fresco* (fresh) or *dolce* (sweet); *stagionato* (aged or matured); *vecchio* (old); or *stravecchio* (extra-old). Mahón, from the Spanish island of Menorca, is sold fresh (within 10 days); *curado,* or medium-ripe (at least 2

A trio of perfectly ripe goat cheeses from the Loire Valley in France: from left, Valençay, Selles-sur-Cher, and Sainte-Maure.

months old); cured (5 months); and *viejo* (old, which has been aged 10 months). Some of these cheeses—Gouda again comes to mind—are frankly not all that interesting until they acquire some age. It is true that the well-made young versions can be delightfully refreshing, in the sense that a glass of pure, unpasteurized fresh milk is refreshing. At the same time they're usually bland and lacking in the more dramatic flavors that come with maturity. Don't let a word like *subtle* fool you; sometimes it's no more than a euphemism for bland.

One of the first things you should consider is a cheese's seasonality. This is a simple calculation involving the animals' grazing season and the amount of time the cheese requires to age properly. If, for example, a certain cheese was made from the milk of goats that go out to pasture from May to September, and the cheese required 4 months' aging, then you could be sure that the best examples would be available from September until January. If you know the cows' optimum grazing season at their high Alpine pastures is the height of the summer and the cheese takes 6 months to ripen properly, then you know it's best consumed in midwinter. Nowadays, due to staggered breeding and other manipulations of the cheesemaking calendar, many fine cheeses are available year-round. The best cheeses, however, are still beholden to the ancient natural rhythms of the animals and their herders, cheesemakers, and ripeners.

There are many degrees of intensity possible from a given cheese as it ripens. At a recent tasting I conducted, a commotion arose when we served Queso de la Garrotxa, the great Catalonian goat cheese, at two very different stages of ripeness. One was so much darker and more honey-colored,

CHEESE AND AMMONIA

SOMETIMES JUST A GASP FOR AIR; SOMETIMES BEYOND THE LAST GASP

A S MENTIONED earlier, ammonia is just one of the by-products of the many chemical reactions that occur during cheese maturation. Early in my cheese education, I heeded frequent urgings to avoid *any* cheese with traces of ammonia odor. It is true that too much ammonia is associated with putrefaction, but in small dosages it is absolutely no problem, and likely indicates a cheese that has reached a mature stage and may even be perfectly ripe. If a tightly wrapped cheese smells of ammonia, it might simply be asking for a breath of fresh air. The ammonia may be coming from the outer layer of the rind and may very quickly dissipate when the cheese is unwrapped. By the same token, there is a point at which a cheese is overly ammoniated—it is dead, gone, suffocated beyond hope for resuscitation. If a cheese remains hard, bitter, and riddled with ammonia even after it's been allowed to air out, this is probably the case. For years, many of the Brie-type cheeses imported into this country featured this soupçon of Mr. Clean, leaving a bad general impression in the public's eye.

drier, and stronger in flavor than its younger, paler counterpart that a few people in the audience were convinced they were two distinct cheeses. The key thing to remember is that as it ripens, a cheese desiccates, hardens, and darkens, and its flavors and aromas are concentrated and intensified.

OVERRIPENESS

Overripe cheeses become sharp, rancid, ammoniacal, or "saponified" (soapy-textured and -flavored). Rancidity comes largely from oxygenation of fats. Washed-rind cheeses such as Epoisses, Munster, and Livarot should be moist and radiant on the exterior. Their rinds should be intact and the cheeses shouldn't be bulging, collapsing, or immutably melded to their wrappers or containers. They should only become spoonable when *à point* and after they've been left at room temperature for at least an hour. If they arrive misshapen or excessively runny, then they're overripe. Their smell should be pronounced, pungent, and immediately noticeable but not rotten, putrid,

SEVEN DEGREES OF RIPENESS

FOR EVERY CHEESE, THERE IS A SEASON (OR A DAY)

DEGREES of ripeness apply to soft-ripened cheeses but are not particularly relevant for the harder, aged ones. With a longer-aged cheese such as Parmesan or Roomano, you won't even see it at Stages 1 and 2; those occurred many months ago when the cheese was quietly resting in the ripening room. Producers of these types, which include hard mountain cheeses and Pyrenées-style sheep cheeses, generally don't release them until they're ready to eat. On the other hand, since peak ripeness for fresh goat's milk cheeses lasts just a few days, we see them mostly at Stages 3 to 5; occasionally you'll see some Stage 2s or Stage 6s, when they are definitely under-ripe and overripe, respectively.

1. Too young. The cheese is fully formed but it's like taking your bread out of the oven when it's still doughy.
2. Beginning to show character, some flavors starting to emerge. A "nice," tender stage where it could be eaten, but you're better off waiting.

Goat cheeses are very moist. Many soft cheeses are spongy or a bit too firm and resistant.
3. The prelude, where the melody is heard but the rich symphonic harmonies haven't yet been introduced. Texturewise, a goat cheese such as Sainte-Maure has too much give; it is still a little too melting or moist to cut properly.
4. Peak, memorable, exemplary. Get it while you can! The Sainte-Maure would be firm yet still moist. Washed-rind cheeses such as Taleggio and Munster start to smell funky, which belies their glorious flavors.
5. Still tasty but past peak. You start to hear some of the minor keys, a hint of sadness in the melody. The Sainte-Maure is hardening. The Lancashire is becoming a bit brittle.
6. Still edible, but definitely fading. An Epoisses or other "stinky cheese" may show some putrescence. The Sainte-Maure is chalky with some harshness.
7. Too far gone, dead, *fuhgedaboudit*. The Sainte-Maure is calcified; the stinkers are unbearable.

CHEESE FAULTS

1. PHYSICAL DEFECTS:
   - bulging, bloating, heaving
   - flat or collapsed shape
   - unwanted interior holes or fissures
   - cracked and/or slimy or drying, pockmarked, rough, leathery rinds
   - unwanted molds, particularly black ones
   - discoloration or uneven coloration of rind or paste (spotty, smeary, mottled)
   - uneven texture, cracking or bulging of paste
   - inappropriate texture of paste, such as brittle, chalky, pasty, greasy or soapy, lumpy, mealy, rubbery (tough or corky), spongy, sticky
   - reddening of paste
   - excessively open texture in hard cheeses or hard texture in soft ones
   - maggots or mites (appearing as a brownish, curry powderlike dust)
2. AROMA:
   - ammoniacal
   - excessively strong, acrid, pungent, sour, putrid, or barnyardy odor
3. FLAVOR:
   - too strong (harsh) or too weak (flat)
   - excessively sour (acidic) or bitter or salty
   - ammoniacal
   - off flavors from tainted milk, that is, flavors that are not normally associated with milk or cheese, for example onion, garlic, metallic, musty, stale, yeasty, weedy, burnt, sulphurous (rotten eggs)
   - oxidation ("cardboardy," rancid)
   - fermented or fruity

or persistently ammoniacal. If at all possible, open their boxes and take a whiff. A definite barnyardy odor is acceptable; the smell of deathly decay is not. The bottom line is they should smell strong but not awful or unpleasant.

With goat cheeses, some blue or gray mold on the exterior is perfectly all right. Fresh goat cheeses are white as the driven snow, moist and soft, relatively bland in flavor. Older aged goat cheeses may become too hard, too dry, or too "goaty" for some people's liking.

Dryness or graininess is usually a bad sign except in a Parmesan or Grana-type cheese. Beware if the cheese is not uniform in texture or doesn't conform to its standards (see Chapter 8)—for example if it's uncharacteristically hard or soft or runny or salty. Also be on the lookout for excessive flavors; black exterior mold; and blue, green, or gray interior mold except in a blue cheese. (Occasionally, some blue will be acceptable, if not desirable, in a nonblue.)

STORAGE

The most common advice from cheese experts is "buy little and often" and "buy only what you need for a given occasion." In other words, the first rule of home cheese storage is—*don't!* Far better to appreciate one precious nugget of gloriously ripened cheese *à point* and finish it than put a leftover in the fridge, forget about it, and go back to it when it's questionable.

Cheeses should be purchased at or near their peak and consumed while they're still peaking. Any delay is essentially a continuation of *affinage;* even under perfect cave conditions, which can be difficult to duplicate at home, cheeses will naturally continue to ripen and eventually deteriorate. If anything, you might buy a cheese when it's a little young. But avoid it if it's a little old since there is, of course, no way of reversing the ripening process. In this respect, selecting cheeses is not unlike shopping for fresh-cut flowers: buy them short of their peak and hope that they'll offer a longer window of appreciation.

The two atmospheric conditions important to cheese storage are temperature and humidity. In general, cheeses are happiest at temperatures of 45 to 60 degrees F and relative humidity of 80 percent or more. Storage conditions should be humid but not too wet with moderate air circulation and temperature. If it's too cold, the cheeses will dry out and crack; too warm and they'll ooze butterfat, smell bad, and feel soft, cloying, mushy, or, as they say in England, "pappy."

One of the main reasons you want to avoid having to store cheeses is that, let's face it, the home refrigerator is *not* the ideal place for them. It is too harsh of an environment—way too dry, cold, and airless for most cheeses. Home refrigerators usually maintain around 30 percent humidity and a temperature of around 38 degrees, give or take a few. Cheese is a living thing, which

SHRINK-WRAPPING IS BAD FOR CHEESES!

The cheeses from some of my favorite artisan cheesemakers, such as Cynthia and David Major, arrive whole, unwrapped, and lovingly packed in old cardboard boxes full of straw. The fragrance is sweet and fresh. Cheeses should be allowed to breathe during shipping, and they should enjoy stable atmospheric conditions—a damp, dark environment with gentle air circulation is ideal. This makes all the difference in the world. (When sourcing a cheese, I ask how it's wrapped.)

is why it cannot survive very long if shut in a cold, airless space like the refrigerator. The key factor regarding lower temperatures, though, is that colder air tends to be drier, and this poses the greatest danger to fine cheeses.

Before you resort to refrigeration, consider that cheeses can be stored in all kinds of places—cellars, garages, sheds, even windowsills—as long as the temperature is moderate, the humidity is high enough, and there is no direct exposure to sunlight. I learned a number of years ago that it's a bad idea to buy milk in glass jars due to the spoiling effect of light exposure (oxidation). Ditto with cheeses: they like the dark. If you have a cool, clean, dark, fairly humid place in your house—the corner of the basement, for example (as long as it isn't right next to a furnace)—it's probably a better place for your cheeses than the fridge. Just make sure there aren't any varmints or household pets that can get at it. In that case, a hanging basket would be an ideal solution, allowing for air circulation while keeping the goodies out of harm's way.

Although any cheese will continue to mature past its prime if left in storage, it will age much more gracefully if it is allowed to breathe a little. Cheese needs ventilation but no drafts. The old-fashioned glass "bells" that cover a plate are lovely ornaments. They keep the flies off the cheese and the smell inside, but they don't let in enough air.

If you must store a cheese in the fridge, the best place is in the vegetable drawer, which contains more moisture, especially when there are vegetables or other cheeses in there. If it's a particularly precious cheese and you want to keep it pristine for a short period of time—say, a few hours or overnight—then consider raising the temperature of your refrigerator.

As mentioned, encasing a cheese entirely in heavy, impermeable plastic for any significant period of time can suffocate it, causing it to become soggy and smelly and to produce off flavors. Any exposed paste, however, needs to be protected against drying. For short-term storage of larger chunks of hard or semihard cheeses, I wrap only the cut surfaces with a light-weight plastic cling wrap, leaving the rind exposed so the cheese can breathe. Smaller pieces and softer, washed- and bloomy-rind cheeses should be wrapped snugly but not too tightly first in some type of lightly waxed, grease-proof paper; then, on top of that, in light plastic cling wrap. This creates enough of an air pocket that the cheese won't suffocate overnight. I change these wrappings every day. But my cheeses do spend the majority of their waking hours sitting on the board exposed to air at room temperature and are eaten as soon as possible.

Like human beings, the younger cheeses have a higher metabolic rate and need to respire more. The older cheeses are less "active" and can be wrapped more tightly for longer periods.

Butcher paper, which is designed to resist blood and fat, is fairly heavy and waxed and can work well for the harder, more dense cheeses. Plain, unwaxed parchment paper is also suitable for harder cheeses. Any cheese where the rind is moist or sticky or where the integrity of the cheese is in

Ideal Storage Conditions

BLUES:
42°–46°F; 85–95 percent humidity

SOFT-RIPENED:
50°–52°F; 80–90 percent humidity

WASHED-RIND:
50°–55°F; 90+ percent humidity

HARD, AGED:
55°–60°F; 80+ percent humidity

"Once the cheese you want is safely bedded down, you might look upon the docile creature and wonder whether you have made the right decision. This is the Robert Mitchum effect. Not a great deal of action on the outside but plenty of seething turmoil within."—DOMINIC COYTE, Neal's Yard Dairy

danger of being compromised calls for some sort of lightly waxed, grease-resistant paper such as pastry paper, which is thinner than butcher paper. New wraps developed for cheese have improved dramatically. Some have a higher paper-to-plastic ratio, making them more permeable. Some wraps have tiny holes large enough to allow for air to pass through but small enough to prevent cheese seepage. Neal's Yard Dairy uses a lightly waxed French paper, specifically designed for cheese, which is glossy on one side to avoid sticking. It allows the cheeses to breathe while retaining more moisture than plain papers, which makes it an ideal wrapping.

Blue cheeses are the notable exceptions and should be wrapped in plastic or foil. Occasionally it's okay to use aluminum foil on other cheeses that are not originally encased in foil, particularly if the cheese is very soft and collapsing or threatening to collapse, in which case wrapping it gently but snugly will help it keep its form.

HOLDING ON TO THE BLUES

THE UNIQUE STORAGE REQUIREMENTS OF THE VEINED CHEESES

GENERALLY, blue cheeses have no protective skin—no washed or moldy rind—and they aren't pressed, which means they carry a lot of water. Many blues, particularly Roquefort, arrive wrapped in foil and quite moist. They drizzle and drool, which is why after I unwrap them I often place them on a cloth napkin to drain. They can lose up to 30 percent of their weight this way (weight which, by the way, you've already paid for).

Because they usually hold more moisture and are susceptible to excessive molding, blues are stored at lower temperatures than other types.

Mature blues should be stored below 42 degrees F. This temperature does expose them to the risk of drying, however. Therefore, they also need to be wrapped snugly. A blue that's been left out for an entire evening, even after it's wrapped and stored overnight, will still taste good but will be much bluer the next day. It will also be drier and not as well balanced. Once it goes further blue it can never go back. Colder storage retards the "blueing," so if you have a blue that's gone about as far as you want it to, this is a good temporary solution.

DO'S AND DON'TS OF CHEESE STORAGE

Don't:
—Freeze your cheeses
—Let them dry out
—Expose them to strong light or temperature fluctuations or to excessively high or low temperatures
—Suffocate them in impermeable plastic wrap

Do:
—Check on your cheeses every day
—Rewrap them if necessary
—Allow them some air exchange
—Give them a bath if they're too dry

Washed-rind cheeses like their humidity levels high—at 90 percent or more. This was their nursery environment, the one that helped them develop their blushing faces in the first place. Cheeses that are drying out should be moved to a damper environment. Some experts report success in protecting these vulnerable types from drying by draping them with a damp cloth or towel and placing them in cardboard boxes. This traps some moisture and creates a more friendly microclimate.

Trying to resuscitate a cheese that has suffered multiple injuries is virtually impossible. If it isn't irreversibly cracked, though, it can be rescued. With a rind that is a little dry or tight or doesn't soften up quickly at room temperature, the cheese may need a bath, either in some water or wine, beer, marc, brandy, or some other alcoholic beverage.

Such washed-rind cheeses as Livarot, Pont L'Evêque, Epoisses, Pavé D'Auge, and Maroilles all come in cute little boxes wherein they enjoy their own personal biospheres. If a cheese comes in a box, whenever possible it should be kept in it. When purchased, however, the box should be opened. Unwrap the cheese and, particularly if the paper is overly sticky or if there is any print (which contains ink) on the label, replace the wrapper with a clean piece of paper.

When I examine a new arrival, I always pick it up, turn it over, and check all its surfaces. If its bottom is wetter than its top, it has probably been resting that way for too long. Then I'm sure to turn the cheese, with the drier side down, so the moisture can trickle down and the cheese can stay as uniformly hydrated as possible.

Always cut a cheese with storage in mind; in other words, try to minimize the surface area that is exposed, especially with softer cheeses. Even if they're properly covered, cut surfaces will eventually dry out, turning hard and crusty. Take your time unwrapping a cut cheese, and be sure to trim off any dried-out surfaces.

EQUIPMENT AND ACCESSORIES

I'm not big on fancy accessories or gimmicks. Rather than acquiring wire cutters, cheese planes, and so forth, I'd like to see aspiring connoisseurs spend their money on cheeses so they can expand their tasting experience. Even if you plan to get fairly serious about cheese, you can manage on a very basic kit: a sharp knife or two and a cutting board.

I find the most useful knives for cutting small- to medium-sized cheeses are the standard sharp, pointy steak knives. It's good to have three or four of those handy if you plan to serve an array of fifteen to thirty cheeses. For medium to large cheeses, you need a larger, sturdier kitchen knife. I recommend a chef's knife suitable for chopping, or the carving type, which has a thinner blade. One or two large kitchen knives will do for a tasting. I always have some clean cloth napkins handy, which I use to wipe my knives in between trimming or cutting cheeses to serve; these cloths are also useful for draining cheeses that weep. In the unlikely event you plan to break open big cheeses—say, a full wheel of Boeren Kaas or drum of Cheddar—you might consider investing in one of those large double-handled cheese knives we call a guillotine. It's one of the few specialty tools I use at the restaurant. There is also a smaller wedged-shaped knife used for prying workable chunks from drums of Parmesan.

For storage, you might buy a few sealable plastic storage containers that fit conveniently in your refrigerator; these can be useful in the event you want to refrigerate a number of cheeses together and there's no room in the vegetable compartment. And, of course, you'll need lightweight plastic wrap or a suitable wrapping paper in case of leftovers.

Other accessories you might want to consider for tastings are larger wooden boards for cutting and serving, trays, marble slabs, and baskets—both for cheese and its accompaniments. Also, I recommend donning an apron, as cheese can be hard on your clothing.

You need to cut a lot of cheese to make this tool a worthwhile investment, but I do: a marble-based wire cutter saves a lot of aggravation when dividing up a full wheel of Valdeón.

SERVING CHEESES

There are a few commonsense guidelines to follow. First, cheese should always be cut fresh. Trust me, there *is* a difference. As mentioned previously, cheese is alive and breathing, and exposure to air can transform it by the minute—through oxidation of its surfaces or dispersion of its aromas. Once cheeses are cut, their surfaces start to dry out. Soft cheeses start to congeal. Recently, many wine lovers have realized that the old convention of "allowing the wine to breathe" by decanting it well in advance is no longer valid. The objective now is to get that wine from the bottle into the glass quickly and observe the miracle of its evolution there. Same thing with cheese.

Try to avoid serving leftover pieces of cheese from a previous plate or presentation, regardless of how well they might have been stored. If you must serve leftovers, trim them carefully.

Cheeses should always be served at room temperature, 62 to 75 degrees F. I recommend presenting them at the middle of that range, say about 70 degrees. Cold masks flavor; therefore, cheeses simply don't taste as good

CHEESE AND MOLD

FROM A LIGHT DUSTING OF BLOOM TO FULL-BLOWN MAGGOTS

A S THE old saying goes, "The mold will find the cheese." If a cheese has the ability to attract the *P. roquefortii* (or whatever indigenous mold strain is lurking around) out of the air, that means it's probably a good one. A little bit of blue mold on the exterior of a cheese is nothing to be alarmed about. Once it invades the interior, however, it can quite easily come to dominate a cheese's flavor and that might not be to your liking. Some cheeses attract just a dusting of light-colored mold—a "bloom"—on their cut surfaces. Again, this is no problem; but if it bothers you, it can easily be brushed or cut off. If too much mold accumulates, it indicates either the temperature is too high or the storage space is too humid and airless, which calls for an adjustment.

Mold spores from a blue cheese will fly around and eventually colonize other pieces of cheese. Some caseophiles actually encourage this blueing; it works beautifully in some non-blues, but horribly in others. British cheese lovers have been known to prick or slightly crack a chunk of their favorite Cheddar or Cheshire which aerates the cheese and encourages the mold. They find an appropriate storage spot, wait a few weeks, and—*voilà*—they have a good "homemade blue." These are the so-called vinney (or vinny) cheeses of British lore. Taking this passion for decay a step further, *fanaticos* of Spanish Cabrales enjoy their cheese with maggots. They allow cheese flies to lay their eggs and the eggs to hatch. Eating maggot-infested cheese is strictly hardcore—*muy macho*.

when they're cold. The rule for home consumption is to give a refrigerated cheese at least an hour to warm up to room temperature before serving it.

How many knives does one need at a given serving? Most hard cheeses can share, but the other categories ought to each have a separate knife—one for the fresh white goat's milks, one for the blue(s), one for the bloomy rinds, one for the washed rinds. I especially recommend a separate knife for each of the "stinky" varieties—or at least a thorough wipe with a napkin after each cheese is sliced.

The harder cheeses need to be sliced thin. This renders their density more palatable, their concentrated textures and flavors more accessible to the taste buds. With crumbly, hard, aged cheeses such as Cheddar, Parmesan, and Boeren Kaas, it is not always possible to carve a delicate thin slice; nevertheless, they should be served in small wedges or chunks due to their formidable impact in the mouth. Soft-ripened cheeses of larger diameter can be served in long, thin wedges. The smaller soft cheeses and their washed-rind cousins should be served in little wedges, no more than an inch long at the outer edge or circumference.

THE CHEESE PLATE

As discussed more fully in Chapter 6, the classic progression in any tasting is from simpler to more complex, younger to older, lighter to heavier, milder to stronger. It works for wines as well as for cheeses. Nine times out of ten, I'll organize a plate this way, beginning at the bottom—in the six o'clock position—and proceeding clockwise. I always recommend first sampling the cheeses in the prescribed order. Then, there's absolutely nothing wrong with jumping around, experimenting, even going backward. Sometimes, you'll experience a pleasant surprise or discover a new preference. Other times, you'll simply confirm why the conventional order makes the most sense.

To plan the sequence of cheeses on a plate, first refer to the section entitled "Progression" on page 109 in the next chapter. This is where you'll find the theory. Then read up on each cheese in Chapter 8 or—if it's not included there, get as much information as possible from your cheesemonger. Think of a projected order for the cheeses. Finally, and most important, taste them to test your progression. Then rearrange if necessary.

When and where should cheese be served? I can't think of any occasion—breakfast, lunch, snack, appetizer, dinner, dessert, formal occasion, casual meal, picnic—that wouldn't be enhanced by cheese. In Chapter 7, "The Cheese Course," you'll find suggestions of cheese plates for numerous occasions.

It's probably fairly obvious by now that I'm a big proponent of the European-style after-dinner cheese plate. This doesn't rule out serving fine table cheeses during cocktail hour or as appetizers. (Obviously, better them than your run-of-the-mill block of Swiss cheese on a toothpick.) I would counsel you, however, to proceed with caution. People are hungry and eager before a meal, and they don't need extra encouragement to eat or drink too much. Presentation and service should be modest and low-key. Keep the portions small, particularly with the more assertive washed-rind types. This said, you can get away with serving rich cheeses such as the triple crèmes. They're mild and, after all, very close to butter, which is often enjoyed with bread at the start of a meal.

For appetizers, serve three to five cheeses, and don't offer any more than 1 ounce of each cheese per person—preferably only half an ounce. If possible, have a designated cheese-server for any stand-up party situation. If not, at least be prepared to clean up and maintain the cheese tray every few minutes. The old standby cocktail-hour method of plunking a few wedges of cheese onto a board, dropping a knife alongside, and inviting everyone to help themselves can get messy. It certainly doesn't flatter your cheeses. I highly recommend separate plates, dedicated knives and forks, and pre-cut portions—regardless of the occasion.

At some point, caseophiles may want to serve fine table cheese as the centerpieces of a meal. For breakfast, I recommend from one to three cheeses, with fruit or bread accompaniments. For lunch or light supper, try three to five cheeses, with a soup or appetizer course and a salad. A full-fledged after-dinner cheese plate can contain from five to ten cheeses, sometimes even twelve. If you want to make a main course of it, select the same number of cheeses and increase the amounts to as much as 1¾ ounces per serving. When planning a cheese meal, make sure your other courses include foods with fiber—really the only essential nutrient *not* provided by cheese.

If you are presenting any more than a few cheeses, I would recommend restraint in all other areas leading up to and following the cheese course. Accompaniments, particularly bread, can be served in pass-around bowls, baskets, or plates. This signals they're optional—as they should be. If you're serving a special accompaniment, such as a small slice or chunk of quince paste, a ripe fig, dates, a small bunch of grapes, or a dollop of chutney, it can be arranged on the plate alongside the cheeses or, on a more crowded plate of five to ten cheeses, placed ceremoniously in the center of the plate. Otherwise, accompaniments should be served separately on the side. If you want to make cheese the centerpiece of a meal, simply serve it as the main course after the soup or appetizer course and followed by a nice green salad.

For a cheese course, choose a plate that is of a solid neutral color. I usually recommend a white plate, but there's nothing wrong with colors as long as you keep it simple. I have a good friend whose eyesight isn't so good and

she likes to serve her cheese courses on dark blue plates. Since cheeses are mostly light-colored—white, yellow, gold, or orange—the darker plate gives her more contrast so she can see the cheeses better.

Most small- and medium-sized cheeses can be cut in wedges, which should be placed with their "noses" pointing to the center of the plate and their rind sides or bases toward the rim. When the cheese comes in oversized wheels—for example, Gruyère—you'll be cutting from a block or wedge and you'll want to make long, thin rectangular slices rather than small wedges. If possible, one of the short ends of this julienned slice should consist of rind. Logs of goat cheese should be cross-sectioned—that is, sliced into buttons or disks. Pyramids should be cross-sectioned vertically—sliced from top to bottom. Sometimes, it's possible to stand these vertical wedges up, a visually arresting presentation. If the cheese is a spoonable soft type, sometimes I'll serve the portion in its own little ramekin and set the ramekin on the plate in its proper position. I always like to present part of the rind, whether or not it's meant to be eaten. It gives the plate visual contrast and also helps distinguish and identify individual cheeses.

The cheeses should be evenly spaced around the plate, on the inside of the rim, in the order you want to present them. Use a regular dinner plate unless the course consists of three or fewer cheeses, in which case you can

One of the more frequently requested cheeses, and for good reason: Parmigiano-Reggiano, usually referred to as Parmesan, is considered by many "The King of Cheeses."

employ salad plates. For utensils, provide a smaller version of a regular dinner knife or a butter knife. You may also offer salad-sized forks, which can be useful for eating accompaniments but are strictly optional for cheese; the small knife is really meant to be the all-purpose cheese-course utensil.

Should you eat the rinds? There's a fair amount of disagreement among experts on this. Steve Jenkins, one of America's great cheese men, doesn't eat the rinds. Patrick Rance recommended at least tasting them. Pierre Androuët, on the other hand, was completely against it. From his *Guide du Fromage:* "*When do you eat the rind of the cheese?* Never. Turn a deaf ear to those who greedily tell you, 'That's the best part!'" True, the rinds contain more potential pathogens, but I enjoy eating many of them anyway (the rinds, that is). In assessing a cheese, I always taste the paste all the way up to the rind. In some cheeses, the surface just beneath the rind can be unappetizing. If it's good, though, I'll often continue through the rind. I can't stand to waste cheese. Plus I'm always curious. The rinds frequently offer an interesting perspective on the rest of the cheese. Often, a lot of a cheese's essential flavor is concentrated in there.

A perfect little tasting, from left: Nancy's Hudson Valley Camembert, Zamorano, and Livarot, served with apple slices.

CUTTING ORDER

PROCEED FROM HARDEST TO SOFTEST AND SAVE THE BLUES FOR LAST

I N SETTING up a cheese board, I always follow an order of cutting, generally beginning with the hardest and proceeding in descending order to the softest. For example, cut the Mimolette before the Fontina since the former will not change as fast. Cut the Roncal before the Cheddar; it holds up better. Here's how I proceed:

1. Hard cow's and sheep's milk cheeses first (Berkswell, Parmesan, Sbrinz, Zamorano)
2. Semihard cheeses in the traditional British farmhouse style (Lancaster, Double Gloucester, etc.)
3. Semisoft cheeses such as Fontina D'Aosta and Tomme de Savoie
4. Bloomy-rind cheeses (Roucoulons, Pierre-Robert)
5. Soft cheeses (Camembert, Munster, Pavé D'Auge, Valençay, and other fresh goat cheeses)
6. Blues

If I were cutting down full wheels of cheese, I would also take into account that, once cut, certain cheeses dry, congeal, or otherwise decompose faster than others. The surface of a Fontina closes up very fast on contact with air; a Lancashire will dry and crumble on its cut surfaces, opening out rather than closing down. Some soft cheeses, because of their relatively higher water count, hold up very well at least in terms of visual appeal—they look fresh. Drafty rooms (or open-air picnics) can hurt, of course. I cut the blues last of all, primarily for two reasons: first, to keep the blue in them and not transfer it to the nonblues (a tiny amount of mold can easily start a growth on an otherwise pristine piece of cheese); second, to control the metabolism of the molds. The only instance where I can see cutting blues early is when the veining might be underdeveloped to the point where the cheese could benefit from the added zing of some further blueing.

THE CHEESE TASTING

If you want to stage a tasting with a generous selection of fine cheeses and matching beverages, you need to keep the focus squarely on the cheese. In other words, don't try to make it a multitiered event with music, dancing, umbrella drinks, and a four-course menu. Keep it simple. There should be few if any accompaniments and no distractions; stick with cheese and possibly a little bit of bread.

You may want to plan a cheese tasting relatively far in advance so as to arrange for all the "extracurriculars"—beverages, accompaniments, service, and so forth. You can select the wines months ahead; you're pretty well assured of when a vintage will be ready and what to expect. With the cheeses, however, be prepared to make last-minute adjustments according to availability and ripeness. Stay flexible! Say you have Berthaut's Epoisses on your tasting roster. The day of the event arrives, you go to the store and discover the Epoisses is either sold out, not ripe yet, or too far gone. Don't despair. There will be other cheeses you can substitute.

Be sure to buy your cheeses—particularly the soft-ripened types—as close as possible to the date of your tasting. If you buy them early, they have a perverse tendency to fade the day of the event or, conversely, they will not have reached their full glory.

At your tasting, you should have a definite plan for doling out the precious morsels. Normally, I'll precut the cheeses and either serve them to each individual on prearranged plates, as we do at the restaurant, or I'll send out a serving plate with the exact number of slices or chunks as there are occupants at each table. Then the tasters can help themselves from the serving plate. The cheeses will have rested at room temperature for several hours and have been sliced within an hour of tasting time. This scenario has one drawback: the tasters miss out on the distinct pleasure of enjoying fresh-cut cheeses.

With all of this in mind, I once tried a tasting for a group of around twenty-five caseophiles. I thought it might be fun to allow the group to cut their own. They seemed to understand my instructions and they obviously enjoyed discovering the different shapes, sizes, textures, colors, and aromas; they did make a bit of a mess, though. Cheese was wasted—a mortal sin. It was difficult for them to judge what size portion to take of each cheese. Some of the initial cheeses they tasted were so delicious they could not resist helping themselves immediately to seconds. Later in the tasting, some of them were in trouble: they were too full. They couldn't possibly stomach another piece of cheese, yet there were several more phenomenal specimens begging to be sampled.

So, realistically, the best way to conduct a tasting is to cut the cheeses

STARTING AT SIX

FOR SOME reason, cheese plates have usually been organized with Cheese Number 1 in the twelve o'clock position. This is the antithesis of the traditional *food* presentation, which places the primary or highlighted element at six o'clock. This is the position closest to the mouth and thus the one most likely to be sampled first. Starting at six o'clock seems to make the most sense to me, practically and intuitively, so it's the system I use.

into small portions and arrange them carefully in the intended order on individual plates. (Remember to place Cheese Number 1 in the six o'clock position on the plate, and make sure you indicate where tasters are supposed to dive in.) Don't underestimate the amount of work this takes, which is another reason to keep the sideshows to a minimum; organizing a proper tasting demands your full attention and energy. If possible, recruit the help of a fellow cheeselover. One or both of you can name and briefly describe the cheeses. A formal speech or announcement isn't necessary, but be prepared to answer questions. Or, if you prefer to be superorganized, you can create a labeling system. When I organize larger tastings, I hand out a list of cheeses, numbered within each flight or course. I make sure to point out Cheese Number 1, holding up my plate. For a one-course tasting, you might consider creating a master plate as a reference, with each cheese labeled.

Another pitfall of cheese tastings is that the tasters have a tendency to get carried away and jump ahead right to the zenith. Due to irresistible curiosity and/or enthusiasm, they may inadvertently ignore the recommended progression. This can backfire. How can even the most discriminating palate divine the nuances in flavor of a Single Gloucester after having snuck a premature nibble of Cabrales? Not to denigrate the fullness of a Smart's Single Gloucester, but it possesses a subtlety that simply can't follow the showstopping qualities of this Asturian blue.

"The thing about traditionally made cheeses is they never tire of laying on a surprise or two. Turn your back for a moment and they'll be up to no good, creating dodgy flavours, ripening quicker than expected, blossoming from the dull to the divine." —DOMINIC COYTE, Neal's Yard Dairy

FIVE | TASTING

WHEN I RECEIVED the mandate in 1994 to transform the three-star Picholine into a major player in the cheese world, I didn't know much more than many of my customers about the world's finest cheeses. I was immediately thrust into the role of expert. People began asking me pointed questions and they expected answers. I didn't have the option of serving an apprenticeship under a great *maître fromager;* I had to learn by experience.

Afuega'l Pitu, made by small farmhouse producers along Spain's north coast, has an assertive flavor that is challenging for most palates.

Even for the world's foremost experts, acquiring cheese knowledge is an ongoing process. It demands a day-to-day, week-by-week pursuit of the flavors and the facts. My education in cheese was a matter of total immersion. I read every printed word I could get my hands on. I tasted as many cheeses as humanly possible. I joined the American Cheese Society and spent many hours talking with cheesemakers, importers, wholesalers, retailers, and cheese enthusiasts of all stripes. Much of my education came from clientele, who often knew a thing or two about certain cheeses. I often found myself disagreeing with conventional wisdom, with what the world's top experts had written. The real experts, it turns out, are the palates of people who taste cheese on a daily basis—mine included.

The first step toward becoming a cheese connoisseur is to pick out a good source of fine cheeses. Find the best local cheesemonger and make regular visits. Sample top cheeses on a regular basis. Start to accumulate an inventory of cheese experiences in your memory bank.

The best person to talk to regarding cheeses at any given establishment—be it restaurant, cheese shop, or gourmet deli—is the buyer, the person responsible for selecting and obtaining the cheeses. Find out who that is and try to pick his or her brain. Shop around and compare, visiting other vendors to see whether they might offer a more attractive Selles-sur-Cher, for example, or Tomme de Savoie.

THE AMERICAN CHEESE SOCIETY

UPHOLDING THE GOALS AND STANDARDS OF ARTISANSHIP

THE American Cheese Society is a nonprofit organization dedicated to the development and appreciation of American-made small-scale and "specialty" cheeses. It was founded in 1983 by Frank Kosikowski (1916–1995), longtime professor of food science at Cornell University, who conducted much research and wrote many articles and several texts on cheese. Among the society's members are artisanal cheesemakers, retailers, importers, journalists, chefs, and cheese enthusiasts. The society puts out a quarterly newsletter, stages tastings across the country, puts on an annual conference, and is heavily involved in lobbying against mandatory pasteurization.

. . . AND IN BRITAIN

The Specialist Cheesemakers Association in Britain was founded in 1989 as an informal group of cheesemakers and cheesemongers. Membership is now approaching 300, including about 120 cheesemakers. One of its primary functions is press communications. With Prince Charles as its patron and sporting the Ministry of Agriculture's stamp of approval, the organization helps create guidelines that allow small producers to stick with traditional methods while also satisfying hygiene inspectors from the Department of Health. (See Appendix page 226 for more information.)

PRINCIPLES OF
CHEESE TASTING

Every piece of fine cheese you swallow has a story to tell. It begins with outward appearance and aroma, continues with a series of momentary taste impressions, and ends with much longer periods of contemplation. The crux of the matter is taste, and the first thing to remember about taste is that the nose does most of the work. The taste buds of the tongue can only detect four basic flavors—sweet, sour, bitter, and salty—whereas the olfactory system can sort out something closer to 10,000 different odors. The physiological reason we are able to detect so many flavors is that, despite the limitations of our taste buds, the nose is connected to the throat at the back of the mouth by a small canal called the retronasal passage. Much of our ability to taste foods is accounted for by what flavor scientists call retronasal aroma, the smells detected through that passage once the food is in our mouths. This is why flavor experts also frequently refer to taste as "flavor by mouth."

Aspiring connoisseurs of fine foods and wines in America are disadvantaged because in this country we're brought up to shun anything that smells strong, pungent, funky—in other words, interesting. Billions of dollars are spent each year by the personal hygiene, cosmetics, and home-products industries developing and marketing products that *mask* natural odors. We are a culture that is out of touch with its nose! So one of the first steps toward enhancing our appreciation of artisanal cheeses is to make a conscious effort to get back in touch with our sense of smell.

Likewise, we need to attune our palates. Whether you're a professional or an amateur, the importance of staying in touch with cheeses cannot be overemphasized. You need to pay close attention and taste them repeatedly. (This was underscored for me during flu season the winter we started writing this book. Due to a prolonged bout with sinusitis, I literally could not smell or taste anything for a good 2 weeks.) When I'm working with my cheeses, I'll often absentmindedly pop a stray morsel into my mouth for a quick taste. Handling the cheeses, smelling them, tasting them is my way of staying in touch with them. I could do my job as a *fromager* by reciting a bunch of facts or recalling a few entertaining anecdotes. But that would be like flying blind. It's one thing to determine that a newly arrived cheese *looks* good and ripe and ready to serve, but without smelling and tasting it you can never honestly swear by it.

One of the more important attributes of the cheese connoisseur is patience. Cheese moves at its own speed. I recommend taking some time to study and learn about it. The more you know, the more fascinating it becomes. Certainly, you shouldn't rush when you're visiting the cheese shop. Always take the time to consider what's available, examine, taste, ask questions, and make appropriate choices according to the particular requirements of the occasion.

Whether you're tasting one or two cheeses or a lineup of fifteen, you need to give your olfactory apparatus the chance to perceive the full depth and breadth of what a cheese has to offer. Superior cheeses almost always deliver multiple combinations of flavors and aromas—a phenomenon we refer to as "complexity," borrowing a familiar phrase from wine-tasting jargon—and they demand contemplation. You can easily taste an assortment of ten or eleven cheeses in a sitting as long as you allow enough time for each to tell its story. Like fine wines, many cheeses have complex aromas that should be savored *before* tasting. Once they enter your mouth, they leave not only an initial impression—the "attack"—but there is an evolution as they are gradually chewed or melt on your tongue. Some of these sensations can linger distinctly long after you swallow, forming a lasting impression called the "finish."

HOW TO TASTE CHEESE

To form a complete and vivid impression of a cheese, we need to perceive every one of its aromas and flavors. The best advice I can give is to take your time and listen to your nose, mouth, and tongue. Ask yourself, what does it taste like? Think in terms of comparison and contrast. Make sure your palate and nose are clear and that you are prepared to concentrate. Cheese is a sensual experience and for that you shouldn't be uptight or fatigued; you want to be at ease and focused. And while casual enjoyment is highly recommended, there is also a time for the systematic, organized approach. In the realm of fine wines, connoisseurs—whether professionals or amateurs—observe a kind of ritual every time they approach a glass of wine for serious tasting. It's a formal protocol that at first may seem a bit overblown or pretentious but really is a valuable tool. I think it's helpful to approach cheeses in a similar manner. Adopting a step-by-step, checklist-type approach helps us slow down, concentrate, contemplate, and get the most out of what a cheese has to offer.

Professional tasters usually compile lists with specific categories and ratings scales to grade and rank cheeses. On the amateur level, most people aren't that meticulous (obsessive?). Yet regardless of how they record their impressions, all serious cheese tasters practice some version of the following.

Look

Before you smell or taste, examine the cheese closely, noting its general appearance including color and texture. Is the rind cracked, fissured, bumpy? Are there any other external faults? Are there molds growing and if so what color? Compare the outward appearance with the standards listed in Chapters 4 and 8. If the cheese is cut, note the appearance of the interior and compare it with the standards.

Does the condition of a cheese's wrapper indicate anything about its taste? A tight or impermeable wrapper suggests asphyxiation; the cheese may not have been able to breathe during its long journey to you. It may have become completely, irreversibly ammoniated (see Chapter 4).

Note any other possible aberrations or flaws. Always give questionable cheeses the benefit of the doubt and try them. Occasionally you'll be pleasantly surprised.

Touch

If the appearance of the cheese doesn't dissuade you, proceed to the feel. You can tell a lot about a cheese's consistency from the outside, before biting into it. Tap the cheese lightly and/or press on its surface. Give it the Pillsbury Doughboy treatment—a gentle poke. Try to determine whether it's brittle, meaty, springy, soft, or any number of other consistencies. Cheese graders or *affineurs* (ripeners)—the experts responsible for ranking and selecting fine cheeses—thump large wheels or drums by hand, gauging their degree of ripeness by sound alone. They instantly recognize the thud of a well-aged cheese. (Parmesan graders are particularly known for this.)

You can also get a sense of a cheese's texture and density by how the blade of the knife or cutting wire slices through it. How soft or firm is it? Again, this depends on what type of cheese it is and its degree of ripeness. For example, for a ripe Loire Valley chèvre, I like the surface to feel soft while the body feels firm but not hard. A Caerphilly should feel solid yet almost bendable.

Cheese graders also often gauge a cheese's body and texture by rolling a small piece of it between thumb and forefinger. Some cheeses should crumble a bit, others should make a smooth, buttery little ball. Depending on the standard for a given cheese, if the ball is overly crumbly or excessively sticky or pasty, this may indicate a defect.

Smell

As noted previously, taste and smell are inextricably linked; the taste buds on the tongue lean heavily on the sense of smell. To smell a cheese properly, it's necessary to hold it right up close to your nose. Waving aromas toward your nose with a hand won't do the trick. I don't suppose putting your nose to the plate would be any major breach of etiquette, but it might look a little silly. Picking the cheese up with your fingers is somewhat of a risk because whatever odors cling to your hands—even the faintest hint of hand soap—could interfere. So the best method is to pick up a specimen with a fork or other utensil, hold it close to your nose, away from other cheeses or aroma sources, and take a good whiff.

Let's talk about stinky cheeses. Many fine cheeses feature an aroma that will practically jump up and bite you the second you walk in the room. You smell them long before you touch or even see them. (In fact, some of them you may not want to touch—let alone taste—after you've smelled them.) Others have aromas so subtle you might have to hold them up close to your nose, sniff, and really concentrate to detect anything at all. Nonetheless, they can still taste incredibly delicious.

A cheese's aroma and its flavor can be very different, both quantitatively and qualitatively. Some of the worst-smelling cheeses taste the best. Yet it is not necessarily true that the stinkier the cheese, the stronger the flavor. Certain cheeses such as Taleggio, Munster, and Alpage Prattigauer are much easier on the tongue than they are on the nose. They might give off very strong barnyardy odors while they taste mild, pure, and milky. Some aromas may be fairly strong, persistent, or pungent; but a cheese should never smell like death, decay, dung, or straight ammonia. Chevrotin des Aravis, a washed-rind goat cheese from the French Alps made in the style of Reblochon, can be one of the stronger-smelling cheeses; its taste, however, is subtle and mild with a long, pleasant, slightly goaty aftertaste. If it tasted as strong as it smelled, it might be hard to take. Epoisses can also have this quality. The aroma of the marc in which it is washed and the effluvium of its bacterial development can give it a powerful stench. But its taste is a lovely chorus of refined flavors, complex yet well rounded.

Taste

Having duly noted all of the visual, tactile, and olfactory qualities of a cheese, it is time to taste it. Take your time; don't gobble and swallow. Be sure to note the "attack," followed by the evolution of flavors, and finally the "finish." Superior cheeses will offer a multitude of changing sensations that can be lost if you rush; they will yield flavors that last anywhere from a few seconds to an hour. Strong blue cheeses and their equals can easily linger for more than an hour.

The smell of this Belgian washed-rind Chimay makes a stronger impact than its taste.

Describing a cheese as flavorful as Ibores is an entertaining challenge—from the color (rusty) and density (semisoft) to the texture (airy with holes) and flavor (salty, bitter, and acidic but also sweet).

Unlike the sloshing, slurping, or air-sucking often associated with wine tasting, there isn't a lot of technique involved in sampling cheese. My main recommendation is to take a small specimen of no more than a teaspoonful—especially if you are unfamiliar with a cheese. (A tablespoon is roughly equivalent to half an ounce; a teaspoon is a third of this.) Look, smell, pop the morsel in your mouth, and close your eyes (this helps you concentrate and shut out distractions). Gently press the cheese to the roof of your mouth with the front of your tongue. Then let it settle on the tongue, filling the entire mouth with its texture and flavors. Before swallowing, allow the cheese to rest in the mouth for a while—say about 5 seconds—so its harmonies can develop.

While the texture of a cheese may be apparent from the way it looks or feels, this aspect can only be fully appreciated after you put it in your mouth. In addition to the taste (sweet, sour, salty, bitter) and "flavor by mouth" (sea breeze, mountain air, piney woods, and hundreds if not thousands of other possible flavors), it's important to take note of the mouth feel of a cheese. What sort of texture are you detecting on your tongue or in other parts of your mouth? Is it astringent or drying, mouth-watering, buttery (rich), smooth, crumbly, heavy or light, gooey or runny?

SUGAR AND SALT

MOST of the flavors in cheeses are associated with aromas, so you can usually get an inkling of them by merely smelling a cheese. Sugar and salt, however, are both nonvolatile substances, meaning they have no aroma. (Volatile substances—the ones that mix with air—are the ones we can smell.) Therefore, to detect the saltiness or sweetness of a given cheese, it must be tasted.

THE LANGUAGE OF CHEESE

You've learned to taste cheeses; now you've got to figure out how to talk about them. Among the numerous parallels between cheese and wine connoisseurship is that description relies largely on analogy. When we're smelling or tasting a wine or a cheese, we're asking ourselves "What does it remind me of?" The answer to this question is usually along the lines of "It smells like strawberries" or "It tastes like caramel" or "It's grassy." A large number of floral, herbal, fruity, animal, and other natural smells, along with chemical ones, have traditionally been evoked to describe wines. The same is true of many gourmet foods, including fine table cheeses. Fruity and nutty, for example, are common cheese descriptors, yet we know there are no fruits or nuts in cheeses. (Whether they share combinations of chemical compounds is an intriguing possibility that I'll leave up to the flavor scientists to explore.)

Terms used to describe wines, cheeses, or any other kind of food can be either quantitative (objective) or qualitative (subjective). Physical descriptions—delineating a cheese's colors or the textures of its rind and paste, for example—are mostly objective. With descriptions of even the most basic tastes, however, there is a degree of subjectivity. What tastes salty to me may be relatively bland to you. A cheese that's tangy to one person may be sour to another; nevertheless, both tasters agree that the cheese possesses a component of acidity. Composite descriptions, qualitative terms, vague adjectives—all fall more clearly into the realm of subjectivity. A cheese that is "lush and luxurious" to one interpreter may be a dull blob of tasteless butterfat to another. (Of course, this is an oversimplification; in real life, there will be differences of opinion over much finer points.) A cheese like Kirkham's Lancashire may seem delicate and ephemeral to one palate, feisty and persistent to another.

My goal as a *fromager* is to offer entertaining, as well as informative, descriptions. This can be difficult. I may find myself using the adjective *rich* thirty times a day; that's when I head back to the thesaurus. Maybe *opulent, sumptuous,* or *plush* will do for a change of pace.

When someone is just starting out with cheese, it's likely they'll grope for the right words. They'll tend to describe cheeses as *cheesy, salty,* or *buttery*—accurate but not particularly illuminating. As they develop their portfolio of cheese experiences, they begin to assimilate a wider vocabulary.

If I'm trying to teach people how to describe cheeses, I think it's a mistake to put words in their mouths. They should be left alone to determine what they feel and taste—as subjective as it may be. What I see as *brick red* you might be convinced is *maroon.* On the other hand, I think it helps to be able to mix and match a few terms, to connect the dots and observe as patterns emerge. The list of words on this page is a kind of cheese thesaurus, meant to open up the possibilities rather than provide a crib sheet. Try to take some of these descriptive words—all used by professionals—and see

CHEESE DESCRIPTORS

COLOR	COLOR MODIFIERS	FIRMNESS OR DENSITY	TEXTURE
aquamarine, blue, brown, golden, gray, green, greenish, ocher (aka ochre, which is darkish yellow or reddish-brown), ivory, orange, orangish, pink, pinkish, purple, purplish, red, reddish, rusty or rust-colored, white (chalky, off-white, pure), yellow, yellowish	bright, bleached, deep, dirty, dull, uneven, uniform, pale, shiny, smudged	compact, dense, firm, hard, liquid, runny, semihard, semisoft, soft, tight	airy, cracking or cracked, crumbling or crumbly, chalky, drying or dry, elastic, fissured, flaky, grainy or granular, greasy, leathery, pasty, resinous, ropey, smooth (satiny), spongy, spreadable, springy, rough, waterless, with holes

if you can legitimately apply them to the cheeses you taste. Or take a "pure" approach: skip this section, start with a blank slate, and simply free-associate. Then go back and compare your descriptors to this list. No doubt you'll discover some matches. You may detect flavors that aren't on this list—and more power to you.

Descriptive terms tend to lose meaning due to overuse. Some are vague, imprecise, or uncommon. They may have different meanings for different people. *Sharp,* for example, very likely means salty to many people. To some, it might mean especially tangy or acidic. Let's clarify sharp right here as synonymous with *pronounced.* This means a cheese could be sharply salty, sour, or bitter. Several sources describe the Spanish cheese Zamorano as having "bite." Bite, to me, indicates the presence of both acidity and saltiness—in appropriate quantities and balanced. A good Zamorano (it's hard to find a bad one) isn't particularly salty or acidic; its pH level averages about 5.6, which is less acidic than most cheeses. It does possess a pungent quality, however, that is not readily apparent due to its oiliness and salinity.

FLAVOR AND AROMA	FLAVOR MODIFIERS (AT LEAST PARTLY SUBJECTIVE)	SUBJECTIVE, QUALITATIVE, OR INTERPRETIVE
acidic, ammoniacal, barnyardy, beefy, bitter, bland, burnt, buttery, chalky, cooked, cloves, farmy, floral, fruity, funky, garlic, goaty, grassy, herbal, meaty, metallic, lactic, moldy, musty, nutty, oily, onion, rancid, salty, savory (or savoury, using the British spelling), sour (sour milk), spicy, sweaty, sweet, tangy, weedy, woodsy, yeasty	harsh, mild, persistent, pronounced, rich, strong, weak	bite (or biting), complex, concentrated, elaborate, gentle, insipid, luxurious, loud, obstreperous, opulent, powerful, rich, robust, sharp, simple, sonorous, stout, timid, unctuous, zesty

> *"Don't be a snob or a blue-stocking. Don't be ordinary either. No literary allusions. Just because you are serving one or two good cheeses do not drag up that old saw of Brillat-Savarin: 'A meal without cheese is like a beautiful woman with one eye.' Know a few facts well and ignore all vague opinions and conjectures."*
> —PIERRE ANDROUËT, *Guide du Fromage*

I like to try out some fairly incongruous adjectives on cheeses; if *sharp* or *biting* can be applied, then why not *loud* or *obstreperous?* Among the cheeses I call *loud* or *boss* are Berkswell, Boeren Kaas, Cabrales, Cheddar, Montenebro, Parmigiano-Reggiano, Roncal, Roomano, Roquefort, Stanser, Stilton.

How about *lactic?* Since cheeses are all made from milk, every one is in some sense lactic. In terms of flavor, though, you can describe a cheese as lactic, which I think is a rather precious term for one that is milky and smooth and has that pleasant bite characteristic of slightly sour milk. (Camembert is a good example of this.) It does not necessarily indicate a soft paste; Queso de los Beyos, for example, is a firm cheese that can also be called lactic.

Strong can be an ambiguous term, too. It's often a matter of comparison. If one cheese is stronger than another, is that analogous to turning up the volume on your stereo? Does Cheese A simply have "a higher volume of flavor" than Cheese B? When is a cheese too strong? It's a matter of opinion. Another more pertinent question might be *when*—that is, at what point during a tasting—is the cheese strong? Some cheeses hit hard up front, then fade fast. Others may build from a timid overture to a smashing crescendo.

DOES *SHARP* MEAN DULL CHEESE?

THE UNFORTUNATE MISUSE OF A PERFECTLY GOOD ADJECTIVE

SHARP is a term commonly applied by marketing types to factory Cheddars. As such, to those in the know, it is a catchword for an acidity that drowns out the wonderful symphony of flavors associated with genuine farmhouse cheeses. It is characteristic of mass-produced Cheddars and it devoids them of whatever complexity or subtlety they might have hoped to achieve. A Keen's, Montgomery's, or Isle of Mull Cheddar, on the other hand, can be sharp without drowning out the symphony.

If you continue to read up, you'll eventually encounter some marvelously esoteric descriptors. In French, two frequently used ones are *nerveux* (literal translation: "nervous"), which indicates a slight acidity or tartness (also used to describe wines), and *noiseté,* which is nutty. *Savoury* is a British term that refers to a small, highly seasoned plate of food served either as an appetizer or at the end of the meal. The American spelling is *savory,* and its definition in common usage is something that is pleasing to the taste *or* spicy and salty, as opposed to sweet. You'll see the term used to describe a cheese whose flavor is rich, deep, and reminiscent of gravy or meat stock.

PROGRESSION

Every meal, plate, or tasting has a sequence of elements that should complement or contrast one another, often making the whole better—or at least more interesting—than the sum of its parts. I always take careful note of the sequences in which I present cheeses, from a humble selection of two to a Wagnerian smorgasbord of sixteen. Sequences provide the opportunity for comparison, which is the best way to begin quantifying and qualifying a tasting experience. Beginning with a plate of just two cheeses, you are no longer tasting each in a vacuum. You have introduced the light of contrast to illuminate the qualities of each. A single cheese might be difficult to describe individually: is it tart, tangy, salty, sweet? But once you've got two cheeses, you can begin to say "Cheese X is smoother and milder," "Cheese Y is drier and saltier," and so forth. Then you move on to a progression of three or more cheeses and the fun really begins.

You'll want to pay special attention to any dissonances or harsh edges that crop up. Is there a bias for or against a given cheese that can be attributed to progression? Has a conflict arisen with whatever cheese (or food or beverage) last visited the palate? Rarely will one cheese transform another into a gustatory disaster; it is more common that the fuller imprint of a more robust type will flatten the nuances of a milder one. This is a situation to be avoided and is why progressions are so important.

Just as the traditional wine progression runs from younger, fruitier, lighter wines to riper, heavier, more tannic ones, so cheeses usually go from milder, softer, younger, fresher ones to stronger, firmer, riper, funkier ones. Androuët calls it the "sacrosanct rule of crescendo": build from mild to strong, simple to complex, small to big, light-bodied to full. The reasoning is that once you progress to a bigger, bolder wine or cheese, you can't go back because it will drown out anything milder. Some "stronger" cheeses may not necessarily be more flavorful but may simply have more persistent, lingering effects or a longer finish. Others may simply have such a volume of flavor that they stun the palate, in which case it takes a while for the taste buds to recover and be prepared to pick up the subtler flavors of a milder cheese.

Is crescendo a holy canon? No. Instead, it's a rule to which we can always expect to find exceptions. I believe it's a mistake to fall into the trap of making categorical pronouncements about most cheeseworthy matters, progression included. Nevertheless, if there is any general rule of progression to which there are very few exceptions, it is that nonblue cheeses should almost never follow blue ones.

Rather than blindly follow the rule of crescendo, I recommend you experiment. On a plate, double back to cheeses earlier in the progression; don't just march from 1-2-3-4 to 5-6-7-8, but try 7 and 8 then go back to 3 and 4, or 5 and 6. Look for significant or interesting comparisons all down the line.

In planning the sequence for a tasting or a plate, there is very rarely one determining factor. Instead, you need to be aware of the nature of each cheese vis-à-vis its potential partners on a plate. Cheeses almost never proceed in strict order of age; for example, I'd usually place a 3-month-old Epoisses after a 6-month-old Vermont Shepherd or a 2-month-old Cashel Blue after an 8-month-old Alben. Other factors that come into play are a cheese's density or firmness and its consistency or texture. While flavors traditionally progress from mild to strong, firmness and texture often simply alternate; for example, soft-hard-soft-hard or smooth-rough-smooth-rough. A plate of all soft cheeses might spell monotony (unless you were guaranteed a tremendous variety and range of flavors); ditto all hard. Without getting too precious about it, the main goal is to mix things up: think variety and alternation. Variety generates excitement; alternation helps highlight and separate different flavors on the palate.

A cheese's stage of ripeness will affect its place in a progression. Depending on how ripe it is, a cheese might go from Position 2 in a seven-cheese plate one week to Position 4 the next week and so forth. Occasionally, a diner will request a lineup of their favorite cheeses that turn out to be all quite similar—for example, Reblochon, Livarot, Munster, and Epoisses. In this case, to determine the order of presentation, I need to be acutely aware of where each cheese is in its development. At their peaks, I would probably put them in this order: (1) Reblochon, (2) Livarot, (3) Munster, (4) Epoisses. Different stages of ripeness, however, could completely shuffle this order.

A perfect progression from delicate to assertive, with contrast or complements at every stage: from ten o'clock, Garrotxa, Durrus, Torta del Casar, Munster, Vacherin Fribourgeois, and Roquefort.

IT'S NOT PEANUT BUTTER

DON'T treat your cheese like peanut butter by spreading or mashing it down. Just lay it on the bread. A fine cheese needs to be tasted as a discrete entity—not mixed into a piece of bread.

SIX | CHEESE PAIRINGS

PAIRING PRINCIPLES

IT'S NOT ALWAYS NECESSARY or even possible to find the perfect food accompaniment for each cheese on a plate. If you follow the principles outlined in this chapter, and remain flexible and open to experiment, you will discover many delightful pairings. But never forget that great table cheeses are perfectly capable of standing alone; pairings with foods other than the occasional piece of bread are optional.

A pairing made in heaven: Pellegrini Finale, a dessert wine made with Gewürztraminer and Sauvignon Blanc, from Pellegrini Vineyards on the North Fork of Long Island, matches beautifully with (left to right) Ticklemore, Roucoulons, Spenwood, and Valdeón.

SIMILARITY OR AFFINITY

Look to pair subtle-flavored or fine-textured cheeses with like foods, rustic cheeses with rustic foods, cheeses with floral or herbal notes with foods that echo those notes. For example, some of the finer sheep's milk cheeses, such as Pecorino Toscano, have deep, warm, fruity flavors that pair well with fruits such as plums and peaches; pears can be matched beautifully with many cheeses, especially firm-textured cow's milk cheeses, of which Lancashire is a good example. The Lancashire has a smooth, sweet, buttery quality that goes along with the clean, refreshing taste of the pears. The cheese also provides an acidity that echoes the pears' flavor—a delectable combination.

COMPLEMENT OR CONTRAST

Nuts and cheeses share similar "nutty" flavors while they also complement one another in several ways. Walnuts, almonds, or nut breads are most frequently chosen to accompany blue cheeses; the oils in the nuts help coat the tongue so that the blue isn't as piercing. Unsalted butter can be used

for the same purpose, its fats tempering some of the stronger, saltier cheeses. Of course, the dry, salty flavors of many cheeses can contrast nicely with the sweet, moist qualities of fresh fruits (especially in the warmer months), as well as sweet jams, preserves, pastes, and fruit tarts (during colder times). Melons in their prime—smooth, moist, and sweet—contrast beautifully with the drier, firmer types of goat's milk cheeses. If your Wabash Cannonball has shriveled up a bit, try it with a ripe cantaloupe. When little chèvres dry up, they can offer the perfect complement for a simple green salad à la vinaigrette.

Bear in mind that pairing principles apply not only to flavor but also to texture and consistency. For texture contrast, try a smooth, runny, spoonable cheese with a crisp, crusty piece of baguette; some of my favorite choices for this are Torta del Casar, Queijo Serra, Vacherin Haut-Rive, and L'Edel de Cleron. Cabrales and raw carrots represent another pair of contrasts: the alkaline root vegetable has a latent sweetness that balances the strong, biting, acidic cheese; there's also a nice texture contrast between the crunchy, juicy carrot and the rich, crumbly cheese.

REGIONAL PAIRINGS

Local foods from a country or region are often matched; for example, Roncal from Navarra is often served with *membrillo* (quince paste) from nearby Catalonia. Caraway seeds, typical of German, Austrian, and Hungarian cuisine, are often paired with Munster, the Alsatian cheese. (The seeds can be sprinkled over the cheese or served as part of rye bread or crackers.) Donna Doel of Doeling Dairy, Fayetteville, Arkansas, likes to pair her Goat's Milk Camembert with the locally grown Arkansas Black Apples or Asian Pears.

ACCOMPANIMENTS

I'm a cheese purist. In my opinion, accompaniments should be kept to a minimum. This is especially true for a tasting or a large meal. At lunch or supper, just a handful of cheeses with a few well-chosen accompaniments will do the trick.

BREAD

This is the old reliable, a no-brainer, cheese's most frequent sidekick. At Picholine, along with a plate of between three and ten cheeses, we serve a dish with two types of fresh bread wrapped in a napkin—usually a plain baguette and a raisin-walnut bread. Nothing beats a classic French baguette—crispy on the outside, soft and fluffy on the inside—or an Italian

The best pairing for cheese is bread— anything from a simple baguette to more adventurous specimens such as this fig-walnut wheel (sliced on plate) and crusty mountain loaf, here served with (from left to right) Valdeón, Beyos, Aged Gouda, Fontina d'Aosta, and Appenzeller, and a bottle of crisp J. J. Prüm Riesling.

pane di casa (home-style peasant bread) to complement fine cheeses. A good piece of crusty bread is the perfect vehicle for transporting a rich, ripe morsel of cheese to your mouth. Bread is also useful as a palate cleanser, especially if you're doing some serious cheese tasting; it can temper some of the more intense flavors.

Be careful not to eat too much bread, however. Even if you're trying small portions of cheese—half an ounce here, an ounce there—the bread adds up. With a cheese plate that progresses in the traditional manner from mildest to strongest, I'd recommend holding off on the bread until you

reach some of the stronger cheeses—the blues, for example—where your palate may want a break.

Although it might seem like overkill, cheese can be served with bread and butter on the side. This is an English custom that is also practiced in Normandy where they make superb butter in addition to excellent cheeses.

A number of bread options go with cheese: classic baguettes, sourdough, focaccia (plain or with onions, herbs, tomatoes, grapes), whole wheat, rye, Tuscan rounds or other peasant-style breads, and olive breads. You can also try wheat or rye crackers, flatbreads, or thin slices of toast to provide texture contrasts. Crackers and flatbreads should be fairly neutral in flavor. Apply the preceding food-matching principles, with an emphasis on compatibility and balance. Some of the more flavorful, multigrain, coarser-textured breads can go well with robust cheeses such as Cheddar and other British farmhouse cheeses. Mild-tasting white breads go best with milder more delicate cheeses. Raisin-walnut bread with a blue cheese is a classic pairing.

FRUIT

Fresh fruits—figs, apples, grapes, peaches, pears, or melon wedges—can be good accompaniments for cheeses. The contrast between the sweet juiciness of the fruit and the dry saltiness of the cheeses works wonders. Pair them on a relatively empty stomach for breakfast, a light lunch, or supper. For a cheese course within a larger lunch or dinner, fresh fruit is unnecessary. At most, offer some dried figs or a Catalonian fig tart or a plum cake. During the winter, I like to offer Medjool dates and/or quince paste, again highlighting the sweet-salty contrast. Dried apricots and apricot preserve can also complement cheeses very nicely, as can chutneys and relishes. Cheddar and chutney is a classic "British Empire" combo.

VEGETABLES

If you want to make a meal or a large appetizer plate of it, serve cheese with fresh vegetables, including carrots, celery, radishes, zucchini, red peppers, and green beans (blanched or lightly steamed). Vegetables can highlight some interesting contrasts with cheeses: crunchy/smooth, raw/fermented, sweet/sour, sweet/salty, juicy/dry, hard/soft, dense/aerated. In Tuscany, a favorite snack or light meal consists of Pecorino and fresh shelled fava beans—a delightful contrast. An Italian-style pickled vegetable salad or marinated roasted red peppers with cheese and bread makes a fine lunch. Green or black olives, with their varying textures and intensities, go well with most cheeses. The sharper-tasting varieties can overwhelm mild cheeses, though, so be mindful of balance.

The sweetness of fruit is the perfect complement to the sharpness of cheeses such as this regal Montgomery's Cheddar.

SPANISH TRADITIONS

IN SPAIN, ewe's milk cheeses are often served alongside quince paste, known as *membrillo*. Cheese with bread is a typical breakfast. Serving cheese as an after-dinner course before the sweet dessert is more of a French custom. In Spain, they're just as likely to serve cheese with a glass of chilled *fino* sherry as an appetizer, or *tapa*. Another wonderful Spanish custom is to drizzle a little honey over a hearty, dense cheese like Zamorano or Roncal.

CURED PORK PRODUCTS

Italian prosciutto, sorpressata, capicola, or salami; Spanish jamon serrano or chorizo; Virginia ham—all go well with cheeses, with the exceptions of delicate, mild, soft types.

NUTS

The fats and oils in nuts, as well as their flavors, are compatible with many cheeses. Try almonds, Brazil nuts, cashews, hazelnuts, pecans, walnuts—raw or toasted. Normally, I would recommend no more than one or two types of nuts to accompany a cheese plate.

BEVERAGE PAIRINGS

Matching cheeses and beverages is a science that is yet in its infancy. Its principles can be tricky; it is an inexact calculus. Anyone who says otherwise is not telling the truth. Cheese-beverage pairings are largely a matter of personal preference. Nevertheless, as with wine, you will encounter a great deal of dogma in the literature. Even the top authorities in cheese and wine have recommended pairings that are questionable.

At times, there will be one predominant rationale for a pairing—a contrast of sweet and salty, a similarity of floral aromas, a balance of complementary or contrasting acidity. Usually, though, it's not that simple. There may be a combination of flavors working for or against each other and no clear-cut rule to explain the pairing. In many cases, you'll have to synthesize principles to create a pairing. If you're looking to match white wines with rich, salty cheeses, for example, you need to find a wine with a high enough acid level to complement the fat content of the cheeses. At the same time, you'll need some residual sugar to balance their saltiness.

Cheese knowledge is arrived at empirically. Apply the principles that follow, try as many pairings as possible, be bold and experiment, then decide which ones work best for you.

WHICH RULES?

In putting together cheese-and-wine (or other beverage) pairings, you need to decide first which one is driving the bus—the wine or the cheese. Often in a restaurant context, diners will look to pair their cheeses with whatever wine is left over from the previous course. Or they have their heart set on a particular beverage. In these instances, the selection of cheeses is beverage-driven; I need to find the cheeses to match. Of course, I would prefer to start over and pick the cheeses, then select wines to match. In my worldview, cheese rules; but not everyone agrees. Once you've determined which rules—the cheese or the wine—you can create some matchups and work out a logical sequence.

BEWARE OF GENERALIZATIONS

One piece of conventional wisdom is that only red wines go with cheese. Not true. In reality, while some cheeses pair well with reds, others go much more happily with whites. Meursault, for example, the classic Burgundian white made from Chardonnay grapes, is an excellent match with certain cheeses as are the wines made from Gewürztraminer or Riesling grapes grown in Germany and Alsace. On the other hand, some cheeses go well with Rhône reds—including the Syrah-Mourvèdre-Grenache blends—which are among the spicier, more interesting wines on the market. Certain cheeses are more versatile; they find pairings across a wide range of wine types. Others have more limited pairing potential.

My first instinct is to get away from traditional notions about pairings. I like to promote pairings of lesser-known, less "serious" or ponderous but nonetheless delightful wines with cheeses. Savennières, Pinot Blanc, and Albariño, for example, can all work well with cheese plates even *after* having a substantial red wine with your meal—again defying convention (see upcoming "Progression" section).

Two other oft-cited maxims are: one, the stronger the cheese, the more powerful, complex, and robust the wine needs to be; two, regional pairings work. As I've discovered, things are not so cut and dried. In some cases, these axioms may be true, but it would be a mistake to rely 100 percent on *any* generalizations regarding cheese-wine pairings. Instead, pairings need to be considered individually.

Within a given varietal or type of wine, you are likely to discover more than enough variation to render some pairing advice moot. Take Sauvignon

Blanc, for example. Sancerre, its famous Loire Valley expression, can be a tart wine; "puckering" is a frequent descriptor. In New Zealand, Sauvignon Blancs are very often termed "grassy" or "vegetal." This same grape, from a different vineyard within the same appellation, can feature either fruity *or* flowery flavors and aromas. Obviously, these differences can drastically affect a cheese pairing. So if you hear that Sauvignon Blanc goes well with fresh goat cheese, you ought to at least inquire, *which* Sauvignon Blanc?; better yet, which fresh goat cheese and which Sancerre or which New Zealand Sauvignon?

A MATTER OF STYLE

Some pairings seem to defy logic or categorization. The most that can be said about them is that they work, but it's not always clear *why*. Why does a Tuscan *vin santo* work so well with the local Pecorino? How does a Garrotxa from Catalonia pair perfectly with a white Burgundy from Chablis or Meursault?

To me, a pairing is akin to a vocal duet. Sometimes when two flavors harmonize or clash, it's simply a matter of style. Two contrasting voices can sound great together— Sonny and Cher, for example. Likewise, two disparate combinations can sound equally good. Frank Sinatra could make beautiful music singing with Ella Fitzgerald; he might create an equally pleasing but totally different sound in a duet with his daughter, Nancy. If he had tried to sing with Janis Joplin, however . . .

BALANCE

One partner shouldn't overwhelm the other. There are some wines—glorious, complex, occasionally overpowering—that should be savored by themselves, leaving the cheese on the shelf. Ditto some cheeses. It would be a disservice to any potential partner to try to conjure a match. I would hesitate to pair a first-growth Bordeaux at its peak with *just anything;* the same for an exceptional vintage Port.

In terms of balance, a strong, powerfully flavored blue cheese such as Cabrales presents a difficult but not impossible pairing puzzle. It calls for an intense, concentrated, sweet, fortified wine. I tried a Coteaux du Layon, which is an excellent late-harvest Chenin Blanc, and the cheese simply overwhelmed it. The Coteaux, however, paired brilliantly with a less powerful Harbourne Blue.

Perfect balance can be difficult to achieve. A well-made, elegant California Pinot Noir from the Carneros zone of Napa, for example, would in theory pair harmoniously with Erhaki, a sheep's milk cheese from the Pyrenées that has rich, mild, nutty flavor notes. I would expect the wine's tannins and acidity to offset the high fat content of that cheese, cutting through it like a dollop of milk in your hot black coffee. When I tried this matchup, however, the wine, in contrast to that cheese's intense richness, was somewhat *under*whelming.

KEEP IT SIMPLE

It's generally not a good idea to pair a complex wine with a complex cheese. Washed-rind cheeses, which develop a multitude of aromas and flavors, aren't going to flatter a multifaceted wine and vice versa. Given a ten-point scale of ratings from simple and easy to complex and challenging, sometimes a Level 1 cheese may correspond to a Level 8 wine or vice versa. For example, a sublime, perfectly ripened, gooey, pungent Munster or Epoisses may demand a young Château-Grillet, a northern Rhone white made from Viognier grapes that has bright floral and slightly metallic notes. Or a pedigreed red Burgundy such as Clos de Vougeot, which can be subtle and sublime, might call for a proud, uncomplicated ewe's milk cheese such as Zamorano.

I almost always recommend keeping the wines relatively simple for a cheese tasting. Pushing a first-growth Bordeaux up against an array of cheeses is courting disaster. Certainly, there are some wonderful possibilities, but why risk muddying a top wine with some obstinate spoiled milk?

SIMILARITY AND CONTRAST OR COMPLEMENT

Choose wines and cheeses that are similar *or* different—for example, spicy cheeses and spicy wines, fruity-tasting cheeses and fruity wines *or* salty cheeses and sweet wines, fatty cheeses and acidic wines. (And with contrast, always be mindful of balance.) Under this category fall many traditional pairings that continue to make a lot of sense. Blue cheeses, with their assertive salty, moldy, long-lasting flavors are often paired with sweet, viscous dessert-type wines for contrast and balance. Sauternes with Roquefort or Tawny Port with Stilton are classic examples. In the former case, the persistent berry flavors of the Sauternes complement the underlying sweet milky essence of the cheese.

When seeking pairings for a range of cheeses, it helps to have more than one wine type.

With a little bit of each—not too much—you achieve the ultimate goal: *balance and harmony!* Buttery cheeses such as Pierre-Robert (a triple crème) can pair well with tannic or acidic wines; the acids and/or tannins absorb the cream of the cheeses, leaving the wines' fruit to shine through. Reblochon, a mild creamy mountain cheese with a satiny smooth paste and refreshing fruity flavors, pairs well with a bright, fruity young wine such as Beaujolais.

REGIONAL PAIRINGS

Tuscan cheese with Tuscan wine, Burgundian cheeses with Burgundian wines . . . regional pairings generally work with wines and other foods, and in theory they should work well with cheese. But we should always be wary of blanket statements. If you're starting with a cheese, review the various wines of the region. Consider the nature of each wine and whether its characteristics justify a pairing with the cheese. Often you'll find that the best matches happen between "lesser" (i.e., not world-class) regional wines and local cheeses.

Among the well-known local pairings that can delight the palate are hard apple cider and the cheeses of Normandy such as Pavé D'Auge and Livarot. Fine handcrafted or artisanal Belgian, or northern French beers and ales can happily accompany the northern French, Belgian, and Dutch cheeses. Loire Valley goat cheeses such as the classic Selles-sur-Cher or Crottin de Chavignol pair extremely well with the famous local white wine Sancerre.

PROGRESSION

As mentioned, it is traditional to proceed in a crescendo from mild to strong, soft to hard, young to old. In other words, once you've gone to a hearty, substantial wine or cheese, it's hard to go back to the subtler, milder, more evanescent ones.

Bear in mind that a sequence of pairings may not follow conventional wine-only or cheese-only progressions. The important thing is that the pairings work, on an individual basis, and that the progression of the ruling element—wine or cheese—makes sense. Here's an example. Recently, I put together a professional wine-and-cheese tasting of about fifteen cheeses (five three-cheese flights with one wine each). I really wanted to showcase what I believed to be an excellent pairing: Beaufort, a superlative hard mountain cheese with a classic dry Blanc de Blancs 100 percent Chardonnay-based Champagne. Now, Beaufort, being a big cheese with a proud bearing, would normally appear toward the *end* of a tasting. But I was also matching a fresh, mild Garroxta and a ripe, buttery triple crème with the Champagne. I figured the Beaufort would complete this trio nicely, and together they would provide a stunning *opening act* to this multiple tasting. This was a wine-driven affair where, for similar reasons of pairing

A classic northern European tradition that brings out the best of all elements: a fine ale and some homemade bread-and-butter pickles are paired with, clockwise from front, Lancashire, Ardrahan, Gouda, and Stilton.

efficacy, the Roquefort-like yet mild Beenleigh Blue preceded the assertive, smelly Azeitão. (Blues normally go last.) These two were in turn succeeded by two seemingly milder albeit profoundly flavorful cheeses, Leon Downey's Llangloffan and Cynthia Major's Vermont Shepherd. From a conventional viewpoint, this was a mixed-up progression; but, due to the wine selections, it had an internal logic that flowed perfectly.

BRANCH OUT

If you're searching for something new and different in the realm of cheese-wine pairings, try a variation on a theme. Think of a pairing that has worked well or one recommended by a trusted expert, then find a *similar* or *related* wine or cheese to substitute. For example, if you're looking for a pairing with Queso de la Garroxta, the rustic Catalonian goat's milk cheese, and you know from experience that it marries well with a Meursault, the superior white Burgundy, try it with another classic Chardonnay-based wine—an elegant, sparkling, dry Blanc de Blanc Champagne. By gradually branching out like this and exploring different pairings, you'll discover some unconventional but beautiful marriages. This is always a thrill.

An example: I know that blue cheeses, for the most part, don't go with red wines, especially big reds; it's a combination that invites the infamous metallic clash. I'd never recommend washing down a Cabrales with a full-bodied, tannic red. Modify that pairing, however, and you can come up with a somewhat surprising but harmonius matchup. Take Beenleigh Blue, a mild, rich, delicately salted unpasteurized sheep's milk cheese from southern England patterned after Roquefort but subtler. Pair it with a big California Zinfandel—the one I tried was a St. Francis Sonoma "Old Vines" blend. Lo and behold, you have an exquisite stew. While the wine was bold, tannic, and supplied plenty of acid, this particular Zin was also rich, fruity, and viscous—so much so that I considered it a "borderline dessert wine." It was no surprise that this big red could balance the smooth saltiness and intriguing moldiness of the Beenleigh.

MISMATCHES

There are many pairings that succeed. Then there are those that either fall flat or create distinct off flavors. Whether it's a chemical reaction or simply a clash of flavors, these mismatches announce themselves loud and clear. Recently, one combination that shouted "No!" was Ibores, a lovely raw goat's milk cheese from the Extremadura in western Spain with Champagne; when the wine came in contact with the cheese, it immediately delivered a sharp blow of unpleasant metallic flavor to the tip of the tongue—as if you'd bitten into a piece of aluminum foil by accident.

While I encourage you to branch out and try different pairings, seeking ones that defy convention, I also caution you to expect a few illogical—and sometimes unpleasant—surprises. For example, I tried a mildly fruity California Pinot Gris with the Portuguese Queijo Serra Monte d'Estrela from Portugal and the Spanish Torta del Casar. This is normally a cheese-friendly wine. Both cheeses are vegetable-renneted, soft-ripened, made from raw sheep's milk, and hailing from the Iberian Peninsula—superficially at least very similar. The Pinot and the Serra worked well together; with the Torta, there was a definite clash. Theoretically, the second pairing should have worked as well as the first; in reality, there was an obvious incompatibility.

As often as not, a flawed pairing will deliver that metallic tinge. Other times, either the wine or the cheese will do nothing more than bring out the most unattractive characteristic of its partner. One partner might amplify a trait in the other that doesn't need amplification. For example, our Pinot Gris made that lovely ripe Torta del Casar taste raunchy. The cheese was already a little raunchy—a good thing, in this case—but it didn't need to be sent over the top, which is exactly what this wine did. It was like having milk and orange juice on your cereal at the same time. On the other hand, the same wine, when paired with a Queso de los Beyos, a dryish, dense, peasant-style cheese from Asturias, highlighted one of this cheese's best character-istics— a scrumptious melt-in-your-mouth quality. It also provided a light, cool, refreshing complement to the cheese's dryness and density.

TASTING WINES WITH CHEESES

To assess potential pairings, first try each partner—the wine and the cheese—separately to get a sense of their individual characters. Next take a moderate-sized bite of cheese and allow its flavors to fill your mouth. Then crumble some of it up against the back of your front teeth and take a sip of wine, creating a nice little sauce in there. Savor the combination, pause for con-sideration, then swallow. How does the pairing work? Sometimes wines and cheeses will seem to meld well at the start then, almost suddenly, the two go to battle. Neither the wine nor the cheese wins, although one or the other may linger. Other times, they just seem to go their separate ways. My favorite pairings are those that harmonize gracefully from start to finish, both wine and cheese improved by the marriage.

In investigating pairing possibilities, a good way to start is to focus on grape varieties or general wine types—for example Champagne or "Bordeaux-style" blends. As you proceed, you will gradually refine the promising ones—narrowing them to ever more specific wines—and weed out the clunkers.

WINE PAIRINGS

I've found the two most versatile red wines for matching with cheeses are the Zinfandels and those made from the Syrah grape. Pinot Noir wines are a close runner-up. My top whites in terms of versatility would have to be Albariños, Rieslings, and Sauvignon Blancs. An old standby for pairings is dessert wines, which are sweet, in contrast to the saltiness of cheeses; this rule is a bit simplistic, though, as you'll discover if you start to experiment.

In general, the red wines with the most versatility for pairings are the fruitier, less dry ones. The dry, steely, more tannic reds—say, the Haut-Medocs from Bordeaux—offer far fewer potential pairings. (As an aside, there are very few good pairings for goat cheeses and red wines.) You'll find many more pairings in the "simple wine" category; the famous, *grand cru,* high-pedigree wines are more difficult to match. For example, a Dão wine from Portugal is a very satisfying red, a good value, nothing to be scoffed at, and an excellent potential partner for cheeses. Beaujolais is another example; it is up front, a little fruity, and very versatile. In choosing any one of these "nonpedigree" wines, however, make sure you select the top of its category—for Beaujolais, choose a Moulin-à-Vent or a Morgon. The same is true of whites: the pricey, top-flight ones can be more difficult to work with vis-à-vis cheese. A Montrachet, for example, would have more limited pairing potential than a Meursault, which in turn would be more constraining than, say a Savennières (Chenin Blanc), a Gewürztraminer, or, better yet, an Albariño. If you're choosing a Gewürz, go for quality—a Trimbach or a Hugel.

In the following list, you'll find some cheese-wine pairings that have been successful at the restaurant or in tastings. It contains only those pairings that I can confirm—no long-accepted ones that many people, including so-called experts, simply *assume* work nicely but haven't tried for themselves. The list is by no means complete but is part of my ongoing pursuit of empirical cheese truth. I discover successful pairings on a regular basis. You will, too, if you put the principles outlined in this chapter to work and experiment a little.

NOTE: ** Denotes the highest-ranked or most successful pairings.

CHEESE-FRIENDLY WINES

WHITES
Albariño
Champagne
Gewürztraminer
Grüner Veltliner
Muscat (dry to sweet)
Pinot Blanc
Pinot Gris
Riesling

REDS
Cabernet Sauvignon
Carignan
Dolcetto d'Albec
Nebbiolo
Pinot Noir
Tempranillo-Garnacha blends
Zinfandel

✦ WHITES

ALBARIÑO: A highly versatile, light, pleasingly acidic varietal from northern Spain that can go with a wide variety of cheeses. It is affordable and shares characteristics with white Burgundy, white Bordeaux, and even white Rhones. Try it with Brin D'Amour, Big Holmes, Ibores, Queso de la Serena, Selles-sur-Cher, Zamorano. It is not recommended with blues.

BORDEAUX: White Bordeaux is made from the Sauvignon Blanc grape (see also separate entry that follows). Recommended pairings: Abbaye de Belloc, Cabécou de Rocamadour.

CHAMPAGNE: I recommend a high-quality dry (brut) or vintage Champagne:

> BLANC DE BLANCS (made mostly from Chardonnay grapes): Beaufort, Doeling Camembert**, Garroxta, Pavé D'Auge**, Pierre-Robert, Vacherin Haut-Rive**.

> BLANC DE NOIRS (made from Pinot Noir grapes): Beaufort, Pierre-Robert, Queso de la Serena, Trade Lake Cedar, Vermont Shepherd**, Wabash Cannonball.

> ROSÉ (pink): Epoisses, Hoch Ybrig, Ibores, Queso de la Serena**.

CHARDONNAY: The Chardonnay grape yields a range of extremely popular wines; however, it can be a difficult match for cheeses.

> BURGUNDY: I've found good pairings with such elegant and refined wines as Corton-Charlemagne (a grand cru), Meursault, or St.-Véran: Beaufort**, Caerphilly, Epoisses, Garroxta**, Ibores, Nancy's Hudson Valley Camembert, Vermont Shepherd, Flixer.

> CALIFORNIA: Fruitier, oakier, not as austere as Burgundies. Try it with Beaufort, Fontina D'Aosta, Mahón, Stilton, Trade Lake Cedar, Vermont Shepherd.

Another rough day at the office, searching for the perfect combinations of wines and cheeses.

CHENIN BLANC: Chenin Blanc is responsible for a couple of very fine cheese-friendly French wines. See Vouvray and Savennières; also Dessert and Fortified Wines. Recommended pairings: Ardrahan, Azeitão, Cheddar, Centovalli Ticino, Durrus, Flixer, Harbourne Blue, Inner-schweizer Weicher, Sainte-Maure, Serena.

CONDRIEU: Made from the Viognier grape, this northern Rhône delight can be sublimely bittersweet with citrusy flavors and full body. Pairings: Caerphilly, Double Gloucester, Epoisses, Fladä, Gubbeen, Inner-Schweizer Weicher, Pavé D'Auge, Peral, Spenwood, Vermont Shepherd.

GEWÜRZTRAMINER: A pleasant, versatile dryish wine with spicy, citrus, and floral aromas. Strong, smelly, washed-rind cheese such as Munster, Epoisses, or Livarot can work with Alsatian Gewürztraminers, the best of this varietal. Also try Appenzeller, Berkswell, Caerphilly, Cheddar, Chimay, Double Gloucester, Durrus, Gubbeen, Harbourne Blue**, Lancashire, Llangloffan, Pierre-Robert, Reblochon, Serena, Taleggio, Vacherin Haut-Rive, Spenwood, Taleggio.

GRÜNER VELTLINER: The pride of Austria, Grüner Veltliner produces fairly dry, floral wines with a pleasing touch of acid. They are also quite versatile with cheeses. Recommended pairings: Appenzeller**, Brin D'Amour, Caerphilly, Cheddar, Chimay au Lait Cru, Double Gloucester, Garrotxa, Harbourne Blue, Hoch Ybrig, Ibores**, Lancashire**, Livarot, Mahón, Mont Briac, Munster, Queso de la Serena, Vacherin Fribourgeois.

PINOT BLANC: A chameleon grape and an unsung hero in the wine world. When well made, the wines from Pinot Blanc show a multifaceted flavor profile restrained by its own grace. Recommended pairings: Cheddar, Fontina d'Aosta, Montasio, Mont Briac, Ossau-Iraty Brebis, Queso de los Beyos, Pierre-Robert**, Pont L'Evêque, Sbrinz, Stanser Schafchäs, Taleggio.

PINOT GRIS (PINOT GRIGIO): Medium- to light-bodied with hints of citrus and some residual sugar, Pinot Gris is a popular, versatile, unassuming wine that pairs well with cheeses. (It is made in Alsace and northern Italy, where it is also known as Tokay and Tocai, respectively, and also in Germany.) Recommended pairings: Chevrotin des Aravis, Gabrielson Lake, Garrotxa, Le Chèvre Noir, Pierre-Robert, Putney Tomme, Queso de los Beyos, Serra, Spenwood.

RIESLING: This multifaceted grape yields beautifully balanced wines within a wide range from dry and almost puckering to sweet and thick. It needn't be very sweet to pair successfully with many cheeses.

ALSATIAN: Ardrahan, Brin D'Amour, Caerphilly, Gubbeen, Hoch Ybrig, Ibores**, Livarot, Llangloffan, Prattigauer, Robiola**, Sbrinz, Vacherin Fribourgeois.**

GERMAN: The Kabinett wines are the lightest and driest; succeeding categories (Spätlese, Auslese, Beerenauslese, and Trockenbeerenauslese) have increasingly more body and residual sugar.

KABINETT: Chevrotin des Aravis, Garrotxa, Lancashire, Livarot, Monte Enebro, Munster, Pavé D'Auge, Pierre-Robert, Reblochon**, Roucoulons, Selles-sur-Cher, Serena**, Vermont Shepherd, Zamorano.

SPÄTLESE: Beaufort, Berkswell, Ibores**, Livarot, Mahón.

AUSLESE: Afuega l'Pita, Ardrahan, Berkswell**, Brin D'Amour, Chimay au Lait Cru**, Durrus**, Hoch Ybrig**, Livarot, Munster

SANCERRE (see also Sauvignon Blanc): The famous Loire Valley wine made from the Sauvignon Blanc grape is often described as flinty or chalky. It also offers herbal and citrus flavors and aromas. It is classically matched with goat cheeses, many of them local. Try it with Brin D'Amour, Chevrotin des Aravis, Crottin de Chavignol, Pouligny-Saint-Pierre, Sainte-Maure de Touraine, Selles-sur-Cher, or Valençay.

SAUVIGNON BLANC: In France, this grape is responsible for wines from Sancerre, Pouilly-Fume, and Graves (white Bordeaux). It also finds expression in fine wines from New Zealand and California. Their main component is tartness; there is also a "grassiness" or vegetal quality, particularly to the New Zealand versions. Cheese pairings: Abbaye de Belloc, Berkswell, Centovalli Ticino, Cheshire, Chevrotin des Aravis, Doeling Camembert, Fladä, Flixer, Garrotxa, Ibores, Le Chèvre Noir, Loire Valley chèvres, Nancy's Hudson Valley Camembert, Peñamellera, Queso de los Beyos**, Roncal, Selles-sur-Cher**, Stanser Schafchäs, Taleggio, Val Bagner, Vermont Shepherd, Wabash Cannonball.

SAVENNIÈRES. Made from the Chenin Blanc grape in a lesser-known Loire Valley appellation; pleasingly acidic and dry. Recommended pairings: Ardrahan, Azeitão, Centovalli Ticino, Cheddar, Durrus, Flixer, Harbourne Blue, Ibores, Innerschweizer Weicher, Pont L'Evêque, Sainte-Maure, Serena, Taleggio, Torta del Casar.

VIOGNIER (see also Condrieu): An intriguing bittersweet grape that has become fashionable in the past decade with some growers in California. Pairings: Caerphilly, Doeling Dairy Camembert, Orb Weaver, Pavé D'Auge, Pierre-Robert, Ticklemore, Timson, Vermont Shepherd.**

VOUVRAY (see also Chenin Blanc): Balanced Loire Valley wines within a range from *sec* (dry) to *demi-sec* (medium) to *moulleux* (sweet). Recommended pairings: Berkswell, Caerphilly**, Double Gloucester, Durrus, Gubbeen, Llangloffan, Spenwood.

✦ REDS

BARBARESCO: See Nebbiolo.

BAROLO: See Nebbiolo.

BEAUJOLAIS: See Gamay.

BURGUNDY: See Pinot Noir.

CABERNET SAUVIGNON: Among the noblest grapes of all; responsible for full-bodied, long-lasting, tannic, yet fruity wines of great subtlety and depth, particularly in Bordeaux and California. Cabernets find a surprising diversity of matchups, mostly with cow and sheep cheeses.

> CALIFORNIA: These big, fruity, fairly forward wines pair nicely with Beenleigh Blue, Cheddar, Durrus, Epoisses, Llangloffan, and Perail.

> BORDEAUX: Complex, tannic wines can complement certain types of cheeses. But beware of the dogma that a big, chewy Bordeaux can go with *any* cheese (not true). Some recommendations: Appenzeller, Brin D'Amour, Cheddar**, L'Edel de Cleron, Llangloffan, Mahón, Montasio, Pavé D'Auge, Perail**, Pierre-Robert**, Reblochon, Roomano**, Roucoulons, Queso de la Serena, Spenwood, Vacherin Fribourgeois.**

CARIGNAN: The most commonly planted grape in southern France, it produces volumes of simple "rustic" wines that can make certain cheeses very happy. Recommendations: Azeitão, Berkswell, Brin D'Amour, Mimolette**, Montasio, Reblochon**, Zamorano.

CHÂTEAUNEUF-DU-PAPE: Usually a blend of the Syrah, Grenache, Mourvèdre and other grapes from this southern Rhône appellation yields full-bodied spicy tannic wines. Cheese pairings: Berkswell, Cheddar, Ibores, Roomano, Vacheria Fribourgeois.

CÔTES DU RHÔNE (see also Syrah): A less-specific Rhône Valley appellation that produces substantial, reliable Syrah-based wines. Try them with Cheddar** and Spenwood.**

CHIANTI CLASSICO: See Sangiovese.

GAMAY (BEAUJOLAIS): The grape is Gamay, the appellation Beaujolais (on the banks of the Rhône near Lyon); together, they yield light, fruity, tasty wines. Try Moulin-à-Vent or Morgon, the two finest *crus* of Beaujolais to complement your cheeses. Recommended pairings: Bra, Reblochon, Durrus**.

MALBEC: Grapey and rustic, this varietal is most successful in Cahors (aka Auxerrois) in southwestern France and in Argentina. Pairing: Bleu des Causses, Evora, Mimolette, Pavé D'Auge.

MERLOT: Historically, this grape is most important as a main component of the Bordeaux blends. In the New World, its accessible, opulent, full-bodied expressions became all the rage. A big fruity California Merlot finds some excellent pairings: Hoch Ybrig, Ibores, Lancashire, Montasio, Pecorino Toscano, Roncal, Roomano, Queso de la Serena.

NEBBIOLO: This king of northern Italian grape varieties is responsible for the great Barolo and Barbaresco wines of Piedmont. It can make big, full-bodied, long-lasting yet well-rounded and very accessible wines. In conventional wisdom, Barbaresco wines are the best Italian reds for cheeses. Suggested pairings for Barolos and Barbarescos: Berkswell, Centovalli Ticino, Montasio, Robiola, Parmigiano-Reggiano, Beyos, Val Bagner, Ibores, Brin D'Amour, Afuega'l Pitu.

PINOT NOIR: Unquestionably one of the most versatile grapes in matching with cheeses. Because of its subtlety, however, it has a tendency to be overwhelmed by strong, smelly cheeses. Pinots can go well with cheeses that

The wide array of fruity, nutty, and butterscotch flavors in a well-aged Mimolette calls out for a rustic red such as Cahors.

have an undercurrent of sweetness such as the Pyrénées-style sheep's milk types. A well-structured Pinot also has the tannins and acids to cut the rich fattiness of dense cheeses.

BURGUNDY: Afuega'l Pitu, Berkswell**, Cheddar, Spenwood**, Vermont Shepherd.**

CALIFORNIA: Azeitão, Beaufort**, Lancashire, Mahon, Reblochon, Spenwood, Vermont Shepherd.**

OREGON: Beaufort, Queso de los Beyos, Ibores, Reblochon, Single Gloucester, Vermont Shepherd, Zamorano.

RIOJA: This most famous of Spanish wines is made from a blend of the Tempranillo and Garnacha grapes, which also goes into the wines of Ribera del Duero, Navarra, and other regions including the Estremadura. It is one of the most cheese-friendly wines, particularly with Spanish cheeses (no surprise there). Try these matchups: Afuega'l Pitu**, Ardrahan, Azeitão**, Berkswell**, Evora, Gamonedo, Garrotxa**, Ibores**, Mahón, Monte Enebro, Peñamellera, Queso de la Peral, Queso de la Serena**, Roncal, Serra, Spenwood**, Torta del Casar.

SANGIOVESE: The star grape of central Italy, predominant in Chiantis and also the Supertuscans (blended along with Cabernet Sauvignon, Merlot, and others). Makes beautiful, balanced medium- to full-bodied wines. Pairings: Afuega'l Pitu, Fontina d'Aosta, Swiss Gruyère, Pecorino Toscano, Queso de la Serena, Roncal, Taleggio, Torta del Casar.

SYRAH: The principal grape in the Rhône reds (Hermitage, Côte Rôtie, Cornas, and St. Joseph). It makes very concentrated, tannic, full-bodied wines with plenty of fruit. There are also some interesting Syrahs coming out of California now, not to mention the excellent Australian Shiraz. Some pairings:

RHÔNE REDS: Beaufort**, Caerphilly**, Double Gloucester**, Gubbeen, Ibores, Llangloffan**, Perail**.

CALIFORNIA: Berkswell**, Le Chèvre Noir, Doeling Camembert, Trade Lake Cedar, Vacherin Fribourgeois, Vermont Shepherd**.

SYRAH-GRENACHE-MOURVÈDRE BLEND: The same blend that goes into Châteauneuf-du-Pape (see separate listing) also produces some less-heralded wines in the Languedoc and other regions of southern France. Pairings: Afuega'l Pitu, Azeitão, Queso de la Serena, Serra**, Vermont Shepherd, Zamorano.

TRINCADEIRA RIBATEJANA: A Portuguese wine, light- to medium-bodied, spicy and reminiscent of Gamay. Pairings: Mahón, Monte Enebro, Serra, Torta del Casar.

ZINFANDEL: With both Zinfandel and Syrah, it is possible to make a big wine with ripe tannins, fruitiness, and residual sugar that provides an excellent complement to the saltiness of cheeses. (Zin is actually a native California

BEVERAGES OTHER THAN WINE

THE overwhelming majority of my pairing investigation has been with regard to wines. It is the beverage accompaniment of choice for most caseophiles. There are others, however, that can match up well. Apple cider—not just the hard kind—as well as grape and berry juices are good possibilities. Coffee pairs well with many cheeses. But tea does not. Also avoid orange and other citrus juices. In fact, I'm quite wary of even the lemon or lime wedge that goes with your sparkling water; it could easily interfere with a good cheese. (More on nonalcoholic beverages to follow.)

varietal.) Pairings: Beenleigh Blue**, Coolea**, Doeling Camembert**, Lancashire, Le Chèvre Noir, Orb Weaver, Queso de los Beyos, Roomano, Trade Lake Cedar, Vermont Shepherd**, Wabash Cannonball, Zamorano**.

✦ DESSERT AND FORTIFIED WINES

BANYULS: Very Port-like; made from the "rustic" varietal Grenache in the very southern tip of France. Pairing: Bleu de Causses**.

COTEAUX DE LAYON: A late-harvest Chenin Blanc wine; the Loire Valley's answer to Sauternes. Try it with Harbourne Blue.

JURANÇON: Made from the Petit Mensang grape in the southwest of France, near the Pyrénées. A sweet white late-harvest wine with some acid—almost a citrus quality. Pairings: Gouda, Prattigauer, Queso de la Peral, Stanser Schafchäs**, Taleggio.

MADEIRA: Toasty, nutty, and well-aged; from the eponymous island off the coast of Morocco. Pairings: Roquefort, Stanser Schafchäs.

MUSCAT DE RIVESALTES: Lighter than some of the other dessert wines, not as viscous and fairly versatile with cheeses—except the heavyweight blues. From an appellation near Perpignan in southernmost France. Recommended pairings: Ardrahan**, Gorgonzola, Harbourne Blue**, Mont Briac, Monte Enebro**, Taleggio**, Valdeón.

TOKAJI: Celestial nectar, Hungarian-style; vies with Sauternes as the world's greatest dessert wine. It is incredibly delicious, balanced, and sweet but never sugary. Pairings: Beenleigh Blue**, Cashel Blue, Harbourne Blue**, Hoch Ybrig, Monte Enebro.

PEDRO XIMENEZ LUSTAU: The famous fortified wine from the south of Spain. This one is not the kind Grandma used to drink for her aperitif but a thicker, more lush dessert wine redolent of raisins. Try it with Cabrales.

For the classic after-dinner cheese course, a dessert wine is a popular choice—for good reason. Here, a superb Bonny Doon Vineyards Muscat is paired with three American masterpieces: from right, Great Hill Blue, Vermont Shepherd, and Wabash Cannonball.

PINOT GRIS (LATE-HARVEST): Probably the best expression of this grape comes in the dessert-wine format. Pairings: Gamonedo**, Harbourne Blue, Queso de la Serena.

PORT: One reason this much-beloved fortified wine is considered to be a prototypical cheese partner is its sweet berry flavor, which contrasts with the cheeses' saltiness. A fine vintage Port can be a course in itself; Tawny Port is usually sufficient to accompany cheeses. Try it with Serra or Stilton.

QUARTS DE CHAUME: One of the distinguished late-harvest Chenin Blanc wines from the Loire Valley. Similar to Vouvray Moulleux and Coteaux du Layon (although a bit thicker than the Coteaux). Pairings: Bleu de Causses, Mimolette.

SAUTERNES: Nectar of the gods; France's foremost late-harvest (noble rot) wine from south of Bordeaux. A classic pairing with blues; also works well with some of the pungent, washed-rind cheeses. Recommendations: Beenleigh Blue**, Epoisses**, Roquefort, Stanser Schafchäs.

WINE-DRIVEN PLATES

My choice is always to let the cheese rule, but there are times when circumstances dictate that the cheeses be selected to match the beverages. Here are some plates tailored to their liquid accompaniments.

CABERNET SAUVIGNON

Some consider it the most magnificent of all grapes. Because it can yield such big, complex and long-lasting wines, you might think it would be limited in its cheese pairings, possibly an overwhelming partner. But there are some really fine matches to be had.

1. PERAIL: Soft-ripened, relatively fresh, smooth, not an elborate cheese, it presents no challenge to all kinds of Cabernet-based wines. It melds easily, offering complement rather than contrast.
2. CHEDDAR: Genuine Cheddar and a fine claret is a classic matchup, a proper British pairing, the kind you'd expect to be served in a traditional London men's club. Real Cheddar, flavorful but not too sharp, has a balanced component of fruitiness that goes hand in hand with a Cabernet. The Cheddar crunch works nicely with the velvety quality of a well-made claret.
3. APPENZELLER: Concentrated, buttery, with a strong undercurrent of sweet milky flavors, the density and intensity of this cheese is softened by the wine. Returning the compliment, the cheese highlights the fruit in the wine.

CHAMPAGNE

Champagne is generally a food-friendly beverage, especially when it has a balanced component of acidity. Texturally, the marriage with cheese is delightful. The Champagne gently dissolves the cheese and gracefully lifts its pungent sour-milk characteristics off the palate. Both of the Champagne types here are fairly dry or "brutish," yet the characteristics of the predominant grapes, Chardonnay for the Blanc de Blancs and Pinot Noir for the Blanc de Noirs, will come to the fore and complement the cheeses.

Blanc de Blancs

1. PIERRE-ROBERT: A glorious cheese that's so rich and buttery it's almost sinful. The Champagne cuts through all that texturally, with its millions of little pinprick bubbles, and chemically, with its component of acidity. The Pierre-Robert coats the tongue like peanut butter; the Champagne refreshes like a soda pop.

2. VACHERIN HAUT-RIVE: The Champagne can moderate some of the woodsy, resinous character of the cheese as well as tame its distinct sour-milk flavor, resulting in an entirely pleasing, mellow harmony.
3. SWISS GRUYÈRE: A well-made Gruyère features hard texture and a myriad of concentrated flavors. Its protein crystals swirl around in the mouth with the bubbly, forming a delightful mix. Gruyère also has a hint of sweetness that agrees nicely with the Champagne.

Blanc de Noirs

1. EPOISSES: A cheese whose flavor is much milder than its decidedly pungent aroma would suggest, Epoisses also has a definite saltiness, which always begs for the refreshing quality of Champagne. The salt also highlights the wine's sweet, fruity undercurrent.
2. BEAUFORT: Although it is made from cow's milk, Beaufort has that particular persistence most often found in fine sheep cheeses. This sparkling Pinot Noir–based wine penetrates the cheese's density, breaking it down into its sweet, nutty, buttery components.
3. QUESO DE LA SERENA: The Blanc de Noirs Champagne is not quite as focused and direct as its Chardonnay counterpart. It forms a successful match with this unctuous cheese because they share full, round, fat flavors. Left alone, the Serena may weigh a bit heavy on the palate; this wine's effervescence stirs it up and melds it into a scrumptious blend.

CHARDONNAY

I admit to being a big fan of Chardonnay wines despite their somewhat dimished reputation. There are some really fine cheese pairings to be found, particularly if you choose an elegant, refined Chardonnay such as the Burgundian *premier cru* and *grand cru* AOC wines.

1. GARROTXA: Should be served firm and moist. Its milky, gentle herbal flavors ennoble Chardonnay-based wines. It's a simple, elegant, delicious cheese that pairs wonderfully with sophisticated Chardonnays.
2. TRADE LAKE CEDAR: This cheese provides flavors that are not so much herbal as they are gently spicy and nutty. It is definitely the backbone of the pairing, giving the Chardonnay something to lean on. In addition, its substantial consistency can round out the austere, angular character of a fine Burgundian white.
3. FONTINA D'AOSTA: A compact chunk of cheese. Although it does possess the buttery, nutty quality of many Gruyère-type cheeses, it also features a clean, fresh-milk taste that matches well with the buttery oak-aged California-style Chardonnays. The vanilla flavors of such a wine work well with the ground-nut ones in this cheese.

If the wine is the driving force behind a tasting, it helps to include some versatile cheeses. For example, this Berkswell is rich enough to stand up to big tannic reds, spicy whites and rich ones, or tart and grassy ones.

CHÂTEAUNEUF-DU-PAPE

This is a big, delicious, and fairly complex wine. There is usually a lot going on in the glass. So a matching cheese should either be quite simple and straightforward *or* one with a full flavor profile and a good balance of sweetness, saltiness, and acidity.

1. IBORES: Spicy and zesty, it brings the Châteauneuf-du-Pape forward on the palate. Without breaking the wine down, it supports its fullness and structure, highlighting its various berry flavors.
2. BERKSWELL: On the other hand, here is a cheese that meets this big wine on even terms. It has substantial texture and firmness on the tongue. It is toothsome and meaty, full and long-lasting but at the same time is an exercise in balance—qualities shared by this wine.

3. ROOMANO: Again, an even match. The hardness and mouth-watering flavors of a 6-year-old Roomano soften the wine's toothsome quality and balance its heft. Roomano has a cooked-curd sweetness to reflect the wine's fruit and create an even, harmonious partnership.

GAMAY

With its simplicity and fruitiness, Gamay doesn't tolerate loud, obstreperous cheeses but instead finds a match with straightforward, softer, less temperamental ones.

1. CHEVROTIN DES ARAVIS: Relatively mild despite a pronounced aroma, the pairing with Gamay is a smooth one that erases any vestiges of the barnyard.

2. DURRUS: Similar to the Chevrotin but made from cow's milk. This matchup is akin to a couple of welterweights dancing in the ring. Durrus is a beautiful artisanal cheese, the kind you might bring home to mother along with your bottle of Beaujolais Villages, for an informal but festive occasion.

3. VALDEÓN: An unexpected match and quite a leap of intensity from the Durrus. As always, the better the specimens of cheese and wine, the more successful the match. Look for a Valdeón with a little goat milk added to it.

GEWÜRZTRAMINER

Spicy, floral Gewürz finds several delightful matches with some of the spunkier, more substantial cheeses. Gewürz is a grape that demands something of its cheese partners; it has versatility and complexity, with acid, residual sugar, and multiple floral aromas.

1. SPENWOOD: A well-crafted wine and a well-crafted cheese that make a tremendous match, with everything in balance. Both have admirable self-assurance and pride. As rich as the Gewürz is in its spiciness and floral character, the nutty Spenwood rounds out the spectrum with equal doses of sweetness and saltiness.

2. MUNSTER: Here is a classic Alsatian regional pairing. The Gewürz is brought to its peak when paired with a Munster. A forceful wine and an emphatically aromatic cheese, each lifting the other to new heights.

3. HARBOURNE BLUE: In my ranking system, this matchup receives the highest mark—a "+2." Both wine and cheese possess a spectrum of flavors, sweet to sour to floral, and they meld well start to finish, highlighting each other's best traits and producing a stunning finish.

MERLOT

A well-oaked Merlot with lush, plummy fruit and ripe tannins seems to find the best pairings with cheeses. In some sense, the bigger the better. Merlot is traditionally considered a blending grape (although a recent New World trend is for the varietals), and that's what it does best with cheeses: it blends.

1. LLANGLOFFAN: Brings out some of the sweeter berry qualities of the wine. Texturally, Merlot is soft, which provides a fitting contrast to the firm texture of this sturdy cheese.

2. PECORINO TOSCANO (AGED AT LEAST 4 MONTHS): This matchup offers a contrast of flavor and texture. Here you have a piquant cheese and a full, fruity wine: Pecorino is peppery; Merlot is berry-like. The Merlot dilutes some of the cheese's piquancy but remains determined enough not to be washed away by it.

3. HOCH YBRIG: Firm but not as dry as the Llangloffan or the aged Pecorino, this cheese is also very smooth on the palate, start to finish, a characteristic it shares with the Merlot. The Hoch Ybrig features a moistness that works well with the lush, juicy qualities of the wine.

NEBBIOLO

Northern Italy's dignified reds, Barolo and Barbaresco, are the marvelous expression of this grape variety. They find successful pairings with cheeses from both near and far.

1. IBORES: This zesty, atypical goat cheese liquifies deliciously with the Nebbiolo, allowing the wine to "wear the pants." The cheese high lights some unrealized flavor components in the wine.

2. CENTOVALLI TICINO: Dignity meets dignity. The Centovalli Ticino tolerates few wines of a lesser pedigree. It harmonizes with the wine, lingering sweetly on the palate.

3. TALEGGIO: Regional affinity justifies this fine pairing. Aromatic and plump but sweet and full, the cheese folds smoothly into the Nebbiolo, tempering its bold pronouncement.

PINOT NOIR

Cheeses to be paired with Pinot Noir wines may have some full, round flavors, but they must also possess some restraint. These wines are known for their agreeable, balanced nature vis-à-vis foods; they can be easily elevated in tandem with many cheeses.

1. SINGLE GLOUCESTER: A gentle, sweet, and unassuming partner for the Pinot. It hesitates, then blends with the wine without overpowering it.

2. REBLOCHON: The cheese's soft texture, a feature matched by some of the best Pinot Noirs, places a greater emphasis on flavor balance between cheese and wine.

3. VERMONT SHEPHERD: Finds many pleasant partnerships with many wine types and one of its most reliable counterparts is a good Pinot Noir. It doesn't matter which one you place on the palate first: a smooth blending is instantaneous.

RIESLING

This noble grape seeks a communicative partner in cheeses; from its driest to its sweetest expressions, it finds many successful matches with nonblue cheeses.

1. CAERPHILLY: Melds gracefully with the Riesling, leaving behind a gentle harmony.

2. PAVÉ D'AUGE: After the Caerphilly; the wine is ready for a greater challenge: the cheese's flavors and aromas are more pronounced and it meets the Riesling on common ground. The wine's acidity stretches the Pavé to show a wider range of flavor components.

3. VACHERIN FRIBOURGEOIS: This is an even stronger challenge to the Riesling. As profound as the cheese may be, the wine penetrates and separates its components, simplifing its complexity.

SYRAH

As a varietal, this grape produces some thick, fruity, purple, juicy wines; "grapey" is the description that most often comes to my mind. For this reason, it can cover a wide spectrum of cheeses. It works particularly well with the butterfats in the following trio.

1. CAERPHILLY: Gentle and subtle in flavor, hearty and substantial in texture, the Caerphilly is like butter to the Syrah's jelly (albeit with a squeeze of lemon).

2. TALEGGIO: Its pungent aroma challenges the Syrah, but the wine holds it own, keeping its focus and complementing some of the buttery flavors and textures this cheese shares with the preceding Caerphilly.

3. QUEIJO SERRA: Neither partner overwhelms the other; this is a marriage made to last. A substantial sheep cheese with full, round, lingering flavors. The focused Syrah lingers on, too, claiming its place in the mouth alongside the remnants of this magnificent cheese.

TEMPRANILLO

Warming, affable, and gracious, Tempranillo is primarily responsible for the great wines of the Rioja and Ribera del Duero appellations of Spain (in tandem with its blending partner, Garnacha). It stands up extremely well to some of the more soulful varieties among the Iberian sheep, goat, and cow cheeses.

1. IBORES: Strikes a lovely balance with the wine.
2. AFUEGA'L PITU: This assertive cheese ennobles the wine; it features an intriguing bitterness that melts away in the face of this wine's fruit and ripe tannins.
3. QUESO DE LA SERENA: Its butterfats match well with the Tempranillo's acids.
4. MONTE ENEBRO: Superficially, this cheese might seem a more likely choice for Position Number 1 on the plate. But its cacophony puts even a robust Tempranillo-based wine to the test. With a good wine, the Monte Enebro will eventually fold, although the finish will lean pleasantly toward the cheese.

A WINE-AND-CHEESE ADVENTURE

SIX FLIGHTS OF WINE WITH TWELVE GREAT CHEESES

1. 1997 SAVENNIÈRES: Ticklemore, Brin D'Amour, Durrus
2. 1998 SANCERRE: Pouligny-Saint Pierre
3. 1998 CONDRIEU: Gorwydd Caerphilly, Pierre-Robert
4. 1995 CORTON-CHARLEMAGNE: Queso de la Garrotxa, Beaufort
5. 1993 VOLNAY: Vermont Shepherd, Keen's Cheddar
6. 1990 SAUTERNES: Berthaut Epoisses, Great Hill Blue

A party of four came in one balmy October evening and asked for a tasting meal of nothing but wines and cheeses. This is what I live for. To begin, I asked the gentleman in charge what kind of wines he liked. Without hesitation, he mentioned Corton-Charlemagne, the superb white Burgundy, and also any *grand cru* red Burgundy. Obviously, he was willing to splurge

a bit. I suggested he also consider some lesser wines and some half bottles to accompany smaller groups of cheese so his party could experience a full spectrum of cheeses and wider range of pairings. He agreed.

I selected six flights of wine with no more than three cheeses to accompany each wine—twelve total. I tried to create pairings that worked not only in terms of flavors but also textures. I also gave attention to the overall progression, trying to alternate textures and types of cheeses.

Clearly, this kind of lineup is very ambitious in the context of home entertaining. If you try it, you'll probably want to limit the remainder of the fare to a soup before and salad during or after. Feel free to pick and choose; cut it down to three flights or even a single one, but do respect the order of presentation.

■ *Flight 1:* The SAVENNIÈRES originates in the Loire Valley and is made from the Chenin Blanc

(CONTINUED)

grape. It is a fairly simple, refreshing, floral wine.

The TICKLEMORE, a semihard goat's milk cheese with a slightly tangy flavor, was on the young side, with a fresh taste, but it nevertheless had that signature crumbly texture. One reason this pairing works so well is the Savennières has a light, a fresh, a springlike quality to balance the cheese's crumbliness. Chenin Blanc also offers a taste of residual sugar to balance the mild saltiness of the Ticklemore.

BRIN D'AMOUR is an uncooked, unpressed sheep's milk cheese encrusted with two herbs, savory and rosemary. I also served a relatively young specimen that was moist, milky, and fairly mild. Brin D'Amour is palatable and easy to digest, which is why it usually works well at or near the starting point of a cheese plate. You can taste a bit of the Mediterranean in it, a slight saltiness, but its strongest attribute is the herbal aroma. The Savennières offered a complement rather than a challenge to the herbal, aromatic qualities of the cheese.

The DURRUS is a rich, smooth, semisoft, washed-rind cow's milk cheese from the western part of County Cork, Ireland. Despite the presence of *B. linens* bacteria in the rind, this cheese retains its milky, grassy, floral cow's milk flavors. The pleasant acid content of the Savennières contrasted nicely with the sweetness and richness of the milk in this cheese.

■ *Flight 2:* The second wine was a crisp SANCERRE, which I paired with a single cheese, the POULIGNY-SAINT-PIERRE, a semisoft, pure, white AOC goat's milk cheese from the Loire Valley. We were fortunate to be able to offer a beautiful specimen of this typical French chèvre at peak stage of ripeness. In mid-October, this selection was a no-brainer, since we knew the cheese had been made when the animals were consuming lush vegetation in late summer. Likewise, the pairing was a gimme: local cheese with local wine. This Pouligny was young, creamy, and moist, not too salty or sharp. The Sancerre was perky and tart like citrus juice, which made for a nice contrast with the cheese. Had the cheese been further along—older and

drier—the pair might not have worked as well. This is a wine to drink young; it is not expected to improve with age.

■ *Flight 3:* CONDRIEU, the great northern Rhône white, is made from the Viognier grape. It has a light and refreshing yet simultaneously luscious quality. It can be quite fruity (with hints of ripe apricots and melons, among other fruits), floral, and slightly bittersweet.

CAERPHILLY is a traditional Welsh semifirm raw cow's milk cheese; Gorwydd is the one remaining farmhouse version. It has a mild, buttery flavor that features hints of lemon and a wonderful soft texture. A good midsummer Caerphilly, matured for about 2½ months, is incredibly satisfying, truly a cheese lover's delight. The Condrieu has a certain viscosity, which helps carry the Caerphilly over the palate. The cheese's subtle saltiness allows it to linger on the tongue past the washing of this intriguing Viognier-based wine; its lemony flavor complements the wine's fruit accents to create a divine pairing.

PIERRE-ROBERT is my favorite among the triple crèmes, a pasteurized cow's milk genre of cheeses from the Île-de-France province that surrounds Paris. These mild-tasting soft cheeses are made with enriched milk and have 75 percent fat in dry matter. Pierre-Robert is a fairly versatile cheese with respect to wines. One of its main characteristics is a buttery richness. In this pairing, we find another good use for the Condrieu's viscosity: it can stand up to the typical richness of the Pierre-Robert.

■ *Flight 4:* The next wine was a 1995 CORTON-CHARLEMAGNE, the world-famous white Burgundy. I made sure to recommend that my diners had some of this wine on its own before tasting it with cheeses. Not only is it brilliant solo but considering the richness of the preceding Pierre-Robert, it was nice to follow with such an expansive wine.

GARROTXA, an old-style rustic goat's milk cheese from north-central Catalonia, has a semisoft paste with a mild herbal flavor. By the nature of the milk alone, this is a more dense cheese than any of the preceding ones. I like it with white Burgundies, and in this case, I was able to fulfill my customer's exact request for a Corton-Charlemagne. This wine possesses an elegance and refinement that offered a gracious welcome to the Garrotxa. Chardonnay wines have a signature buttery flavor while the Garrotxa has an herbal quality; these two aspects marry very well here, as they do in several classic herb-butter culinary combinations such as Bearnaise sauce and *maître d'hôtel* butter. Garrotxa is a relatively subtle goat cheese, especially in comparison to the stronger ripened Loire Valley goats—say, a mature Crottin de Chavignol. So it's a fitting match to a wine that is both subtle and complex, refreshing and profound.

The second cheese with the Corton was "The Prince of Gruyères," BEAUFORT, which is made in the mountainous Haute-Savoie region of France from raw cow's milk and is pressed and cooked. If you want to know what a classic mountain cheese should taste like, try this. It is rich and concentrated and redolent of all the best qualities of cow's milk, a regal cheese that stands up to this noble wine. Beaufort has a relatively high butterfat content and exceedingly tasty hints of spoiled milk. A good Beaufort avoids the burnt-milk taste of many inferior "Swiss-style" cheeses and instead exhibits a sweetness and a nuttiness that pairs well with a magnificent Chardonnay.

■ *Flight 5:* The 1993 VOLNAY is a fairly big red Burgundy. VERMONT SHEPHERD is a semihard raw sheep's milk cheese made in the style of the Ossau-Iraty Brebis from the French Pyrenées. The preceding cheese, Beaufort, occupies an extremely elevated cow's milk plateau. I felt that if you didn't proceed to a blue or a strong washed-rind cheese, you had to go to a completely different plane. The Vermont Shepherd came in a wheel made from summer ewe's milk—on June 12—so although it was younger than the Beaufort, it was every bit as substantial. The Volnay was a big enough Pinot Noir from a good enough vintage that its tannins and heft could stand up to a big cheese. A lesser Pinot might not have fared so well. Vermont Shepherd has herbal,

grassy, nutty flavors, which are a complement to this wine's fruit, while at the same time the cheese provides the butterfat to balance the wine's acidity. Pyrenées-style cheeses such as this one are often paired with white Bordeaux wines, which supply the acid to cut the richness of the sheep's milk. In this case, I liked the pairing of this complex, well-rounded cheese with a worthy red Burgundy.

KEEN'S is a traditional raw cow's milk farmhouse Cheddar from southwestern England. The cheese we sampled on this October evening was over a year old. After the Vermont Shepherd, with all its flavor character, this well-aged Cheddar would not be drowned out. Keen's holds back in the face of something as full and lush as the 1993 Volnay. The Keen's is a straightforward workmanlike "cheesy cheese," not some complicated Gallic art form that might, in tandem with this multifaceted wine, tend to overwhelm your senses.

■ *Flight 6:* CHÂTEAU RIEUSSEC is a fine example of Sauternes, France's most celebrated dessert wine.

EPOISSES is a soft, richly flavored, washed-rind AOC cow's milk cheese from Burgundy; Berthaut is its best producer. This was a very mature, soft-textured, strong-flavored but not over-the-top specimen. It was cut fresh at room temperature and still wonderfully milky. Although not a conventional pairing, this worked very well because the Epoisses was tangy enough to go hand in hand with the nectarlike qualities of the Sauternes. After the Cheddar, you could easily justify putting either the Epoisses or the Sauternes in your mouth. There was certainly no letdown in either case.

GREAT HILL BLUE is a raw cow's milk blue from the Great Hill Dairy in Marion, Massachusetts, by the shores of Buzzard's Bay. With this late-harvest sweet wine, I felt obliged to present a superior blue cheese. The flavors of the Great Hill had been very well balanced over the previous 2 months, and I felt it would pair effortlessly with the Sauternes. It did, confirming conventional wisdom.

SEVEN | THE CHEESE COURSE

THE AVERAGE SIZE OF THE PLATE I offer in restaurant service is five cheeses; I've served as few as one or two and as many as fourteen or fifteen. In assembling a cheese course, I always try to mix up the textures, the animals, the provenance: a cow, a sheep, and a goat; some mild, some strong; some soft, some hard; some smelly (you may prefer the term aromatic), some inert. Sometimes, based on curiosity or personal preference, I'll use a theme—a country or region, perhaps, or a particular category of cheese—but it's generally best to mix 'em up.

The quintessentially romantic cheese course: Champagne and strawberries with Beaufort (top) and Pierre-Robert, both rich *fromages* that pair fabulously with the effervescent tartness of a Blanc de Blanc.

What follows in the chapter are some of my favorite plates. When you go to the store, not every one of the cheeses on every one of the plates will always be available. Some are easy to find, others relatively rare. The key is that none of these plates is set in stone. You can very easily substitute similar cheeses *or* simply eliminate a cheese or two. For substitutions of any cheese, refer to Chapter 8 under each entry where I've included sensible alternatives.

Many of the plates in this chapter contain six or more cheeses, which may be beyond your means or your motivation. So delete a cheese or two, even three, as you see fit. In general, I'd try to maintain a basic structure, though, by keeping at least the first and last cheese of a plate. Remember that while all of these plates have been carefully conceived to provide maximum enjoyment in terms of variety and progression—they're all real and tested—you don't need to take them for anything more than inspiration. Feel free to mix and match, to create your own combinations through experimentation. (See the "mix-and-match" chart on page 161, created to encourage your experiments.)

Beginner Plate

To get started, I feel it's valuable to include at least one goat and one sheep cheese as well as the usual cows—that is, as long as you can obtain good specimens. Should a cheese novice taste a bad example of a given cheese, this experience will very likely create a bias that may be hard to overcome. For a beginner plate, I'd lean toward the milder, less-ripened types of cheeses. Some of these can be soft and some hard. Some people start heading for the exits when they see a cheese that's so soft it seems to be running off the board. So I'd tilt slightly in favor of the harder varieties.

A good beginner plate should have a few reference points—familiar names such as Cheddar, Roquefort, or Parmesan. Often I find that novices are more willing to be adventurous if they have some ancestry in a cheese's country of origin. Or perhaps they've vacationed there or have just read a book that takes place there. My suggestions for a beginner plate might include:

1. Fresh Wabash Cannonball
2. A plump, soft, young cow's milk cheese such as Reblochon or Pierre-Robert
3. Manchego that hasn't been shrink-wrapped
4. Cheddar (I have my favorites; see Chapter 8) or a fruity Parmesan
5. A crisp Roquefort (Carles or Vieux Berger), Cashel Blue, or Mont Briac

BREAKFAST

At breakfast, I need my cup o'joe to jump-start the day, so my first thought is of coffee-friendly cheeses. I wouldn't recommend anything too strong, certainly not a blue. Perhaps some hearty, substantial cheeses, even something a little salty if you're going to have it alongside toast and jam or other fruit preserves, which have plenty of sugar, to provide balance. Some of the hard, "rustic" sheep's milk cheeses—Zamorano comes immediately to mind—could go very nicely with fresh seasonal fruit on a breakfast plate. They are eminently digestible and also provide plenty of energy to start your day.

Breakfast Plate #1

1. Plum, peach, apple, or pear
2. Gruyère or Fontina d'Aosta which are coffee-friendly.
3. Possibly Caerphilly or Lancashire, which tastes a little like scrambled eggs anyway.
4. Croissant (optional).

Breakfast Plate #2

1. Fresh berries or melon, if available.
2. A mild, friendly goat's milk cheese such as Trade Lake Cedar or Ossau-Iraty Brebis.
3. Tomme de Savoie or Timson. Timson is made from 100 percent Jersey cow's milk and pairs well with fresh fruits.

Breakfast Plate #3

1. Baguette slices, jams, or preserves.
2. Roncal or an authentic Manchego. I'd go for the Roncal with some honey, either spread on the bread or directly on the cheese, Spanish-style, highlighting the balance between the saltiness of the cheese and the sweetness of the honey.

Additional Breakfast Possibilities

Loire Valley goat's milk cheeses; Wabash Cannonball; Mary Falk's Big Holmes or Gabrielson Lake; Brin D'Amour; Le Chèvre Noir; Hoch Ybrig; Queso de los Beyos, also a coffee-friendly cheese, albeit a firm or semi-hard, not a rock-hard, one.

The Big Board

WHEN we first started offering cheeses at Picholine, we had about fourteen of the best available in New York City at the time. Regular customers would come back and say, "Well, we had those fourteen cheeses, what do you have for us this week?" Our inventory has grown to between sixty and eighty cheeses at a given time. Out of that number, we'll pick at least fifty for "The Big Board." My cheese assistants and I assemble one or two of these daily; it is our *magnum opus*.

LUNCH

For lunch, my first choices are cow's milk cheeses in a range from the traditional British farmhouse cheeses to Parmigiano-Reggiano. To me, the ideal lunch is a plate of three or four cheeses accompanied by a green salad and some good bread. An alternative is a plate of seasonal fruits, other than citrus or bananas, alongside the cheeses: berries, apples, pears, plums, and peaches all work well. If you want to expand the meal a bit, consider serving a first course of soup or appetizer and possibly a plate of vegetables to accompany the cheese main course. Lunch and supper or light dinner are virtually interchangeable except that you may want to give extra weight to the criteria of digestibility when it comes to a meal very close to bedtime (see next section).

For lunch, I wouldn't recommend anything too challenging—no "boss" Cabrales, for example, where the mold has taken over and there's not so much as a memory of the sweet lactose. You could try some substantial, flavorful cheeses, though. I suggest no more than one blue—if any—and none of the more assertive washed-rind cheeses. You might prefer to save those for the after-dinner course or a more formal tasting.

Lunch Plate #1:
Classic British Ploughman's Lunch

1. A large piece of Cheddar, about 4 ounces.
2. A chunk of crusty bread, either whole wheat or white.
3. Chutney or pickled onions, and butter.
4. Nowadays, possibly a salad on the side.
5. A pint of ale or cider.

Possible cheese substitutes: Double Gloucester, Caerphilly, Cheshire—any of the traditional British farmhouse cheeses. (You *might* have Stilton.)

Lunch Plate #2: Cheese and Salad

1. Wabash Cannonball or a Loire Valley goat's milk cheese such as Pouligny-Saint-Pierre or Selles-sur-Cher.
2. Fontina D'Aosta or Bra. Fontina offers some beefy flavor, something to sink your teeth into without becoming overly aggressive or challenging. It also matches well with some of the crisp white wines, which are likely choices at lunch.

3. A green salad. Salads always present a difficult pairing with wines because of the acid in the vinegar. The chalky, basic nature of the goat's milk cheese, however, provides the perfect foil; a fresh one will melt in your mouth, too, its soft texture delightful in contrast to the crunchiness of the lettuce.

Other Suggested Lunch Cheeses

One reason I really like Garrotxa at lunchtime is that the most frequently requested wine for lunch is Chardonnay, which can present difficult pairing puzzles; it sings a beautiful duet with this Catalan goat cheese, however. Brin D'Amour works well at lunch, too; it is a sheep's milk cheese that is at once digestible and different, with its intriguing herb coating. I'd also recommend two other sheep's milk cheeses, Serra and Evora. If you want to go for a different goat at lunch, I'd serve a nice plump, soft Chevrotin des Aravis (not one that's too smelly or past its prime), a relatively mild but tasty and intriguing enough cheese to be perfectly suitable for the midday meal.

LIGHT SUPPER OR LATE DINNER

For a late-evening meal, digestibility is an important criteria: you don't want to go to bed full of challenging cheeses. In the cow's milk category, this means leaning toward the firmer-textured, more aged cheeses. Both sheep and goat cheeses are more accessible in this respect so they would be natural candidates for a late supper.

1. TICKLEMORE: Moist, semisoft, fairly mild, goat's milk, always a good place to begin. Ticklemore is variable but almost always delicious. Alternatives: Cabécou de Rocamadour or a Loire Valley chèvre.
2. KIRKHAM'S LANCASHIRE or some other firm-textured, buttery cow's milk cheese, except of the extra-aged variety. A younger cheese like this—less than 6 months old—falls nicely into place after the goat. It can be bloomy rind, natural rind, or clothbound, as is the Lancashire.
3. OSSAU-IRATY BREBIS (Pyrénées-style) or similar hard, nutty sheep's milk cheese. Berkswell, Spenwood, Tyning, Vermont Shepherd,

A perfect lunch: frisée in a light vinaigrette plus a quartet of, from left, Brin d'Amour, Caerphilly, Garrotxa, and Coolea.

THE one-cheese
plate or the one-
cheese meal: a
piece of bread, a
hunk of
Parmigiano-
Reggiano, a glass
of wine. Rabelais
called this the
"Holy Trinity"
of the table.

or one of the other Iberians—Manchego, Roncal, or Zamorano—will all do. With the first three cheeses in this progression, you have a goat, a cow, and a sheep. Regardless of their respective stages of ripeness, it is hard to go wrong with this order; the different species assure distinct flavors. Following these, the sheep's milk cheeses provide the fuller, sweeter flavor profile to follow the cow's milk. Here, I prefer the firm to hard types as they give the succeeding cheese type an appropriately sensuous intro.

4. TALEGGIO: A melting, yeasty dollop of hedonism, sufficiently extravagant to follow the fullness of Cheese Number 3 in this progression.

5. SWISS GRUYÈRE: Preferably one of the venerable sort—that is, aged over a year to a hard texture wherein crystals have begun to form. The glory of this cheese is revealed in its opulent finish.

6. FOURME D'AMBERT: There are a few blues to choose from after the Gruyère. A well-made raw-milk Fourme D'Ambert can succeed, one that is typically balanced in flavor and firm yet moist.

PICNIC PLATE

If you're taking a cheese in your day pack for a hike in the mountains or in your basket for a *déjeuner sur l'herbe,* make sure it's one that holds up well. Anything that's creamy, pasty, runny, slimy, or crumbly—this includes blues along with many of the soft-ripened or washed-rind cheeses—might be better served at home. Very hard cheeses may also be difficult to deal with since you don't necessarily have a stable cutting surface. To me, Caerphilly is the ideal picnic cheese: it's moist, durable, and portable—you can even carry it in your pocket like the Welsh miners did.

Pick three of the following and bring along some bread or fruit as accompaniment: Abbaye de Belloc, Beaufort, Caerphilly, Coolea, Erhaki, Evora, Gubbeen, Lake Gabrielson, Peñamellera, Queijo de Nisa, Queijo Feliciano (a Portuguese cheese similar to Azeitão but firmer), Single Gloucester, Spenwood, Timson, Tomme de Savoie, Trade Lake Cedar, Zamorano.

There are also several goat's milk possibilities for picnics, including Selles-sur-Cher, Crottin de Chavignol, and Wabash Cannonball. The Cannonballs are eminently portable at about 4 ounces, and the aged Crottins are even smaller. Some of the soft varieties could also work as long as they aren't jostled too much; I wouldn't rule out a small L'Edel de Cleron, for example.

APPETIZERS

For appetizer plates, I recommend an emphasis on the softer, whiter types of cheeses. Any of the soft, bloomy-rind cheeses can work well, beginning with VCN (Véritable Camembert de Normandie—that is, *real* Camembert) or Coulommiers and progressing all the way up to Pierre-Robert. Washed-rind cheeses on the milder side are also suitable for appetizer plates, say a young Reblochon or a Durrus. Lancashire, with its buttery crumble, would also be appropriate; it's light and airy enough not to fill up your guests excessively, and it's tasty enough to stimulate the appetite and start the digestive juices flowing.

Appetizer Plate #1

1. WABASH CANNONBALL: Mild and creamy with a bit of tartness.
2. ZAMORANO: Nutty, melts in the mouth.
3. CENTOVALLI TICINO: Buttery, smooth, balanced. (If you can't find it, Fontina D'Aosta is a good alternative.)
4. LANCASHIRE: With its acidulous character, it prepares the mouth for successive spicier courses.

Appetizer Plate #2

1. TICKLEMORE: Sublime; an excellent "first food."
2. PERAIL: A runny, mild-flavored cheese, though its aroma might suggest something altogether different.
3. STANSER FLADÄ: Eminently satisfying; smooth, sweet milky flavors.
4. SPENWOOD: Full, round, complex, and nutty. Why proceed to other foods after this masterpiece? Just have more cheese!

FULL DINNER

Although it's by no means an everyday occurrence, I do have the occasional request to put together a full cheese dinner. If you want to create a very special meal for guests, I'd encourage you to do the same. Ten of the world's greatest cheeses served with a little pomp and ceremony are guaranteed to make a tremendous impression. For this type of cheese dinner, I'd recommend a full soup or appetizer course to precede the main cheese course; light seafood dishes or anything vegetable-based works best. Avoid filling, high-carbohydrate foods or anything with a heavy, cream-based sauce. Even caviar can work —just skip the sour cream blini; they're too rich. To make a full meal of it, serve a green salad after the cheese and then proceed to dessert and coffee or after-dinner drinks.

1. POULIGNY-SAINT-PIERRE: A good place to start, it offers the mildness and accessiblity of a goat cheese. It works best if well developed and focused, with a little zesty tartness.

2. REBLOCHON: A nice, plump, oozing cow's milk cheese, soft and more luxurious when at its best.

3. VERMONT SHEPHERD: I'm happy to stand this cheese up against any of its European cousins. It can fit well in a number of spots in a progression and is equally versatile with many wines. Here it provides a break between the richness of the Reblochon and the smoothness of the Vacherin.

4. VACHERIN HAUT-RIVE (A WELL-MADE BRAND OF VACHERIN MONT D'OR): We have moved from the soft, subtle Reblochon to the equally subtle but firm Vermont Shepherd and then back to this meltingly rich, sweet delicacy. Pour some of the Vacherin over your chunk of crusty baguette, close your eyes, and savor this incredible delicacy.

5. CENTOVALLI TICINO: This regal cheese could at first be a little lost following the sumptuous Vacherin, but it waits patiently and its finish shows the cheesemaker's mastery. A beautifully balanced cheese with no rough edges, no affronts to the palate—grace with dignity. Fontina D'Aosta is a good alternative.

6. LIVAROT: There are few cheeses quite like an aromatic and provocative Livarot served *à point*. Once cut, its paste starts to ooze slowly. It ushers us into the pungent zone.

7. QUESO DE LOS BEYOS: Chalky (it feels and tastes a bit like clay), but its finish is remarkable, an unexpected delight. In this sequence, it provides a welcome barricade between two generous cheeses. In fact, the Beyos can pop up in a number of plate positions.

8. TORTA DEL CASAR: After the dry chalkiness and delicious afterglow of the Beyos, this unusual cheese announces its presence immediately. It is soft, oily, and a little sheepy, taking the crescendo up another notch from the preceding cheeses.

9. COOLEA: With its long aging, the sweet Coolea follows the Torta del Casar effectively. It is a balanced, rich, hard, abundantly flavorful cheese that owes its character in equal parts to its aging and to the diversity of vegetation upon which those cows graze in County Cork.

10. CASHEL BLUE: A memorable last stop on this little odyssey. When the Cashel is good—and it almost always is—it is the choice blue, very buttery, tangy, and firm but moist. It settles all the other lingering nuances in one clear, conclusive statement.

AFTER-DINNER COURSES

Theme Plates

What I call "theme plates"—all-blues, all-sheep, and so forth—are often a perfect opportunity to demonstrate texture and flavor contrasts. Tasting a lineup of similar cheeses can be more illuminating than tasting decidedly different ones: it helps you sort out their subtler distinctions. Cheeses from similar recipes in different parts of the world, for example, will allow the variations due to *terroir* or breed of animal to shine through. If you're just getting acquainted with the world's great cheeses, this thematic approach may seem a bit fussy or gimmicky; but once you've acquired a broad cheese experience, such "vertical tastings" make a lot of sense.

All-Goat

Contrary to popular belief, all goat cheeses are not chalky white and relatively bland. In fact, there is a tremendous range and variety in this category—more than enough to put together an exciting plate.

1. WABASH CANNONBALL: A fairly fresh, milky, mild goat cheese with a little bit of tartness. The rind needn't be perfectly white, and the paste should be slightly yielding to the touch.

2. MINE GABHAR: A rare delicacy, recognizably goaty but not at all chalky or soapy. If you can't get it, substitute Ticklemore; if that's not available, skip ahead.

3. CHEVROTIN DES ARAVIS: Best when soft and oozing, this is a unique soft goat's milk cheese. The smell may be a little barnyardy but don't let that scare you off; its flavor is much milder.

4. SAINTE-MAURE: This is a more assertive chèvre than most. It should be firm, but not hard or cracked. Its success and reliability are due in large part to the straw in the center, which acts as a trachea, allowing the paste to breathe and ripen from the inside as well as the out.

5. LE CHÈVRE NOIR: A Cheddar-style crystalline-textured goat cheese. Possessed of texture and intensity from extensive aging, it has the substance to take the penultimate place on this plate. It also has a wonderful undercurrent of sweet milk flavor. (A good alternative: Doeling Dairy Goat Gouda.)

6. MONTE ENEBRO: With its intriguing surface molds, this is the most complex member of this lineup.

All-Sheep

Why all-sheep? To demonstrate the range in a category that is at once digestible, nutritious, stimulating, and profoundly satisfying.

1. PERAIL: Young, fresh, very soft and mild.
2. TRADE LAKE CEDAR: Versatile, a bit spicy, this cheese could be placed further along in the plate, but given the heft of some of the others this might be its best opportunity to show well.
3. AZEITÃO: Getting sheepier but still fairly mild and milky when at its best.
4. ABBAYE DE BELLOC: A hearty, dense, nutty-flavored mountain cheese made by an ancient method.
5. QUESO DE LA SERENA: A teaser of an interlude, sensuous and round, this one can be a banquet in itself.
6. PECORINO TOSCANO: Peppery and biting when aged 6 months or more; acts as a coda after the Serena.
7. STANSER SCHAFCHÄS: In a word, persistent—some might say obstreperous. Its aromas and flavors are intense, pungent, memorable.
8. BEENLEIGH BLUE: Plenty bold enough to follow the Stanser yet with a sweet spectrum of flavors that spells "dessert."

All-Blue

For the adventurous caseophile, an all-blue indulgence, from eight o'clock: Beenleigh Blue, Queso de la Peral, Great Hill Blue, Cashel Blue, Harbourne Blue, a very aged Stilton, and the pièce de résistance, Roquefort.

On a standard plate, I wouldn't normally encourage customers to have more than one or two blues. For some people, once they get some of that mold in their mouths, it's hard to taste anything else. Others like strong flavors and can detect the subtle variations—in texture, flavor, and intensity. This is the plate for them.

1. BEENLEIGH BLUE: Sweet and delicate.
2. QUESO DE LA PERAL: Intriguing, tart, and a little pungent, but not fully blue.
3. GREAT HILL BLUE: More direct and in focus—a "true blue" American classic.
4. CASHEL BLUE: Diffuse, tangy, and round.
5. HARBOURNE BLUE: Warm, pretty, and mouth-filling.
6. STILTON: Magnificent depth, like rolling thunder.
7. ROQUEFORT: The pièce de résistance. No other cheese I know can successfully follow a good Roquefort.

All-French

You don't have to be an avowed Francophile draped in the *tricouleur* celebrating Bastille Day to justify an all-French course. They make so many great

cheeses in France, in fact, that the challenge is in limiting the choices to six or seven. Note the progression of milk types for the first five cheeses in this plate: sheep, goat, cow, sheep, cow—a good mix. The plate ends with three cows in a row, but they are all sharply contrasting: a smelly, soft, washed-rind cheese (Pavé D'Auge); a hard, cooked, aged one (Mimolette); and a blue.

1. BRIN D'AMOUR: Best enjoyed young, moist, and semisoft; as such, it's a good starting point for a plate. I often like to start with a fresher-ripened, approachable sheep's milk cheese like this one.
2. CHEVROTIN DES ARAVIS: A goat cheese that, served at peak, will have a stronger smell than its taste. It should be supple and creamy and only mildly goaty.
3. L'EDEL DE CLERON: The first cow's milk cheese on the plate. It doesn't quite have the complexity of the Chevrotin, but its richness dictates that it follow the first two cheeses.
4. ABBAYE DE BELLOC: For contrast after the l'Edel, we move back into the realm of sheep. The Belloc is firmer in texture and quite concentrated in flavor. With a soft, sweet cheese such as the l'Edel, you might not have enjoyed a washed-rind cheese to follow; it probably would have tasted somewhat bitter.
5. MUNSTER: After an interval with the Abbaye de Belloc, we can move on to a ripe Munster, which will now happily deliver its full, pungent aromas. The Belloc will have shown the most character to date; now the Munster offers a diversity of flavors and a smooth richness that ups the ante.
6. MIMOLETTE: Well-aged, dense, and hard, with concentrated flavors, the Mimolette provides a good textural contrast and brings the Munster experience to a close on the palate.
7. FOURME D'AMBERT: A refreshing, definitive blue. There's no other cheese needed. Unless you'd prefer a Roquefort, this is a classic finale to *any* plate.

WHAT? NO GOAT?

THE caveat I hear most often from customers is "No goat cheeses." I'm not quite sure why. One reason could be that there are a lot of inferior goat cheeses—soapy, bland, dried out—that, literally and figuratively, leave a bad taste in people's mouths. Some diners are nervous about goat cheeses because they're fresher, or because of the old wives' tale that pregnant women or very young children shouldn't eat them (although I doubt many people even recall where they heard that one).

A pair of great Italians—
Montasio (top) and
Pecorino Toscano—with
honey, fig log, and
tomato confit.

All-Italian

Hardly anybody is surprised at the glory of French cheeses, but they will be
delighted to discover that Italy its own masterpieces. Serve a plate like this
to culminate a full-fledged authentic Italian feast.

1. MONTASIO: Fairly mild and somewhat firm in texture with a lingering gentle, sweet finish. It is a fitting prelude to the Taleggio.
2. TALEGGIO: A washed-rind cheese that will offer intriguing aromas and somewhat more forceful flavors than the Montasio.
3. PECORINO TOSCANO: A well-aged Pecorino di Pienza, at 6 to
9 months, will close out the Taleggio and lead in to the next cheese.
4. FONTINA D'AOSTA: Should offer a distinct, tangy taste of fermented milk while holding onto some of its lactic sweetness.
5. PARMIGIANO-REGGIANO: A glorious center-cut chunk of midsummer Parmesan (I like mine about 2½ years old) might convince you
to call it quits, but there's another great Italian waiting to be heard
from . . .
6. GORGONZOLA: A good creamy Gorgonzola Naturale with a bit
of a bite is the perfect closer, providing the Italian answer to France's
magnificent Roquefort finale.

All-British

Everybody has *heard* of Stilton and Cheddar, but have they experienced these two cheeses to their nth degree? And did they know about the other artisanal gems of the British Isles? Serve this plate and open their eyes.

1. TICKLEMORE: A logical place to start—mild, balanced, and subtle.
2. DURRUS: In second position, this cheese might possibly switch with the Caerphilly (third), depending on their relative ages. At times, the Caerphilly can be the more refined of the two, so it might beg to go first. Yet the Ticklemore and the Caerphilly share such similar textural qualities that the progression is probably more interesting with the Durrus in between.
3. CAERPHILLY: Generally possesses a slightly acidulous flavor, and this progression gives it an opportunity to show its true colors. Its loose, airy texture provides a welcome contrast to the full mouth-coating effect of the Durrus.
4. SPENWOOD: Although it's a somewhat unconventional placement, the inherent sweetness of this beautiful sheep's milk cheese can be accentuated here by following the delicate citrus flavors of the Caerphilly.
5. MONTGOMERY'S CHEDDAR: The Montgomery's can follow just about anything you want. While some might say it's like having your pudding before your meat, this progression is quite successful. The Spenwood's flavors, though subtle, cover a broad spectrum. If it were a cheese meant to age longer, it might even belittle the Montgomery's a bit, but the sumptuousness of the latter makes both cheeses shine.
6. COLSTON-BASSETT STILTON: At first, the Stilton seems like a refreshment; a cheese of this pedigree, however, won't settle for a subservient role. It is provocative and triumphant—the perfect ending for this intriguing assortment.

All-Spanish

Spanish cheeses seem to represent something a little exotic and out of the ordinary for most North American gourmets. This plate includes a couple of cheeses that will definitely raise eyebrows.

1. IBORES: Should be served young enough so that it retains a fair amount of moisture; it has the distinctive flavor of a rustic raw goat's milk cheese but is mild enough to qualify for the leadoff position.
2. QUESO DE LOS BEYOS: Dense, lactic, made from cow's milk. (It can also be made with goat's milk, but unfortunately we don't see that version in America.) It may seem a bit flat on the attack after the Ibores, but it melts deliciously on the palate, offering unique flavors and an intriguing mouth feel.

MIX AND MATCH

T AKE one from Column A, one from Column B, and so forth to make your own cheese courses. Once you've made your choices, arrange them in proper order; as with any cheese plate you devise, if you're looking for a strategy, consult the final sections of Chapters 4 and 5. Taste the progression—and adjust if necessary.

MILD	STRONG	SOFT	HARD	WASHED-RIND
1. Selles-sur-Cher	1. Lancashire	1. Perail	1. Bra	1. Durrus
2. Bethmale	2. Torta del Casar	2. Durrus	2. Vermont Shepherd	2. Chevrotin des Aravis
3. Caerphilly	3. Fontina D'Aosta	3. Chevrotin des Aravis	3. Montgomery's Cheddar	3. Taleggio
4. Roucoulons	4. Livarot	4. Pierre-Robert	4. Mimolette (aged 18 months)	4. Livarot
5. Abbaye de Belloc	5. Berkswell	5. Torta del Casar	5. Boeren Kaas	5. Vacherin Fribourgeois
6. Taleggio	6. Boeren Kaas	6. Munster	6. Bleu de Gex	6. Stanser Schäfchas
7. Mimolette	7. Valdeón	7. Mont Briac		

3. QUESO DE LA SERENA: After the dryish Beyos we move to this ewe's milk cheese, with grassy flavors and a soft, luxurious texture that offers a nice contrast to the Beyos.

4. AFUEGA'L PITU: A good Afuega'l Pitu will be piercing and fiery. With this forceful cheese, the Spanish plate is showing spunk.

5. RONCAL: Of all the Spanish hard sheep's milk cheeses, this is probably the boldest. Lacking the subtlety of, say, a Manchego, it makes a big stamp on the palate and has the necessary impact to follow the fiery Afuega.

6. MONTE ENEBRO: From sheep, we return to this wonderfully complex, dense, and flavorful goat cheese.

7. CABRALES: For the clincher, it's got to be Cabrales, preferably the real thing—that is, one made from mixed milk (cow's, sheep's, and goat's). Be careful: Cabrales can get mean if allowed to go too far.

All-American

Stand up and salute the Stars and Stripes. Show your guests how far American cheesemakers have come and where they are going. They're on the right trajectory and going strong. There's no question that these hardworking artisans deserve our support and encouragement. The best thing we can do is buy their cheeses, taste them, and spread the good word. Here is a representative plate of some of my favorite Americans.

1. DOELING GOUDA: My choice for first position is this firm, moist, sweet, goat's milk cheese.
2. ORB WEAVER: Should be firm, thick, herbaceous.
3. TRADE LAKE CEDAR: A sheep's milk cheese aged a minimum of 3 months and featuring spicy, nutty flavors with a hint of sweetness.
4. SONTHEIM'S TILSIT: Semisoft and tangy.
5. GRAND CRU GRUYÈRE: A very good American imitation of the famous Swiss original, with full, nutty flavor.
6. BERKSHIRE BLUE: Made from cow's milk, this American finale has a nice zing, but like a good Stilton or any other world-class blue, it should never overwhelm the palate with saltiness. It is well balanced and crisp.

TASTING BOARDS

For lunchtime restaurant service, we generally offer an abbreviated version of our big board. If you want to create a relatively large, festive cheese tasting for an office party or other institutional function, I suggest you put together something approximating one of these boards. It should feature a representative variety of cheeses but not so many that tasters are overwhelmed and can't recall numbers 1 through 5 by the time they're on 15. No one is expected to taste this many cheeses at once; but by offering all these choices, you have a much better chance of satisfying a greater number of palates.

TASTING BOARD 1. Beenleigh Blue; 2. Trade Lake Cedar; 3. Brin D'Amour; 4. Azeitão; 5. Monte Enebro; 6. Valençay; 7. Queso de la Garrotxa; 8. Chevrotin des Aravis; 9. Pavé D'Auge; 10. Tomme de Savoie; 11. Pierre-Robert; 12. Mimolette (18-month-old); 13. Fontina D'Aosta; 14. Cashel Blue; 15. Appleby's Double Gloucester; 16. Taleggio; 17. Montbriac; 18. Gorwydd Caerphilly; 19. Munster (Alsatian).

Note that the first four cheeses are all made from sheep's milk but are completely different in composition and character: the Beenleigh is, of course, a blue; the Trade Lake, a hard Pyrenées-type cheese; the Brin D'Amour a soft, herb-encrusted one in the style of many goat's milk cheeses; and finally, the Azeitão, a soft natural-rind cheese with a gentle sheepy flavor. They are from England, the United States, France, and Portugal, respectively.

Next come four goat's milk cheeses, two French and two Spanish. The Monte Enebro, Valençay, and Garrotxa are all interesting variations on the standard chalky white goat's milk type while the Chevrotin des Aravis is completely apart—a mild, washed-rind mountain cheese in the style of Reblochon. Following these are examples of classic British cheeses (Double Gloucester and Caerphilly), aged hard Dutch-style cheese (Mimolette), triple crème (Pierre-Robert), classic alpine semisoft (Fontina D'Aosta), washed-rind (Taleggio, from Italy; Munster, from Alsace), a couple of blues (Cashel, from Ireland, and Montbriac, a unique French delicacy). Possible substitutions: 2. Ossau-Iraty Brebis (Pyrenées mountain sheep cheese), Roncal, aged Pecorino Toscano or Zamorano; 12. aged Boeren Kaas; 14. Gorgonzola, Great Hill Blue, or Roquefort; 18. Cheshire; 19. Livarot or Epoisses.

The following "Around the World" boards can also work well for larger tastings.

 AROUND THE WORLD #1: *England:* 1. Harbourne Blue, 2. Montgomery's Cheddar, 3. Spenwood, 4. Colston-Bassett Stilton; *France:* 5. Mont Briac, 6. Munster, 7. Pierre-Robert; *Ireland:* 8. Coolea; *Italy:* 9. Montasio; *Netherlands:* 10. Roomano; *Portugal:* 11. Evora; *Spain:* 12. Ibores, 13. Queso de la Serena; *Switzerland:* 14. Appenzeller; *United States:* 15. Crocodile Tear.

AROUND THE WORLD #2: *Canada:* 1. Le Chèvre Noir; *England:* 2. Berkswell, 3. Montgomery's Cheddar, 4. Ticklemore; *France:* 5. Chevrotin des Aravis, 6. Selles-sur-Cher, 7. Epoisses, 8. Roquefort, 9. Brin D'Amour, 10. Beaufort, 11. Pierre-Robert; *Ireland:* 12. Durrus; *Italy:* 13. Taleggio; *Netherlands:* 14. Boeren Kaas; *Portugal:* 15. Serra; *Spain:* 16. Cabrales, 17. Monte Enebro, 18. Torta del Casar, 19. Zamorano; *Switzerland:* 20. Vacherin Fribourgeois, 21. Stanser; *United States:* 22. Great Hill Blue, 23. Vermont Shepherd, 24. Wabash Cannonball; *Wales:* 25. Llangloffan.

SEASONAL PLATES

A superior food experience will reflect the change of seasons, highlighting the fresh, ripe fruits of the earth, constantly reminding us of nature's cycle. Sure, it's an exotic treat to have tropical fruits in the dead of winter, but the true challenge is to fashion a cuisine, at any given time of the year, with what's naturally available. Both cheeses and their accompaniments vary with the seasons. If you had fresh Loire Valley goat's milk cheese year-round, then it wouldn't be so special anymore, would it?

Spring Plate

There aren't as many types to choose from at this time of year, but if you're able to source from a wide range of cheese-producing regions, you can come up with some interesting combinations.

1. PIERRE-ROBERT: Soft and lush. At its best, the sides should be bulging slightly. Once cut, a choice specimen should virtually collapse under the weight of a fork. Available in this state year-round, when many other French soft-ripened cow's milk cheeses are in short supply.
2. SERRA (FULL NAME QUEIJO SERRA DA ESTRELA): Spoonable, oily, with a pleasant sourness, it has a flavor reminiscent of ground walnuts. This is one of the first of the Iberian soft-ripened sheep cheeses to arrive in top form each year.
3. SWISS GRUYÈRE: A reliable choice year-round, well-aged Gruyère features a crystalline texture that thrills the palate from the start. It also delivers a lingering round, buttery finish.
4. BEENLEIGH BLUE: While the tart Roqueforts have begun to fade, the Beenleigh remains at the top of its game well into the spring. A fine, firm, dignified blue, with a soft chorus from descant to profundo.

Summer Plate

A new crop of the fresh, soft-ripened cheeses begins to appear, many of them made over the previous 2 months. The Loire Valley goat's milk cheeses are coming into fine form around now. Other goats—Chevrotin des Aravis and Garrotxa among them—work well as first cheeses; ditto the Perail (sheep), Reblochon, and Saint-Marcellin (both cow).

1. SELLES-SUR-CHER: Firm but moist with a little mold on the ashed rind and a little tartness to its flinty flavor.
2. REBLOCHON: Pink and plump and oozing, the bacon and eggs of cheeses—over easy.
3. QUESO DE LA SERENA: Very soft, fat, full and provocatively flavored with no rough edges on the palate.
4. QUESO DE LA PERAL: Soft, moist, and yellow with a little bit of blue beginning to appear. A great summer-party blue, it features some of that unique Asturian bitterness.

Fall Plate

A season when it's almost hard to find a cheese that's not in good form. There's a huge range of possibilities; these are four of my favorites for the fall—none of them a wallflower.

1. LIVAROT: Plump, slightly oozing, and smelly (almost ammonia-cal). To place this cheese at the beginning of a plate might seem a bit radical, but its flavor and texture are sufficiently smooth and mild to make an appropriate opener.

2. BERKSWELL: Stalwart, firm, nutty, not overly sheepy and beautifully balanced—a quality the hard sheep cheeses possess in varying degrees.

3. MONTE ENEBRO: Preferably fairly solid with the paste white and homogenous right up to the brown rind; fresh-tasting but with a well-developed mouth-filling, almost puckering flavor—a delicious anomaly. Few goat cheeses can be this successful late in a grouping, particularly after the kind shown in the first half of this quartet.

4. GREAT HILL BLUE: Crisp, sprightly, and light on the palate with a true blue zest and no residual "cowy" flavor—a refreshing finale.

Winter Plate

I think of cheese as a traditional winter food—for the times when other sources of nutrition are in short supply. It is still a fabulous season for fine table cheeses; some are at their peak, others are just beginning to show, a few are fading.

1. VACHERIN MONT D'OR (OR VACHERIN DU HAUT-DOUBS OR VACHERIN HAUT-RIVE): So sweet, milky, velvety, and luxurious—it hardly seems like cheese at all.

2. VERMONT SHEPHERD: A nugget for sustenance on a blustery day; coal for my inner furnace; so satisfying without bragging about itself.

3. TALEGGIO: Looks innocent enough but it is full and unabashed on the palate; so delicious when peaking, it's hard to stop eating it.

4. ROQUEFORT: The zenith when at its best. Must be a prime specimen to make its point—in this case an exclamation point.

ASSORTED CHEESE COURSES

All of the following are adopted from actual courses I've served as a *fromager*. Feel free to shorten them or substitute similar cheeses, but note the basic strategy or progression. Although they may seem a bit random—some of them are all over the map—this is what my customers most often ask for. They want variety, diversity, an eclectic cheese experience. So, while always remaining mindful of progression, that's what I give them.

Assorted Plate I

This plate clearly demonstrates a progression of complexity and intensity of flavors. With various textures, animal types, provenances, and ages, here we have an eclectic and tasty mix. Note the relationship of the first and the last cheeses and then compare the second and fourth: the Ibores acts as a coda between the similar second and fourth ones. The Trade Lake tops off the Taleggio—a hard act to follow. Capricious Monte Enebro, able to stand off just about any rival with its mouth-filling intensity, finally surrenders at the Caves of Combalou.

1. PERAIL
2. DURRUS
3. IBORES
4. TALEGGIO
5. TRADE LAKE CEDAR
6. MONTE ENEBRO
7. ROQUEFORT

Assorted Plate II

A well-moderated progression that helps the palate adapt as the crescendo builds. Given a collection of well-ripened cheeses, this progression goes by increasing age—until the final cheese, a tart youngster. Then it's back to Iberia where we find a rustic modern blue from the hallowed ground of Spanish cheese, Asturias.

1. VALENÇAY
2. REBLOCHON
3. CAERPHILLY
4. TORTA DEL CASAR
5. APPENZELLER
6. QUESO DE LA PERAL

Assorted Plate III

I don't always start a plate with the mildest cheese in the group. In this case, the Camembert isn't as strong as the Llangloffan, albeit equally subtle and delicious. I recall our diners had some Cornas—a hearty Rhône red—left in their glasses from the main course. So they sipped that with the distinguished Welsh cheese, then enjoyed a tranquil interlude with the Camembert before moving on to the rest of the plate, which I matched with a Riesling Auslese. Building toward the finale, the Coolea provides an eloquent recitative between the brash Munster and the audacious Stanser Schafchäs. Then, with one fell swoop, the Valdeón sends that Swiss stalwart packing.

1. LLANGLOFFAN
2. NANCY'S HUDSON VALLEY CAMEMBERT
3. CHEVROTIN DES ARAVIS
4. MUNSTER
5. COOLEA
6. STANSER SCHAFCHÄS
7. VALDEÓN

Assorted Plate IV

Here is a selection of firm-textured cheeses that will stand up without running all over the plate. It works well if you're plating them in advance—say, at the beginning of a meal—and serving them somewhat later . . . or simply if you have a preference for firmer cheeses. Though not a *hard* cheese, the Ticklemore, at its prime, is moist yet firm enough. If it's not hard enough for you, try a Garrotxa or Le Chèvre Noir. Although the textures are quite similar, this plate provides some delightful color contrasts. Note the stealth of the Évora following the stark, dark Mimolette. The Évora is not patient and the Beenleigh is all the sweeter for it.

1. TICKLEMORE
2. ABBAYE DE BELLOC

A little mix-and-match plate, from left, quince paste, Spenwood, Abbaye de Belloc, and Mahón, with a beautiful wheel of Trade Lake Cedar on the side.

3. Fontina d'Aosta
4. Mimolette
5. Evora
6. Beenleigh Blue

Assorted Plate V

Is it their aristocratic bearing or is it because you don't have to chew them that soft cheeses are so popular? The triple-crème Pierre-Robert offers a richness sufficient to follow the Reblochon (depending on their relative ages). The Fladä is voluptuous, and then the Little Colonel steps up and makes his presence known . . . Oh, for a moment of serenity, and on to the intriguing Mont Briac.

1. Reblochon
2. Pierre-Robert
3. Fladä
4. Livarot
5. Queso de la Serena
6. Mont Briac

Assorted Plate VI

Often, the sky's the limit, as long as there's no blue in it. The Orb Weaver is so sweet—well-made and without elaboration. The Roucoulons does have a little more pretense; it's a bit of a flirt. Zamorano, the lone sheep in the mix, knows exactly where it belongs—in the middle. We can all go home after the superb Cheddar. But didn't we say, "The sky's the limit"? Yes, and so, as though it was necessary, in walks the original party animal—Vacherin Fribourgeois. Loud, even obnoxious, but we love it all the same.

1. Orb Weaver
2. Roucoulons
3. Zamorano
4. Cheddar
5. Vacherin Fribourgeois

EIGHT

MY FAVORITE CHEESES: A SELECTION OF THE WORLD'S FINEST

WHAT FOLLOWS is my personal pantheon of cheeses, all of which I have purchased, ripened, and served at one time or another. They are cheeses across a broad spectrum, all gourmet table cheeses, mostly artisanal, many of them discussed in the preceding chapters; they are not necessarily the *only* cheeses appropriate for your cheese course at home, but certainly every one listed is worthy. (Apologies to the many deserving entries—and their producers—that have been inadvertently left out.)

An important note on availability: In cases when you can't get the specific cheese *type* you want, we are supplying a category of "Similar Cheeses" for each entry—whenever possible. As mentioned in connection with the cheese plates in Chapter 7, whether you are serving one or more cheeses, you can simply substitute a similar cheese for your original choice *or* simply delete that choice and move on. If the particular *brand* you'd like is unavailable, simply ask your cheesemonger to supply something equivalent or similar. Make it clear that while you'd prefer the superior brand, you're not averse to trying the next best thing. Then judge for yourself whether the alternate is up to snuff.

Some of the cheeses have an additional category, "Seasonal Note," listing their windows of availability and desirablity. If there is no such note, assume the cheese is available and good year-round.

British Isles

E NGLAND, Ireland, and Wales are geographically and climatically ideal for cheese. It doesn't take a rocket scientist—or even a weather forecaster—to tell you that these closely allied countries offer an excellent combination of soil, climate, and dairy production that spells great cheese potential. The British Isles are industrial, true, but they are also dotted with green pastures peopled with hardworking farmers who still tend sheep, goats, and cows the old-fashioned way.

True to national character and as necessitated by climate, British cheeses are harder, more stolid, and they occupy a narrower spectrum. Nevertheless, they represent a rich legacy, dating back to Roman times. Unfortunately, today only a fraction of the authentic regional farmhouse cheeses of the British Isles survive. They experienced a late-twentieth-century revival, however, fed by the increasing national and international demand for gourmet delicacies.

Some people think British cheeses are boring. That statement may be true about a Wensleydale or your run-of-the-mill Cheshire, but it's not a fair generalization. There are British cheeses that may have an unspectacular, even stodgy appearance and reputation, but still offer exquisitely subtle, smooth, and long-lasting flavors. A luxurious soft French cheese—with its milkiness, creaminess, velvet texture, and perfect balance will melt on your palate and tug at your heart. No question, it's love at first taste. On the other hand, if you take some time to discover the cheeses of the British Isles, especially the ones listed here, I guarantee you will not be disappointed.

ARDRAHAN

A pungent, monastery-style expression of western Irish terroir.
- TYPE: Pasteurized cow's milk.
- ORIGIN AND MAKER: County Cork, southwestern Ireland. The Burns family have been dairy farmers at Ardrahan for generations. Eugene and his wife, Mary, began making cheese in the early nineties; he passed away in 2000, but Mary continues the cheesemaking.
- PRODUCTION AND AGING: Washed-rind. Made from milk produced on the farm.
- APPEARANCE: 2-pound cylinders, 8 inches across and 1½ inches high. Orange rind and a golden paste.
- CONSISTENCY AND TASTE: A rich, soft, curdy, sticky paste. The flavor is pungent, savory, smoky, and lactic. Full and satisfying.
- RECOMMENDED PAIRINGS: Alsatian Riesling, Muscat de Rivesaltes, Rioja-style Tempranillo-Garnacha blend, Bonnezeaux, Chardonnay.
- SIMILAR CHEESES: Durrus, Gubbeen, Livarot, Milleens, Munster.

BEENLEIGH BLUE

A unique cheese made by the very accomplished Robin Congdon, no doubt one of the top twenty cheesemakers on the planet. Part of the British New Wave, Robin is a soft-spoken, cerebral former bank employee. His partner, Sarie Cooper, runs their retail operation, the Ticklemore Cheese Shop, in nearby Totnes.
- TYPE: Raw sheep's milk blue.
- ORIGIN: Sharpham Barton, South Devon, southwestern England.
- PRODUCTION AND AGING: Artisanal, all local milk. Aged 4 to 8 months.
- APPEARANCE: 8-pound cylinders with naturally moist rinds wrapped in gold foil; ivory-colored

paste with evenly distributed threads of greenish blue.

■ CONSISTENCY AND TASTE: Semisoft; fudgy yet can tend toward flaky. Beenleigh combines the typical sweet, caramelly, mildly herbaceous depth of flavor of artisanal sheep's cheeses with the salty bite of a blue. (Dom Coyte of Neal's Yard Dairy on Beenleigh: "The blue is to the sweetness what the Bogey was to the Bacall.")

■ SEASONAL NOTE: Fall to spring.

■ RECOMMENDED PAIRINGS: Late-harvest Chenin Blanc (Coteaux de Layon), Muscat de Rivesaltes, late-harvest Riesling, Sauternes, Hungarian Tokaji; a full-bodied, fruity California Zinfandel or Cabernet.

■ SIMILAR CHEESE: Roquefort.

■ ADDITIONAL CHEESES: Robin makes two other superior cheeses: Harbourne Blue, the goat's milk version of this cheese, and Ticklemore (see below).

BERKSWELL

Created by the Fletchers at their beautiful Elizabethan farmhouse Ram Hall in the mid-1990s, this cheese is most definitely a masterpiece. It boasts remarkable density, concentration, and myriad flavors that can really take your breath away. To me, it's the cheese that Manchego wishes it was . . .

■ TYPE: Raw sheep's milk.

■ ORIGIN AND MAKER: Stephen Fletcher and family. Berkswell, Forest of Arden, Warwickshire, a little enclave of charming English countryside sandwiched between the sprawling urban industrial areas of Birmingham and Coventry, northwest of London.

■ PRODUCTION AND AGING: Made in the style of the sheep's milk cheeses of the Pyrenées (e.g., French AOC Ossau-Iraty Brebis). Aged 6 to 12 months.

■ APPEARANCE: A "basket" or compressed sphere, weighing 5 to 9 pounds, with a natural orangish-brown rind.

■ CONSISTENCY AND TASTE: The paste is firm but slightly pliant. Its taste is somewhat reminiscent of a fine Tuscan Pecorino—some say of Parmesan—but with a marvelous long-lasting caramel-like sweetness, both fruity and savory.

■ SEASONAL NOTE: Fall to spring.

■ RECOMMENDED PAIRINGS: Berkswell is quite versatile and possesses enough butterfat to stand up to a big tannic wine such as Barolo or Bordeaux or a Rhône Valley red. Also try it with a red Burgundy, a Châteauneuf-du-Pape, a German Gewürztraminer Spätlese, a Ribera del Duero (Tempranillo-Garnacha Rioja-style blend), a German Riesling Auslese, California Syrah, Barbaresco, Barbera d'Alba, white Bordeaux, Malvasia Della Lipari, Sauternes.

■ SIMILAR CHEESES: Pecorino Toscano, Spenwood, Trade Lake Cedar, Tyning, Vermont Shepherd.

CAERPHILLY

I like cheeses that talk to me, making a bold statement. But I also like the subtler ones such as Caerphilly. It is simple, direct, and incredibly delicious— a cheesy cheese in the best sense of the word. Most people, on first trying it, exclaim something along the lines of, "Now *that's* real cheese!" The enduring image I have of Caerphilly is of the Welsh coal miners descending to the bowels of the earth with a piece of it stashed away in their pockets for a quick snack as they toiled.

■ TYPE: Raw cow's milk.

■ ORIGIN AND MAKERS: Originally from north-northwest of Cardiff, Wales, genuine Caerphilly is now made by Martin Trethowan of Gorwydd ("Gorewith") Farm, Ceredigion, Wales. Martin is a former archaeologist who pursued his cheese apprenticeship under the master Chris Duckett in Somerset.

■ PRODUCTION AND AGING: Martin Trethowan and his family have been making Caerphilly since 1996, reviving the family legacy of his grandmother. Caerphilly can age up to 4 months.

It was traditionally consumed young and fresh, after just a few weeks of maturing. At this early stage, it is drier, more crumbly, and acidic; as it ripens from the outside in, the paste becomes softer and smoother in texture while the flavors get stronger and more integrated. At age 3 months, which is when we receive it from Neal's Yard Dairy, there is a definite contrast between the ripened paste toward the crust and the fresher portion toward the core. Allowed to ripen all the way through, it becomes quite funky.

■ APPEARANCE: 8-pound millstones with natural rinds.

■ CONSISTENCY AND TASTE: Firm, smooth, and creamy, approaching the consistency and weight of a farmhouse butter, albeit with more palpable texture. Tastes clean, mild, and buttery with hints of lemon.

■ RECOMMENDED PAIRINGS: Châteauneuf-du-Pape Blanc, Cornas or St. Joseph (Northern Rhône Syrahs), Grüner Veltliner, German Riesling Spätlese, Mersault or Alsatian Riesling, Vouvray (demi-sec)

■ SIMILAR CHEESES: Llangloffan, Single Gloucester.

CASHEL BLUE

The Grubb family, who were driven from England in the late eighteenth century for being Anabaptists, settled in Tipperary where they became millers and butter makers. In the mid-1980s, Jane and Louis Grubb created this, the first Irish farmstead blue cheese.

■ TYPE: Pasteurized cow's milk blue.

■ ORIGIN: Beechmount, Fethard, near Cashel, County Tipperary, south-central Ireland.

■ PRODUCTION AND AGING: Farmhouse-made; aged from 6 months to a year.

■ APPEARANCE: 3- to 4-pound cylinders about 6 inches across and 5 inches high with naturally wet rinds that come enclosed in gold foil.

■ CONSISTENCY AND TASTE: Moist, creamy, semisoft; has been described as "voluptuous." Cashel can turn almost runny when perfectly ripened, and it will definitely melt in your mouth. It is relatively mellow tasting for a blue, featuring a distinct sweetness along with the expected salty, sharp, tangy notes.

■ RECOMMENDED PAIRINGS: Madeira, Tawny Port, Hungarian Tokaji.

■ SIMILAR CHEESES: Compares favorably to the great Italian blue Gorgonzola.

CHEDDAR

More than 95 percent of all the cheese made in Britain is sold under the name Cheddar. Unfortunately, the name was never legally protected, so for much of the so-called civilized world "Cheddar" covers all kinds of abominations. As far as I'm concerned there are only three real British Cheddars left: Keen's, Montgomery's, and Reade's (from the Isle of Mull), superb examples of what a raw-milk farmhouse cheese *can* be. Montgomery's is a cheese that has truly earned brand recognition. Like the French triple-crème Pierre-Robert or the double-crème Roucoulons, it can and should be referred to by its proper name rather than its type.

■ TYPE: Raw cow's milk.

■ ORIGIN AND MAKERS: The Montgomery's Manor Farm is located in North Cadbury, Somerset, southwestern England, just 10 miles or so from the Keen's Moorhayes Farm near Wincanton. The Reade's farm is on the Isle of Mull off the southwest coast of Scotland.

■ PRODUCTION AND AGING: Classic farmhouse manufacture; 10 to 18 months aging, sometimes more. Cloth-wrapped and aged at higher temperatures and humidity than standard Cheddars.

■ APPEARANCE: Montgomery's comes in drums weighing up to 56 pounds; Keen's are 60 pounds. Keen's also makes a 28- to 30-pound cheese for the export market as well as a smaller "truckle" of around 3 pounds. The Reade's are up to 58 pounds.

- CONSISTENCY AND TASTE: Hard paste with a range of fruity, sharp, and nutty tastes. Montgomery's offers a complex spectrum of flavors and aromas with a touch of sweetness and the occasional suggestion of a Sunday roast. Its consistency is dry and subtle. Keen's is a classic full-flavored, sharp, firm-bodied Cheddar with a smoother texture and that familiar "bite." If Keen's is deemed sharp or tangy, Montgomery's is generally characterized as "rounder tasting." The Reade's cheddar has a bit of bitterness, not as fruity as the Somerset Cheddars.
- RECOMMENDED PAIRINGS: A fairly bold Pinot Noir (Burgundy) or some type of Cabernet-based red, especially classified-growth Bordeaux or comparable California Cabs; also a Côtes du Rhône red (Syrah), a German Gewürztraminer Spätlese, a Bonnezeaux, Nebbiolo, Tawny Port, or Grüner Veltline.
- SIMILAR CHEESES: While there are some credible Cheddars made in the United States, they are not the same as the genuine British farmhouse ones.

CHESHIRE

Timeless and exemplary. England's oldest, and one of its most revered, cheeses.
- TYPE: Raw cow's milk.
- ORIGIN AND MAKER: While most of Cheshire consists of factory-made imitations, there is one surviving genuine cheese made by the Appleby Family, Abbey Farm, Hawkstone, near Whitchurch, Shropshire, in west-central England.
- PRODUCTION AND AGING: Genuine farmhouse; pressed and cooked (but less than Cheddar).
- APPEARANCE: Clothbound tall cylinders weighing 18 pounds; orange paste.
- CONSISTENCY AND TASTE: Semihard but moist, with a flaky, crumbly texture; a slightly salty full-bodied tang and lingering finish.
- RECOMMENDED PAIRINGS: A light, young, fruity red wine such as Beaujolais or Dolcetto; a white such as Sauvignon Blanc or Muscat; ale.
- SIMILAR CHEESES: Double Gloucester, Llangloffan.

THE GREAT CHEDDAR HEIST

SCOTLAND YARD: NO MATCH FOR BRAZEN CHEESE THIEVES

WHILE memories of the Great Train Robbery have faded with the years, the Great Cheddar Heist is fresh in the minds of many. It remains *the* major unsolved crime in the world of cheese.

Only days before the British Cheese Awards, in the hours before dawn on Saturday, September 26, 1998, thieves driving a delivery truck pulled up to the cheese barn at the Montgomery's Manor Farm. They hastily loaded up 274 heavy cheeses and drove off into the night. The total value of their loot was more than £30,000, unin-sured. It included two pallets of cheeses specially selected by Neal's Yard Dairy and bound for the United States. None of the cheeses was ever seen again; most likely, they were cut up and sold in prepackaged blocks to unsuspecting or incurious merchants. Other than some tire tracks in the mud, which were washed away by the rain before Scotland Yard could properly examine them, the thieves left no evidence. While the heist dealt the Montgomerys a serious blow emotionally and financially, they did not allow it to put them out of the cheese business.

COOLEA ("COO-LAY")

A superb Gouda-style cheese made by a family of transplanted Dutch restaurateurs, it has won competitions back in Holland on Gouda's home turf. Coolea measures up to any of the best Boeren Kaases (Dutch aged farmhouse Gouda; see below), which are hard-pressed (pun intended) to achieve their creaminess and sweetness.

■ TYPE: Cow's milk.

■ ORIGIN AND MAKERS: Manufactured in Coolea, in the northwest of County Cork, southwestern Ireland, by Dick and Helene Willems and their son, Dickie.

■ PRODUCTION AND AGING: Cooked, pressed, and aged 4 to 8 weeks (young); or 9 to 12 months, sometimes up to 2 years (aged).

■ APPEARANCE: Three sizes of round-edged millstones (17 pounds, 9 pounds, and 2 pounds) with shiny orange rinds.

■ CONSISTENCY AND TASTE: Semihard to hard paste with a mild and creamy flavor when young; when aged, well-rounded nutty, piquant with a lingering aftertaste that features hints of butterscotch.

■ RECOMMENDED PAIRINGS: A well-rounded substantial red wine such as an Australian Shiraz, a Rhône red, or a California Zinfandel.

■ SIMILAR CHEESES: Aged Gouda (Boeren Kass); Mimolette.

DOUBLE GLOUCESTER

A quintessentially English cheese that was traditionally made in many farmhouses across Gloucestershire; the real thing is now a rare delicacy.

■ TYPE: Cow's milk.

■ ORIGIN AND MAKERS: The Applebys of Shropshire, who also make traditional farmhouse Cheshire, and the Smart Family (Diana and Jamie) of Old Ley Farm, Vale of Gloucester, Gloucestershire, west of London.

■ PRODUCTION AND AGING: Made from whole milk, as opposed to the Single Gloucester, which is made from skimmed milk.

■ APPEARANCE: 14-pound clothbound cylinders.

■ CONSISTENCY AND TASTE: Hard with a silky smooth texture and rich, creamy flavor accentuated by a tangy nuttiness. The orange paste, colored with annatto, has a buttery, crumbly consistency reminiscent of a farmhouse Cheddar.

■ RECOMMENDED PAIRINGS: Tawny Port, Zinfandel, Cornas, Grüner, Veltliner, Gewürztraminer Spätlese.

■ SIMILAR CHEESES: Cheshire, Single Gloucester.

DURRUS

Pretty in pink. Complex yet subtle—and a true farmhouse artifact.

■ TYPE: Raw cow's milk washed-rind.

■ ORIGIN AND MAKER: Jeffa Gil from Coomkeen in Bantry, the western part of County Cork, southwestern Ireland.

■ PRODUCTION AND AGING: Jeffa began making cheeses in her kitchen in the late 1970s. She started out using the milk of her eight cows but now buys it from a "very particular" farmer 6 miles away.

■ APPEARANCE: 2-pound cylinders, 8 inches across and 2 inches high. Pink-gray mottled rind and pinkish-yellow paste.

■ CONSISTENCY AND TASTE: Durrus has a rich, smooth, creamy semisoft paste with small air holes in it; the typical texture is oozy rather than runny. Its flavor is milky, sweet, fruity, and very approachable.

■ RECOMMENDED PAIRINGS: Albariño, Beaujolais, California Cabernet, German Gewürztraminer Spätlese, German Muscatel, German Riesling Auslese, Vouvray (demi-sec), Savenièrres, Beaujolais.

■ SIMILAR CHEESES: Durrus is like a slightly milder version of Reblochon; it is also reminiscent of Tomme de Savoie, although somewhat more vegetal.

GUBBEEN

Expresses its wild *terroir:* forward, outgoing, and definitive but with appropriate restraint.

- ■ TYPE: Pasteurized cow's milk washed-rind.
- ■ ORIGIN AND MAKERS: Tom and Giana Ferguson, western County Cork, Ireland.
- ■ PRODUCTION AND AGING: Farmhouse; the rind is washed with salt water.
- ■ APPEARANCE: The rind has a distinctive uneven, slightly amorphous, wavy, fuzzy surface that is a peachy-pink color. Even with some fairly scary-looking exterior growths and funky odors, this is a cheese that definitely tastes wholesome.
- ■ CONSISTENCY AND TASTE: Semisoft paste with a silky smooth, pliable texture and fresh, milky taste with a mild buttery, nutty flavor and smokey accents. It also gives off an aroma recalling mushrooms or a pleasantly musty, earthy old cellar.
- ■ RECOMMENDED PAIRINGS: Cornas (northern Rhône red), German Gewürztraminer Spätlese, Alsatian Riesling, Vouvray (demi-sec)
- ■ SIMILAR CHEESES: Ardrahan, Chimay, Durrus, Pont L'Evêque.

HARBOURNE BLUE

An enthralling, unconventional "hybrid" sort of cheese that, albeit somewhat finicky, can be sublime when at its peak.

- ■ TYPE: Raw goat's milk blue.
- ■ ORIGIN AND MAKER: Robin Congdon, Sharpham Barton, South Devon, southwestern England.
- ■ PRODUCTION AND AGING: Since they don't utilize staggered breeding, the cheese is made from spring to fall and is generally available in fall and winter. Aged from 4 to 8 months.
- ■ APPEARANCE: 8-pound cylinders with natural wet rinds.
- ■ CONSISTENCY AND TASTE: Bright white paste with an evenly spread web of blue-green veins; semisoft, creamy, almost fudgy in texture with a pleasingly dry mouth feel. The flavor is sharp, pro-

nounced, and lingering yet it maintains a certain mellow sweetness and complexity, which cannot be said of many blues. It is also not oversalted. It is probably the most "desserty" of the blue cheeses, yet it can be quite fierce when older than 8 months.

- ■ SEASONAL NOTE: Fall to spring.
- ■ RECOMMENDED PAIRINGS: Dessert wines such as a Muscat, Sauternes, a late-harvest Coteaux du Layon, Amarone di Valpolicella, or a Hungarian Tokaji; a German Gewürztraminer Spätlese or a Grüner Veltliner.
- ■ SIMILAR CHEESES: Beenleigh Blue, Bluette by Jacquin, Monte Enebro, Cayuga Blue.
- ■ ADDITIONAL CHEESES: Beenleigh Blue, the sheep's milk version of this cheese, and Ticklemore.

LANCASHIRE

Not much authentic farmhouse Lancashire is being made, but I can unequivocally recommend the one made at the Kirkhams farm since 1977. Mrs. Ruth Kirkham is a third-generation cheesemaker, having learned the recipe from her mother and grandmother. The Kirkhams are British cheese heroes. Their son, Graham, has joined the family business. Lancashire is what I like to call one of the "Boss Cheeses." It manages to stay simultaneously subtle and delicate, hardy and robust.

- ■ TYPE: Raw cow's milk.
- ■ ORIGIN AND MAKERS: John and Ruth Kirkham and their son, Graham, at Beesley Farm, Goosnargh, Lancashire, northwest England.
- ■ PRODUCTION AND AGING: The farm's out-

> # TRADITIONAL BRITISH CHEESES: SIX CLASSICS
>
> Caerphilly, Cheddar, Cheshire, Double Gloucester, Lancashire, Stilton

put is generally four or five cheeses a day. Some are waxed, but the ones destined for Neal's Yard—have the natural buttered, cloth-covered rinds, a telltale sign of a genuine British farmhouse cheese. Key to the Kirkhams' method is the blending of curd: day-old curds, which have higher acidity and drier texture, are carefully combined with fresh, milky sweet ones to achieve proper balance. The cheeses are aged 4 to 8 months in the Neal's Yard caves.

- APPEARANCE: Comes in cylinders of 50 pounds, 25 pounds, 6½ pounds, or 3 pounds. (*Note:* The smaller cheeses tend to dry out faster.)
- CONSISTENCY AND TASTE: A good Lancashire features a texture described locally as "buttery crumble," a sumptuous almost breadlike consistency, creamy and flaky at the same time. Its flavor should be mildly acidic with a lemony tang, buttery and full but not strong or overpowering. It maintains a sublimely light, airy, moist consistency, at times almost as if it were a hardened version of cottage cheese.
- RECOMMENDED PAIRINGS: A pint of traditional British beer or ale (no surprise there); a hearty, flavorful wine such as a big, fruity Cab, Merlot, Syrah, or Zinfandel; a quality Pinot Noir, a German Riesling Kabinett, Carignan, Amarone di Valpolicella, Barbera d'Alba.
- SIMILAR CHEESES: Cheshire, Double Gloucester, Llangloffan.

LLANGLOFFAN

Leon Downey retired as principal viola for the Halle orchestra and now he and his wife, Joan, make beautiful music with their cheese.

- TYPE: Cow's milk.
- ORIGIN AND MAKERS: Leon and Joan Downey at Ty Uchaf, Llangloffan, Pembrokeshire, on the western coast of Wales.
- PRODUCTION AND AGING: Made according to essentially the same recipe as a traditional farmhouse Cheshire, Llangloffan has an additional richness due to the creamier milk the Downeys use. Aged 2 to 6 months.
- APPEARANCE: 10-pound millstones with natural rinds that are greenish brown to brown.
- CONSISTENCY AND TASTE: Firm with a light, pleasantly flaky texture reminiscent of Cheshire, yet it remains full-bodied, buttery, and luxurious, with concentrated flavor due to its aging.
- RECOMMENDED PAIRINGS: Red Bordeaux, California Cabernet, Cornas (northern Rhône Syrah), German Gewürztraminer Spätlese, Alsatian Riesling, Vouvray (demi-sec), Port, Malbec, Barbera d'Alba.
- SIMILAR CHEESES: Cheshire.

SINGLE GLOUCESTER

The milder, lower-fat cousin of Double Gloucester.

- TYPE: Cow's milk.
- ORIGIN AND MAKERS: Smart Family (Diana and Jamie) of Old Ley Farm, Vale of Gloucester, Gloucestershire, west of London.
- PRODUCTION AND AGING: Farmhouse.
- APPEARANCE: 7-pound millstones with a natural cream-colored rind that may develop some green mold.
- CONSISTENCY AND TASTE: Hard paste that features a sublime, smooth, slightly crumbly texture and gentle, clean flavors.
- RECOMMENDED PAIRINGS: A soft Pinot Noir, German Muscatel, Sancerre Rouge, Syrah.
- SIMILAR CHEESES: Caerphilly.

SPENWOOD

Cheesemaker Anne Wigmore is a technical wizard, and her cheese simply has an incredibly satisfying depth of flavor.

■ TYPE: Raw ewe's milk.

■ ORIGIN AND MAKERS: Anne and Andy Wigmore, Risely near Reading in Buckinghamshire, west of London (named after the village of Spencers Wood in Berkshire).

■ PRODUCTION AND AGING: Pyrénées-style; aged 6 to 7 months. Made from March to October; coagulated with vegetable rennet, like many sheep's milk cheeses.

■ APPEARANCE: 5-pound millstones with a natural rind that has a delicate grayish powdery mold and a hint of *B. linens.*

■ CONSISTENCY AND TASTE: Its paste is firm and, with age, it develops a dense, dryish flaky texture and offers a clean flavor that has been described as deep, rich, caramelly, seductively sweet, nutty, and savory. How's that for complexity? A visiting Australian cheesemaker who tasted it was heard to exclaim: "Vegemite!" (High praise from Down Under . . .)

■ RECOMMENDED PAIRINGS: Versatile with wines: try it with Albariño, red Bordeaux, red Burgundy, California Pinot Gris, Merlot, German Gerwürztraminer Spätlese, northern Rhône reds (Cornas, Côte Rotie, Hermitage, St. Joseph), Rioja-style Tempranillo blends, Vouvray (demisec), Sangiovese.

■ SIMILAR CHEESES: Spenwood's flavors are mellower, rounder, and sweeter than an aged Tuscan Pecorino; it doesn't fall back on saltiness. If you compare Spenwood it to its Spanish cousin, Zamorano, you'll find it can carry on a more eloquent discourse. I also liken it to Vermont Shepherd.

STILTON

The most celebrated cheese in all of England, Stilton has been known as "The King of English Cheeses" for the past three centuries and more recently as "King of the Blues."

■ TYPE: Pasteurized cow's milk blue.

■ ORIGIN AND MAKER: From central England, named after the market town in Leicestershire where it was originally sold. Colston-Bassett, from Nottinghamshire, is the best brand for my money—really the *only* one. It has been made by Ernie Wagstaff and Richard Rowlett and their dedicated team at Colston-Bassett & District Dairy for many years.

■ PRODUCTION AND AGING: For the past century, all the milk for Colston-Bassett Stilton has come from five farms within about a 2-mile radius. The creamiest and most succulent blue, Colston-Bassett is matured for between 9 and 14 weeks. Stilton is Britain's only protected cheese—its production zones, standards, and specifications are defined by law. Although its makers are, ironically, forced by protective legislation to utilize pasteurized milk, Colston-Bassett retains a surprising richness and depth of flavor. Significantly, Stilton's ripeness is judged by how creamy it is, not how far the interior blueing has progressed. Stilton made from summer milk is considered superior; its paste is slightly yellower and, due to its 3- to 4-month aging period, it is best in the fall and winter.

■ APPEARANCE: Upright cylinders about 8 inches in diameter, 12 inches tall, and weighing around 18 pounds. (Smaller 5-pound drums or "mini-Stiltons" are produced for the holidays, but they don't offer the same depths of flavor or rich consistency as the full-sized ones.) The paste is

---

REAL CHEESE, REAL ALE

A GOOD pint of British ale goes very well with almost any traditional British farmhouse cheese—even Stilton!

cream colored and full of greenish-blue veins, and the rind is moist and reddish-brown with mold. You can see prick marks on the exterior where steel needles were inserted to help the mold spread.

- CONSISTENCY AND TASTE: Semihard with a rich, minerally tang reflecting its *terroir*. Its texture is buttery and its flavor is mellow, fruity, deep, and syrupy. Colston-Bassett is *never* oversalted as is often the case with other blues. Its flavor is strong and full without being unpleasantly sharp or overpowering.
- SEASONAL NOTE: Fall to early spring.
- RECOMMENDED PAIRINGS: Madeira, Tawny Port, Vintage Port, Jurançon.
- SIMILAR CHEESES: Fourme D'Ambert, Gorgonzola, Jersey Blue, Shropshire Blue.

TICKLEMORE

True to its name, this cheese's tantalizing dryish texture is guaranteed to tickle your taste buds.

- TYPE: Goat's milk.
- ORIGIN AND MAKER: Robin Congdon, South Devon, southwestern England. The cheese is actually named after Robin and his partner Sarie Cooper's store, the Ticklemore Cheese Shop, Ticklemore Street, Totnes.
- PRODUCTION AND AGING: Artisanal.
- APPEARANCE: Has a bumpy rind as a result of being drained in a colander.
- CONSISTENCY AND TASTE: Firm and pleasantly creamy with a superb light, somewhat tangy flavor. With age, it develops a dry, slightly crumbly texture that nevertheless melts in your mouth.
- RECOMMENDED PAIRINGS: Albariño, a dry Riesling, Viognier.
- SIMILAR CHEESES: (Queso de la) Garrotxa.
- ADDITIONAL CHEESES: Robin, one of the most gifted cheesemakers alive, also makes Beenleigh Blue and Harbourne Blue.

TYNING

Fruity, sweet, and definitely to be counted among the world's greatest sheep's milk cheeses.

- TYPE: Raw ewe's milk.
- ORIGIN AND MAKER: Mary Holbrook farms 80 acres at her Sleight Farm in the Mendip Hills south of Bath, southwestern England. She produces a truly exceptional lineup, including this delight.
- PRODUCTION AND AGING: Made in the style of Tuscan Pecorino; aged 4 to 12 months.
- APPEARANCE: A unique 5- to 7-pound "basket" shape (like a flying saucer with rounded edges) featuring a natural grayish-brown moldy rind.
- CONSISTENCY AND TASTE: Hard, fine-grained, even somewhat brittle due to the scalding of its curds. Tyning is chock-full of flavors—not infrequently, notes of Del Monte's pineapple chunks have been detected—yet is uncannily able to maintain its integrity and deliver a subtle, full, rounded impression.
- RECOMMENDED PAIRINGS: Merlot, Sangiovese (e.g., Chianti, Brunello di Montalcino, or California).
- SIMILAR CHEESES: Berkswell, Tuscan Pecorino.
- ADDITIONAL CHEESES: Mary also makes a Valençay-style soft raw goat's milk cheese called Tymsboro (the ancient name of the village near Mary's farm), which unfortunately is not currently exported to the United States as it simply couldn't survive the trip. She makes two other raw sheep's milk treasures, Emlett and Little Ryding, which are also currently unavailable in the United States.

France

T HE FRENCH possess a unique and profound appreciation of the good things in life. It's deeply embedded in the national psyche. Wine, cheese, food, art, architecture . . . all are expressions of the French soul, of that certain sense of style and *joie de vivre*. And so, without prejudice toward any other country, it must be stated that when it comes to cheese, France is king. Although there are individual Spanish, Italian, and British cheeses that achieve—and occasionally exceed—the high French standard, the crown goes to the Gallic nation. There is no match for its powerful combination of attributes—tradition, inventiveness, quality, and flavor. Furthermore, for sheer numbers and variety, nothing comes close to French cheese, a multiplicity that reflects the country's tremendous geographical diversity and cultural depth.

France is divided into ninety-six *départments*, "enlightened" political boundaries made during the Revolution that don't always represent ancient cultural divides. It has twenty-two provinces, which define the more traditional "spiritual" boundaries (there are between three and eight *départements* within every province). Each province has distinct characteristics that are reflected in its principal products, including cheese. The cheeses of the south-central highlands are as different from those of the northern plains

as British farmhouse cheeses are from, say, their Italian counterparts.

France has the oldest and most extensive system of standards to authenticate wines, spirits, and dairy products, to protect their names and guarantee quality. These so-called AOC laws are administered and enforced by the Institut National Appellation d'Origine (INAO), which is a division of the Ministry of Agriculture. For each cheese, detailed AOC regulations specify precise place of origin (zone of production of milk and of cheese), breed of animal (in some cases), farming practices, and milk type. They also spell out the composition and attributes of the cheese itself, including physical appearance, sanctioned ingredients, and methods of production. Violation of these regulations is punishable by fines and imprisonment; it is a form of fraud that is taken very seriously in France.

The French AOC laws define four categories of cheese production, and many cheeses are labeled accordingly:

1. *Fermier*, or "farmhouse," where an independent owner-operator uses traditional methods and milk from a herd raised on the property.
2. *Artisanal*, a term we're appropriating in English-American usage, which means the cheeses are handmade by an independent farm or small dairy owner but the milk can come from outside sources.
3. *Frutière*, *cremier*, or *cooperative*, where the milk is bought from local farms and made in the small local dairy.
4. *Industriel*, or factory, cheeses, where the cheese is made by factory-style methods and milk can come from afar.

In general, look for the *fermier* label or, if not available, a *frutière* or co-op one. Seek out cheeses that are handmade and cured or ripened in their place of origin. (*Laitier* is another term that may appear on a cheese label; it means dairy-made.)

There are currently thirty-six cheeses that have been granted AOC status (Tomme de Savoie is pending):

Abondance

Beaufort

Bleu d'Auvergne

Bleu de Gex

Bleu des Causses

Bleu du Vercours-Sassenage

Brie de Meaux

Brie de Melun

Brocciu

Cabécou de Rocamadour

Camembert de Normandie

Cantal

Chabichou de Poitou

Chaource

Comte

Crottin de Chavignol

Epoisses de Bourgogne

Fourme d'Ambert (or de Montbrison)

Laguiole

Langres

Livarot

Maroilles

Mont D'Or (Vacherin du Haut Doubs)

Munster

Neufchâtel

Ossau-Iraty Brebis

Picodon de la Drôme (or de l'Ardeche)

Pont L'Evêque

Pouligny-Saint-Pierre

Reblochon

Roquefort

Sainte-Maure de Touraine

Saint-Nectaire

Salers

Selles-sur-Cher

Valençay

You'd think that every French AOC cheese would automatically make it onto my list of favorites. Frankly, though, many of them just don't blow me away. The washed-rind and soft mold-ripened cheeses are the real French forte.

Strong worldwide demand for such household names such as Camembert or Munster can lead to a lowering of standards—even stringent ones such as the AOC regulations. Sometimes, the AOC label may only signify that a given cheese is not a blatant commercial imitation. Certain AOCs may allow for "industrial" practices such as collection of milk from multiple sources, pasteurization, use of synthesized starters and rennets, centralization of production, loss of traditional animal breeds, and artificially induced rinds. Simply put, the AOC stamp is a reliable indicator of good—even very good—cheeses; but it does not *guarantee* an authentic, superior farmhouse-type product.

Many fine French cheeses, ironically, have become victims of their own stellar reputations and success. Homogenized factory-made imitations are exported in huge quantities. French cheeses have been coming into America in such large quantities for such a long time that there was bound to be a loss of character. The cheeses selected in the following pages are the ones that, in my experience, have been able to maintain top quality and character.

All caveats aside, France offers superlative examples in every major category: hard mountain cheeses such as Comté and Gruyère; smelly washed-rind ones such as Munster, Epoisses, and Livarot; lush triple crèmes such as Pierre-Robert, a uniquely French product; soft, fresh, mold-ripened cheeses such as Camembert and Brie; and numerous pure-white goat cheeses.

HOW MANY CHEESES
IN FRANCE?

PROBABLY MORE THAN 600; NOBODY KNOWS FOR SURE

G ENERAL CHARLES DEGAULLE, the savior of modern France and its most famous statesman, supposedly made the following pronouncement: "How can anyone be expected to govern a country with 325 cheeses?" According to some reports, he uttered these oft-quoted words during a meeting with Churchill. In his *Guide du Fromage,* Pierre Androuët indicates that it was actually Churchill who remarked to DeGaulle, "A country that produces 325 varieties of cheese cannot be governed." Bartlett's *Familiar Quotations* attributes the statement to DeGaulle as follows: "Only peril can bring the French together. One can't impose unity out of the blue on a country that has 265 different kinds of cheese." Patrick Rance, in his *French Cheese Book,* reports DeGaulle's count as 324. Yet Rance promptly goes on to estimate that there are more than 750 cheeses in France. During his 50-year career as a professional cheese connoisseur, he certainly hunted down and tasted a huge number of them. In his book, he makes an earnest attempt to come up with an exact number but finally throws up his hands: "There is one certain fact about French cheeses: practically speaking, they are innumerable. I should like to have produced a more comprehensive book, but life is too short." (As it was, he managed to fill 550 pages.)

The heart of Gallic farmhouse cheese artisanship includes the mountainous provinces of Franche-Comté and Rhône-Alpes, bordering on Switzerland and Italy and encompassing the French Alps. The mountains of the Massif Centrale, a region also known as the Auvergne, and the Loire Valley also produce excellent cheeses. While cows, sheep, and goats graze the pastures of the Alps, sheep are prevalent in the rugged central mountains and Pyrénées. The Loire Valley is home to the most celebrated of French goat cheeses, including Crottin de Chavignol, Sainte-Maure de Touraine, Pouligny-Saint-Pierre, and Valençay. Meanwhile, up in Normandy, which is famous for its butter and cream, cows rule.

ABBAYE DE BELLOC

Never a braggart, this ancient cheese is smooth, reliable, and endlessly satisfying.

■ TYPE: Pasteurized sheep's milk.

■ ORIGIN AND MAKERS: Ossau-Iraty Brebis Pyrénées AOC, southwestern France, along the Spanish border; farmhouse-made and ripened in the Abbaye de Belloc, a Benedictine abbey. The Ossau-Iraty Brebis cheeses are the Pyrénées sheep's-milk equivalent of the great alpine cheeses Beaufort and Comté.

■ PRODUCTION AND AGING: The best Pyrénées sheep's milk cheeses are all made by essentially the same recipe, one that is more than 3,000 years old, and so their differences reflect terroir.

■ APPEARANCE: 8-pound cylinders with rounded edges and an orangish, hard rind with dustings of white mold.

■ CONSISTENCY AND TASTE: Semihard paste with a fairly dense, concentrated consistency and delicious sweet, fruity, nutty, lactic flavors.

■ RECOMMENDED PAIRINGS: White Bordeaux, Cahors (made with the Malbec grape in southwestern France), Sancerre Rouge, Pinot Blanc,

Dolcelto d'Alba, Barbera d'Alba, Chardonnay, Cabernet Sauvignon, Pouilly-Fumé, Carignan.
■ SIMILAR CHEESES: Berkswell, Spenwood, Vermont Shepherd, Zamorano.

BEAUFORT

Famous far and wide since Roman times, Beaufort, along with Tomme de Savoie and Reblochon, is one of the noble cheeses of the French Alps. It is frequently referred to as the Prince of Gruyères.

■ TYPE: Raw cow's milk.

■ ORIGIN AND MAKERS: Haute-Savoie, in the mountains of east-central France, south of Lake Geneva, Switzerland; the best cheeses are made by small independent producers. Many very fine Beaufort cheeses are also made in the *frutières* or co-ops. Look for the AOC label.

■ PRODUCTION AND AGING: The best Beaufort, labeled Haute-Montagne, is made from the milk of cows that graze in the high-mountain pastures during the summertime (mid-June to mid-September) and is therefore available in winter. Under Beaufort's AOC rules, cheeses may be labeled *alpage* only if they are made in a chalet in the summer from the milk of a single herd. *Été* (summer) cheeses are made in a dairy, June to October. Beaufort is categorized as a cooked-curd cheese, but its curds are not heated as hot as other classic Gruyère-type cheese—Emmental, for one—so it retains its melt-in-the-mouth character and avoids the very firm consistency and "cooked" flavors of its Gruyère cousins. All Beauforts are cured in cellars for at least 6 months.

■ APPEARANCE: Large wheels, about 2 feet in diameter, 5 inches thick and weighing from 85 to 130 pounds, which have characteristic concave sides. Beaufort has yellowish ivory-colored paste, with some small holes and horizontal fissures *(lenures)*.

■ CONSISTENCY AND TASTE: A fairly dense, concentrated, buttery consistency, a fruity aroma, and rich, nutty flavors with a hint of sweetness. (The summer cheeses feature additional herbal and flo-

ral tastes.) As Beaufort ages, it takes on a pronounced flavor of spoiled milk, borderline rancid, that is, for most people, an irresistible taste. Avoid any Beaufort that has a cracking rind, any trace of mold on the interior, or a large number of air holes.

■ RECOMMENDED PAIRINGS: Versatile with wines; try it with a good dry Champagne, a fine Chardonnay (California or Burgundy), California or Oregon Pinot Noir, German Riesling Spätlese, St. Joseph (northern Rhône red).

■ SIMILAR CHEESES: Gruyère is a more general term encompassing the hard cheeses of the provinces of Franche-Comté and Haute-Savoie, which include Emmental, Comté (aka Gruyère de Comté) and also Beaufort. Swiss Gruyère (see below) and Emmental (aka Emmentaler) are also related; Beaufort is like an aged Fontina D'Aosta.

BLEU DE GEX

One of the oldest cheeses in France, it survives in close to its ancient form.

■ TYPE: Raw cow's milk blue.

■ ORIGIN AND MAKERS: Local cooperatives in the Juras region of Franche-Comté Province, around the town of Gex, to the north of Geneva, Switzerland. Both Bleu de Gex and another blue, Bleu de Septmoncel, are protected under the same AOC, which is also sometimes referred to as "Bleu du Haut-Jura."

BEAUFORT'S SHAPE

LEGEND has it that Beaufort was made with concave sides to facilitate winding a rope around its sides. All you had to do was sling a wheel of it on one side of your horse or donkey, do the same thing with a second wheel on the other side, and you were ready to transport them on the steep mountain paths from chalet to market in pretty good balance.

- PRODUCTION AND AGING: Made in cooperatives from the milk of cows who graze in the Jura Mountains. Aged 1 month; air injected into paste to promote growth of *P. glaucum* mold.
- APPEARANCE: Large rounds.
- CONSISTENCY AND TASTE: Has a rich, relatively mild but tantalizing taste for a blue, with a pleasant mineral quality. It is somewhat reminiscent of Stilton but not as firm.
- SEASONAL NOTE: September through February.
- RECOMMENDED PAIRINGS: Banyuls, LBV Port, Muscat de Rivesaltes.
- SIMILAR CHEESES: Fourme D'Ambert, Stilton.

BRIN D'AMOUR

How could you object to a cheese whose name means "a breath of love" in the Corsican dialect? It can also go by the name of Fleur du Maquis ("Flower of the Maquis"), the *maquis* being the local term for the typical thickets of rough underbrush where highway robbers and guerrilla fighters used to hide out.
- TYPE: Ewe's milk.
- ORIGIN AND MAKERS: The island of Corsica, in the Mediterranean off the south coast of France; look for cheeses from Antoine Ottavi in Ghissonaccia or a comparable producer.
- PRODUCTION AND AGING: Farmhouses and cooperatives. An uncooked, unpressed artisanal cheese that is sometimes made with goat's milk or mixed milk; but we only see the 100 percent ewe's milk version in the United States.
- APPEARANCE: A moist, smooth whitish paste and grayish natural rind with a dusting of bluish mold that is encrusted with rosemary or savory.
- CONSISTENCY AND TASTE: Soft, mild, and aromatic. Honestly, I'm not a fan of herb-crusted cheese, but this is truly an exceptional one. The flavors of the best Brin d'Amours are subtly enhanced—not overwhelmed—by their herbs.
- SEASONAL NOTE: Brin d'Amour shows

well year-round but best June to September.
- RECOMMENDED PAIRINGS: This is not a complex or challenging cheese so it's very versatile with wines. Try it with Albariño, red Bordeaux, Nebbiolo, Syrah, Carignan, Grüner Veltliner, Alsatian Riesling or German Riesling Auslese, Chardonnay, Sancerre Blanc, Sherry (Oloroso). It is also coffee-friendly.
- SIMILAR CHEESE: Sally Jackson's leaf-wrapped sheep's milk cheese.

CHEVROTIN DES ARAVIS

This is a goat cheese with a difference—most definitely *not* your typical chalky white Loire Valley chèvre.
- TYPE: Goat's milk washed-rind.
- ORIGIN AND MAKERS: Laitiers. From the Haute-Savoie region, along the Swiss border, south of Lake Geneva, named after the Aravis mountain range near Megève.
- PRODUCTION AND AGING: Made by a recipe similar to that of Reblochon—that is, uncooked and lightly pressed.
- APPEARANCE: The washed rind has a pinkish to orangish-yellow color with some whitish powdery mold. Comes in rounds about 4 inches in diameter, weighing about half a pound, with a smooth, supple off-white paste.
- CONSISTENCY AND TASTE: Soft; mild flavor with a pleasant, somewhat musty, goaty finish.
- RECOMMENDED PAIRINGS: As with the chèvre-style cheeses of the Loire Valley a good, crisp Sancerre; also try it with an Alsatian Tokay Pinot Gris, a German Riesling Kabinett, a northern Rhône Syrah, white Bordeaux, or Sauternes.
- SIMILAR CHEESES: Consider this a goat's milk version of Reblochon.

CROTTIN DE CHAVIGNOL

One of the world-famous and quintessentially French Loire Valley chèvres.
- TYPE: Goat's milk.

- ORIGIN AND MAKERS: An AOC cheese from the Berry region of the Loire Valley around Sancerre. One of the best brands is from the *affineur* and *négociant* Jacquin, which also makes superb Sainte-Maure de Touraine and Valençay.
- PRODUCTION AND AGING: Its rind starts out cream colored and gradually attracts blue or white mold with age, eventually shriveling and turning brownish-black. Unfortunately, the AOC for this cheese allows for the use of frozen curds and as little as 10 days' ripening. It also doesn't sufficiently pinpoint the cheese's provenance.
- APPEARANCE: The word *crottin* means "dung" or "turd," and the cheese is so named because it is a small flattened sphere (up to about 2 inches in diameter).
- CONSISTENCY AND TASTE: Semisoft to semihard, creamy and mild to sharp and salty, depending on its degree of aging. The younger cheeses are called *mou* or "wet"; their flavor is less pronounced.
- SEASONAL NOTE: May through November.
- RECOMMENDED PAIRINGS: Albariño, Sancerre Blanc, and other dry Sauvingon Blanc wines.
- SIMILAR CHEESES: Pouligny-Saint-Pierre, Selles-sur-Cher, Valençay, Wabash Cannonball.

L'EDEL DE CLERON
See Vacherin du Haut-Doubs.

EPOISSES DE BOURGOGNE (OR SIMPLY "EPOISSES")
One of the more frequently requested cheeses on any fine board, Epoisses was probably developed by Cistercian monks in the environs of Dijon during the late Middle Ages. It became an established delicacy during the reign of Louis XIV and is said to have been one of Napoleon's favorite cheeses. (Of course, that's said about plenty of French cheeses.) The great food scribe Brillat-Savarin called Epoisses "The King of Cheeses." It nearly went extinct in the 1930s and was dormant throughout the World War II years but was revived in the 1950s.

- TYPE: Cow's milk washed-rind.
- ORIGIN AND MAKERS: An AOC cheese from Burgundy, particularly the area west-northwest of the city of Dijon, it bears the name of the village where it originated. Unfortunately, the Epoisses we're getting in the United States are pasteurized. Berthaut is the best authentic brand; Germain is also excellent.
- PRODUCTION AND AGING: An uncooked, unpressed cheese, its rind is built up from repeated baths in brine then in wine or marc. Epoisses is ripened for a total of 5 to 6 weeks and should be eaten à point; otherwise, it doesn't do justice to its exalted reputation.
- APPEARANCE: Comes in two sizes of flattened cylinder or disk—small (about 4 inches in diameter, weighing 9 ounces) and large (about 7½ inches in diameter, weighing 1 pound). I much prefer the smaller size. Its rind has a pronounced orangish tinge that can turn darker, bordering on brick-red with aging.
- CONSISTENCY AND TASTE: A smooth and pliant pâte that becomes gooey and spoonable at room temperature when ripe. Although "pungent" can be a generous description of the aroma of a ripe Epoisses, it offers a remarkably diverse spectrum of soft, rich, and mouth-watering flavors. It's amazing how it can smell so funky and yet taste so balanced and well rounded.
- RECOMMENDED PAIRINGS: White Burgundy, California Cabernet, Condrieu (Viognier), Coteaux du Layon, Rosé Champagne, Jurançon Petit Mensang, Sauternes.
- SIMILAR CHEESES: L'Ami du Chambertin, which is essentially a brand of Epoisses that comes in a 9-ounce size; Livarot; Munster.

FOURME D'AMBERT
France's answer to Stilton.
- TYPE: Raw cow's milk blue.

- ORIGIN AND MAKERS: Cooperatives in the Auvergne region of the Massif Central, south-central France; AOC protected.
- PRODUCTION AND AGING: Similar to Stilton but pressed, so it comes out less crumbly.
- APPEARANCE: Like Stilton, Fourme D'Ambert comes in a rather large upright cylinder or drum, albeit a bit smaller at about 4 inches across and 8 inches tall, weighing 5 pounds. This is the shape of the *fourme*, or mold, into which the curds are poured.
- CONSISTENCY AND TASTE: The paste is semisoft, smooth, rich, creamy—not dry or crumbly. The flavor is buttery and tangy, not salty or bitter.
- RECOMMENDED PAIRINGS: Banyuls, Tawny Port, Oloroso Sherry.
- SIMILAR CHEESES: Fourme de Montbrison comes mainly from the Loire and is essentially the same cheese under a different name; also Bleu d'Auvergne and Bleu de Causses.

LIVAROT

An ancient and noble cheese dating back more than 700 years and originating with the monks, a fine Livarot is worthy of its lofty reputation.

- TYPE: Cow's milk washed-rind.
- ORIGIN AND MAKERS: From the region of southern Normandy also known as the Pays d'Auge (see also Pavé d'Auge and Camembert). Livarot takes the name of the principal market town in the Calvados zone where it was originally sold; it was also traditionally sold in nearby Vimoutiers. Look for the AOC label. Eugéne Graindorge is the best brand available in the United States. There are superior artisanal ones in France.
- PRODUCTION AND AGING: Washed-rind; aged 2 to 3 months. Unfortunately, Livarots often arrive in the States suffocating, and their windows of ripeness can be fairly small.
- APPEARANCE: Livarot is also known as "The Little Colonel" because of the five strips of sedge or raffia that traditionally encircle the cheese. It comes in small- to medium-sized rounds about 2 inches high that are wrapped in paper and packed in a box. Its rind should be smooth and moist, not sticky or slimy, and pinkish-brown with reddish-yellow or orange shading. Graindorge's Livarots come in two sizes: regular, which is about 5 inches across and 2 inches high, weighing 17½ ounces; and Petit Livarot, just over 3½ inches in diameter and weighing 9½ ounces.
- CONSISTENCY AND TASTE: Although it has an assertive aroma and nutty flavor, it doesn't taste nearly as strong as it smells. Livarot's paste is semisoft, creamy and smooth in texture, with small holes. The paste can get quite runny when ripe at room temperature.
- RECOMMENDED PAIRINGS: Grüner Veltliner, hard cider, Alsatian Riesling, German Riesling (Kabinett, Spätlese, Auslese), Gewürztraminer, Malvasia delle Liparia, Sherry (Oloroso), Tokay Pinot Gris d'Alsace, Hungarian Tokaji.
- SIMILAR CHEESES: Epoisses, Munster, Pont l'Evêque.

MAROILLES

A little bit of this one goes a long way!

- TYPE: Cow's milk washed-rind.
- ORIGIN AND MAKERS: An AOC cheese from Eastern Flanders in the Ardennes forest near the border with Belgium, it was created by monks at the abbey of the same name at least 1,000 years ago. Now made by various dairies and creameries. My favorite version is called Gris de Lille, a cheese that is nicknamed, aptly, *Puant de Lille,* which translates literally as "The Stinker from Lille."
- PRODUCTION AND AGING: The raw-milk version is aged less than 2 months.
- APPEARANCE: Within the Maroilles AOC, there are numerous cheeses made in different shapes—from little 5- to 7-ounce heart shapes to larger 1½-pound bricks—according to the same recipe. They have smooth, reddish-brown rinds, and most of them come in square wooden boxes.

- CONSISTENCY AND TASTE: Typical of the cheeses of its region, Maroilles has a very pungent aroma and a strong, salty taste.
- RECOMMENDED PAIRINGS: Gewürztraminer.
- SIMILAR CHEESES: Livarot, Munster.

MIMOLETTE

A cheese whose name comes from the word *demi-molle* ("semisoft"), Mimolette is also traditionally known as Boule de Lille, after its rounded shape and the fact that its original ripening caves were in the northern city of Lille. I call it a dangerous cheese for a couple of reasons. First, after more than 2 years, not only does the Mimolette look like a cannonball, it's hard enough that you could use it as one in a pinch. Second, it once sent me to the hospital for stitches. It takes a sharp knife to gouge flaky wedges out of a partially consumed cannonball of Mimolette. If the knife slips, you can get a nasty cut.
- TYPE: Pasteurized cow's milk.
- ORIGIN AND MAKERS: Flanders, primarily the northernmost *département* of Pas de Calais, south and west of Belgium. Factory-made by the firm of Issigny-Sainte-Mère.
- PRODUCTION AND AGING: A pressed, cooked cheese. Its degrees of aging are: young (*jeune*, 3 months), half old (*demi-vieille* or *demi-etuvée*, 6 months), old (*vieille* or *etuvée*, 12 months), and very old (*extra-vieille*, 24 months).
- APPEARANCE: Comes in the shape of a cannonball, about 8 inches in diameter with a flattened top, weighing about 7 pounds with a hard orangish-brown natural brushed rind and orange-hued paste.
- CONSISTENCY AND TASTE: Young Mimolette is a pedestrian, bland, undistinguished cheese with a semihard interior. Properly aged, upwards of 18 months, it hardens, turns a deeper orange on the interior, and takes on an exceptionally mouthwatering array of fruity, nutty flavors, with notes of butterscotch and caramel. It's lip-smacking, jaw-clacking flavor!
- RECOMMENDED PAIRINGS: Rustic reds

such as Cahors (made with the Malbec grape in southwestern France) and Carignan; also Quarts de Chaume (late-harvest Chenin Blanc) or Cabernet Sauvignon.
- SIMILAR CHEESES: Mimolette is essentially a French version of Dutch Edam, so a substitute would be an aged Edam or Gouda (Boeren Kaas).

MONT BRIAC

This is a spectacular and unique cheese, a real eye-opener when perfectly ripened—not because it bowls you over with an explosion of flavor but because of its subtlety and originality.
- TYPE: Cow's milk double crème.
- ORIGIN AND MAKER: From the rugged Auvergne region of south-central France, it is actually a brand of cheese and a relatively new one at that. Factory-made; Roche Baron is the producer.
- PRODUCTION AND AGING: Made from the milk of the local Salers cows; similar to a fine Brie but with some interior blueing.
- APPEARANCE: Thin, crusty rind covered with ash.
- CONSISTENCY AND TASTE: A soft, mild tasting, gentle blue with a silky smooth, creamy paste that goes gooey soft at room temperature.
- RECOMMENDED PAIRINGS: Muscat de Rivesaltes or some other late-harvest Muscat or Semillon-based wine. Pinot Blanc or Grüner Veltliner.
- SIMILAR CHEESES: Gambozola, a soft, creamy blue from Germany.

MUNSTER

Authentic Munster is a far cry from the bland supermarket cheeses that we Americans might associate, for example, with a liverwurst sandwich on rye. It is another ancient cheese that traces its roots back to monastic life in the early Middle Ages; in fact, the word *Munster* is said to be a contraction of "monastery" in the local dialect. The original Munster cheeses had bloomy rinds; their modern form, with washed rinds, evolved about 800 to 1,000 years ago. At peak, this is an exquisite cheese; in fact, it has been known to fool connoisseurs and be mistaken for a ripe Epoisses!

■ TYPE: Cow's milk washed-rind.

■ ORIGIN AND MAKERS: From the mountains of the Vosges region, in Alsace, northeastern France, bordering on Germany. There are unpasteurized *fermier* (farmer) and pasteurized *laitier* (dairy) versions of Munster; unfortunately, the raw-milk versions are illegal in the United States. Recommended brands are Hexaire (which makes an organic version), Valdeweiss, and Marcillat. Another favorite is the Petit Munster/Geromé called La Fleur Vosgienne, which comes in 200-gram rounds from the *affineur* La Maison Fischer. Munster is AOC-protected; its sister, Geromé, a nearly identical but larger cheese that comes from the neighboring province of Lorraine just to the west, is covered under the same AOC. (Unfortunately, Geromé has been almost completely overshadowed by the Munster name; many cheeses that could or should be called Geromé are referred to as Munster for expediency's sake.)

■ PRODUCTION AND AGING: Made from mountain pasture milk in the summer, farm milk in the winter, and aged 2 to 3 months in cellars at high humidity. (Fresh, unripened Munster, which is a fairly bland cheese, is sold and consumed mostly within its zone of production.)

■ APPEARANCE: Comes in two basic round sizes: regular (7½ inches in diameter and 1 to 3 inches high) and small (3 to 5 inches in diameter and about 1 inch high). The rind is a beautiful sight, with its bright pinkish-orange color that turns progressively darker and more reddish/orangish with age. As with all washed-rind cheeses, its exterior should be moist but not slimy or cracked.

■ CONSISTENCY AND TASTE: The pâte goes from semisoft when young to soft and runny at peak; it has an assertive, deep, rich, tangy flavor and a strong, barnyardy aroma.

■ SEASONAL NOTE: June through October.

■ RECOMMENDED PAIRINGS: Alsatian

HOW TO GIVE A CHEESE A BATH

WASHED-RIND CHEESES SHOULD BE RESUSCITATED BEFORE DRYING OUT

F OR A small- to medium-sized washed-rind cheese, use a big dish or small bowl large enough to hold the cheese along with 1 to 2 cups of water. Fill the bowl with enough water at room temperature to submerge the cheese about halfway. Add a little salt (I like to use Kosher style), mix well, and then set the cheese in the dish for a minute or two, basting it occasionally by rubbing the salt solution on using a gentle circular motion. The cheese's surface will probably begin to feel slimy and some of the pink blush may wash away. Don't worry, that phlegmlike coating won't hurt you. For the time being, the smell won't be too bothersome, since the cheese is partially submerged in water.

Turn the cheese over; bathe and baste for at least 2 or 3 minutes and as much as an hour if its rind still seems tight. Allow the cheese to drain, leaving a slight even coat of moisture on its rind. It probably won't need to be patted dry except possibly on its bottom to keep it from sliding around on its plate. Rewrap the cheese for storage or present it for serving.

Gewürztraminer, Grüner Veltliner, German Riesling (Kabinett or Auslese), Alsatian Tokay Pinot Gris, Sherry (Oloroso).

■ SIMILAR CHEESES: Epoisses, Livarot, Maroilles.

PAVÉ D'AUGE

The word *pavé* means paving stone or slab and this cheese is essentially a larger, more rustic version of the more famous Pont L'Evêque, originally a monastic cheese that dates back over a thousand years.

■ TYPE: Cow's milk.

■ ORIGIN AND MAKERS: Creamery-made in the Pays D'Auge at the northern base of the Normandy peninsula to the west of the town of Pont L'Evêque. Local pavé cheeses are often known by more specific place names such as Pavé du Plessis and Pavé de Moyaux.

■ PRODUCTION AND AGING: Aged 2½ to 4 months.

■ APPEARANCE: Square-shaped bricks with rounded edges, 4½ inches at the base and up to 2½ inches high, weighing 1½ to 1¾ pounds. The rind is straw colored or yellowish beige and is scored with a basket pattern.

■ CONSISTENCY AND TASTE: The paste is semisoft to soft, rich and flavorful, with a strong, woodsy flavor.

■ SEASONAL NOTE: Available year-round but best May through December.

■ RECOMMENDED PAIRINGS: Red Bordeaux, Blanc de Blancs Champagne, Condrieu (Viognier), hard cider, German Riesling Kabinett, Cahors (made from the Malbec grape in southwestern France) Gewürztraminer, Chardonnay, Merlot, Cabernet Sauvignon.

■ SIMILAR CHEESES: A genuine Pont L'Evêque would be a viable substitute. Graindorge makes an excellent one in two sizes: standard (14 ounces) and small (8½ ounces). Pavé D'Auge also recalls, for many, its other famous cousin, Camembert.

PERAIL

A very pleasant little cheese, ideal for consumption by one person in one sitting.

■ TYPE: Raw ewe's milk.

■ ORIGIN AND MAKERS: Made in several dairies. From the Causses du Larzac in Rouergue, in the center of southern France, near Roquefort country. The Causses is a high, rugged plateau, made of chalky soil and calcareous rock, that is the perfect natural habitat for sheep (Patrick Rance calls it "primeval sheep country").

■ PRODUCTION AND AGING: Artisanal and aged at least 1 week.

■ APPEARANCE: Medium-small disks about ½ inch high and 3½ to 4 inches across. A natural rind with imprints of the basket in which the curds were drained.

■ CONSISTENCY AND TASTE: Gives off barnyard surface odors but has a soft, smooth, creamy paste that is aromatic and mild.

■ SEASONAL NOTE: Best March through September.

■ RECOMMENDED PAIRINGS: Red Bordeaux, California Cabernet, northern Rhône red (Syrah), Viognier.

■ SIMILAR CHEESES: Cabécou de Rocamadour, Pavé D'Affinois, Saint-Marcellin.

PIERRE-ROBERT

This splendid delicacy is actually not a cheese type but rather my favorite brand of triple crème.

■ TYPE: Pasteurized cow's milk.

■ ORIGIN AND MAKER: These cousins of Brie come from the Seine-et-Marne *département* of Île-de-France, the province surrounding Paris. Pierre-Robert was named by its inventor, Robert Rouzaire, after himself and a good friend named Pierre.

■ PRODUCTION AND AGING: Molded, lightly pressed, and made with the addition of extra cream to achieve the required 75 percent fat content. Cured for about 3 weeks.

■ APPEARANCE: A miniature drum about 5

inches in diameter, 2 inches high, and weighing about 1 pound, with Brie-like rind—white, bloomy, and slightly moldy. The rind can become fairly thick, hard, and crusty with age.

■ CONSISTENCY AND TASTE: A triple crème is soft and moist with a rich, buttery, creamy, mild flavor—imagine a perfectly blended mixture of butter and cream cheese. Its texture is luxurious and divine; its flavors are, in a word, salt and butter. I like to ripen this cheese to the point where its rind turns brownish in color and its paste becomes so meltingly soft that it virtually collapses when you cut it.

■ RECOMMENDED PAIRINGS: Red Bordeaux, Blanc de Blancs Champagne, Pinot Gris, German Riesling Kabinett. Can also pair with white Rhône wines such as Châteauneuf-du-Pape Blanc and Condrieu; or with Chardonnay and Gewürztraminer.

■ SIMILAR CHEESES: Rouzaire's Gratte-Paille is a double-crème cousin of Pierre-Robert, with 60 to 75 percent fat content rather than the 75 percent of a triple crème. Rouzaire also makes Bries as well as Coulommiers, a related but larger cheese. The original triple crème was Brillat-Savarin, which was named after Anthelme Brillat-Savarin, the great gastronome of the late eighteenth and early nineteenth centuries, by the cheese merchant Henri Androuët in the 1930s. Another famous triple crème is Explorateur, which was devised in the early 1960s and named in honor of the French explorer Bertrand Flornoy, a cheese lover. It has a picture of a Sputnik-type rocket ship on the label.

POULIGNY-SAINT-PIERRE
A classic Loire Valley chèvre made in a distinctive four-sided conical shape and thus nicknamed the Pyramid or the Eiffel Tower.

■ TYPE: Goat's milk.

■ ORIGIN AND MAKERS: Loire Valley, west-southwest of Paris. Various farms and local dairies; AOC protected. Jacquin is one of the more reliable *affineurs/negociants*.

■ PRODUCTION AND AGING: Aged 4 to 6 weeks. The AOC minimum is 2 weeks; among the better cheeses, 4 or 5 weeks is common.

■ APPEARANCE: Pouligny has a beautiful, somewhat rough surface to its rind, which deepens in color to reddish-brown with grayish-blue tinges of mold due to the application of *P. glaucum*. It is about 3 inches square at the base and 4 inches tall and weighs 7 to 9 ounces.

■ CONSISTENCY AND TASTE: The paste is a very pure white, moist, and semisoft, with a well-balanced, full flavor that offers complex sweet, sour, and salty notes. The sweetness of a fresh Pouligny gives way to a sharper, saltier, more intense flavor as the cheese ages.

■ SEASONAL NOTE: Best May through November.

■ RECOMMENDED PAIRINGS: For the traditional Loire Valley goat cheeses, the local white wine, Sancerre; also other dry Sauvignon Blanc–based wines and Albariño.

■ SIMILAR CHEESES: Crottin de Chavignol, Sainte-Maure de Touraine, Selles-sur-Cher, Valençay.

REBLOCHON
Mountain cheeses are generally superb, and Reblochon is among the best. It may be the single most requested one in my restaurant experience. Interestingly, the name of the cheese derives not from a place-name but from a verb, *réblocher*, which is the local word for "second milking." Legend has it that the herders and dairy workers would milk the cows, stop and give the proprietor his milk, then finish the milking later. They'd use that thicker, richer milk to make cheeses for themselves.

■ TYPE: Cow's milk washed-rind.

■ ORIGIN AND MAKERS: The Haute-Savoie region of east-central France, near Geneva, Switzerland, primarily around the Chaine des Aravis mountain range and its surrounding valleys, near the towns of Megève and Chamonix. (See also Chevrotin des Aravis, essentially a goat's milk version of Reblochon.) Farmhouse, artisanal, and creamery production; look for the summer *fermier* and *chalet* versions, which peak in the early fall; the *fermier* cheeses have a green label.

■ PRODUCTION AND AGING: Uncooked, lightly pressed, and made from the milk of the venerable Abondance breed of cow, which also yields Beaufort and Abondance cheeses as well as Vacherin d'Abondance. Aged 4 to 5 weeks.

■ APPEARANCE: Flattish rounds or disks about 5 inches in diameter and 1 inch high, weighing about 1 pound. (I recommend these over the smaller half-pound versions.) Its washed rind is smooth and beige or gold in color with an orange or pink tint and a natural dusting of white mold.

■ CONSISTENCY AND TASTE: The paste is very smooth, creamy, almost shiny, with some holes and a soft, pliant, springy consistency that can range from somewhat rubbery to slightly sticky or gluey. It offers mild, fruity flavor. I sometimes describe it as the "bacon and eggs" of cheese, as there is an eggy hint to its milk flavors and it also features a baconlike saltiness.

■ SEASONAL NOTE: Best June through January.

■ RECOMMENDED PAIRINGS: Red Bordeaux, Beaujolais, California or Oregon Pinot Noir, Carignan, Riesling, Gewürztraminer, Chardonnay.

■ SIMILAR CHEESES: Durrus, Taleggio.

ROQUEFORT

If this isn't France's most famous cheese, it is certainly its most historically prominent. The Romans, who conquered the area in the first century B.C., extolled its virtues; it has been celebrated ever since. Caesar, Charlemagne, the popes of Avignon, and Louis XV of France were all Roquefort aficionados. It has been mentioned in the writings of Pliny the Elder, Rabelais, and Casanova, not to mention Brillat-Savarin and Collette, all cheese lovers. Like many prized cheeses, it was used to pay rent and settle other debts in feudal times. In the late seventeenth century, specifications for Roquefort production were enacted as laws, the precursors of the

modern AOC regulations. In a tasting, there's almost nowhere else to go after this amazing cheese. I couldn't imagine returning to a Stilton, although you might progress to a Cabrales.

■ TYPE: Raw ewe's milk blue.

■ ORIGIN AND MAKERS: Roquefort-sur-Soulzon in the southern portion of the Rouergue region, central southern France. There are but twelve producers of authentic Roquefort. Société des Caves et des Producteurs Reunis de Roquefort (Société, for short) was founded in 1842 and makes the majority of the Roqueforts today. Other recommended brands are Gabriel Coulet, Le Papillon, and especially Le Vieux Berger and Carles, two of my favorites that are less salty, from two of the smaller producers.

■ PRODUCTION AND AGING: Among many other specifications, AOC rules dictate that the cheeses must be ripened in the caves of Mount Combalou for at least 3 months and as many as 9. The milk used to come from sheep reared all over the southern *départements* of France, but it is now primarily from the local breed of Lacaune sheep, organically raised on the limestone plateau of Larzac in the Rouergue. Like most traditional blue cheeses, Roquefort was made only from ambient molds; now the *P. roquefortii* is added to the curds during cheesemaking. The AOC specifies, however, that the mold must come from the caves of Combalou. It also outlaws pasteurization, homogenization, and *thermisation* (heat treatment) of the milk.

■ APPEARANCE: Rounds approximately 8 inches in diameter and 4 inches high that weigh approximately 5½ pounds and are wrapped in light foil. As it ages, the pale green mold evolves to a blue-gray, and holes and fissures appear in the cheese.

■ CONSISTENCY AND TASTE: Roquefort has an ivory-colored paste that is soft, spicy, and tart; it is known for its rich, mild creaminess. Its flavors should not be dominated by saltiness, acidity, or bitterness.

■ SEASONAL NOTE: October through March.

■ RECOMMENDED PAIRINGS: Pairs well

with Banyuls, Madeira, Muscat de Rivesaltes, Sauternes, Tokai Pinot Gris—sweet, full-flavored, full-bodied dessert wines.

■ SIMILAR CHEESES: Bleu des Causses, Beenleigh Blue.

ROUCOULONS

Many connoisseurs, especially European-educated ones, feel Roucoulons is nothing spectacular and don't pay it much mind. For me, it is delightful and versatile, a good starting point for a cheese plate.

■ TYPE: Pasteurized cow's milk.

■ ORIGIN AND MAKER: Fromagerie Milleret, Charcenne, in the Franche-Comté region, east of Burgundy and on the western border of Switzerland.

■ PRODUCTION AND AGING: *Industriel* production. Aged 3½ weeks.

■ APPEARANCE: It has a light beige, slightly orange-tinted bloomy rind with a basket mold imprint and a coating of *P. candidum.* It comes in a round 8¼ inches by 1⅜ inches high, weighing just under 3 pounds. (There is also a mini-Roucoulons of about 250 grams or close to 9 ounces.)

■ CONSISTENCY AND TASTE: The paste is soft and melting at room temperature and features an amazingly smooth, satiny consistency. Its flavor is mild, salty but subtle, and offers a faint taste of wild mushrooms.

■ RECOMMENDED PAIRINGS: Red Bordeaux, German Riesling Kabinett.

■ SIMILAR CHEESES: Camembert, L'Edel de Cleron.

SAINTE-MAURE DE TOURAINE

The most goaty of Loire Valley goat cheeses at peak.

■ TYPE: Goat's milk.

■ ORIGIN AND MAKERS: From the areas around Touraine and Poitou in the central Loire Valley, west-southwest of Paris. Sainte-Maure comes in both *fermier* (farmhouse) and *laitier* (dairy) versions. The *laitier* cheeses come encased in paper; always go for the unwrapped farmhouse ones if possible. Look for the Jacquin brand.

■ PRODUCTION AND AGING: Like other

Loire Valley goat cheeses, best to buy this one from June to October.

■ APPEARANCE: Made in distinctive logs about 5½ inches long and 1½ inches wide, weighing about 9 ounces, that are pierced lengthwise by a narrow straw. This helps hold the cheese together, particularly when fresh and still very moist, and also lets air into the center to encourage ripening. There is a light exterior dusting of ash that helps promote the development of beneficial grayish-white mold.

■ CONSISTENCY AND TASTE: The paste goes from soft when fresh to semisoft and creamy at peak ripeness and has a full nutty flavor.

■ SEASONAL NOTE: May through November.

■ RECOMMENDED PAIRINGS: Albariño, Sancerre Blanc, or California Sauvignon Blanc.

■ SIMILAR CHEESES: Pouligny-Saint-Pierre, Selles-sur-Cher, Valençay.

THE COLOR OF THE BLUES

THEY'RE called blue cheeses when in reality much of the mold is closer to green, gray, purple, or black than blue. How does the coloring in Roquefort compare with that in other "blue" cheeses? It's greenish.

SAINT-MARCELLIN

The legend of Saint-Marcellin is that when King Louis XI was still the Dauphin (prince-in-waiting) he spent a good deal of his time in the Dauphine region; in fact, it was his extended playground, hence the name. One fine day in the mid–fifteenth century, he became separated from his hunting party. While trying to find his way home through the forest, he was confronted by an ornery, hungry bear. The prince yelled for help and two woodsmen rescued him. They took him back to their hut and gave him a simple meal of peasant bread with the local cheese, which he never forgot. The cheese was Saint-

Marcellin, and since that day it has been famous all over France. Louis didn't forget the woodsmen, either; he rewarded them with land and titles.

■ TYPE: Cow's milk (once made with goat's milk).

■ ORIGIN AND MAKERS: Farmhouse production. From the Isère *département* of the mountainous Dauphine Province, an area just west of the city of Grenoble, southeastern France.

■ PRODUCTION AND AGING: Farmhouse production; traditionally (but no longer) leaf-wrapped.

■ APPEARANCE: Small rounds about 3 inches in diameter and ½ inch thick, weighing about 3 ounces. Natural rind, which turns from white to brownish or caramel-colored and develops a dusting of white mold.

■ CONSISTENCY AND TASTE: The paste is soft and fairly mild but rich.

■ SEASONAL NOTE: Late spring through late fall.

■ RECOMMENDED PAIRINGS: Try it with Condrieu (from the Viognier grape) and Syrah-based wines (e.g., Rhône reds).

■ SIMILAR CHEESES: Banon.

SAINT-NECTAIRE

A *tomme*-style cheese with a broad following. Be sure you pick a good raw-milk example; otherwise, you may be disappointed.

■ TYPE: Cow's milk.

■ ORIGIN AND MAKERS: An AOC cheese from the town of the same name in the northern Auvergne, south-central France. The raw-milk *fermier* versions are illegal for import into the United States. There are some acceptable small-dairy versions and many inferior factory-made ones. The summer high-mountain cheeses, which peak in fall, are the best.

■ PRODUCTION AND AGING: Brushed-rind; mold-ripened.

■ APPEARANCE: Comes in disks about 1½ inches thick and 8 inches in diameter with an ivory to straw-yellow interior.

LES TOMMES

BY SOME COUNTS, there are nearly 100 French cheeses that bear the name *tomme*. The root is the Greek *tomos,* meaning part or fraction; tomme cheeses are frequently made from partial milkings. The term originally referred to the smaller alpine cheeses, usually a pound or less. After hundreds of years of usage, it now applies to many different smallish round cheeses from various parts of the country, particularly the soft young cheeses of Dauphine Province around Grenoble, which encompasses the *départements* of Hautes-Alpes, Drôme, and Isère. The most famous of them is Tomme de Savoie. Italy's nearby province of Piedmont produces a number of cheeses under the name *toma.* In Italy, the cheeses generally come in smallish flat disks, but it is even more of a loose category.

■ CONSISTENCY AND TASTE: Semisoft paste with occasional small holes. The flavors are fresh, buttery, fruity, grassy, and not too salty.

■ RECOMMENDED PAIRINGS: Gamay-based wines (Beaujolais) and light Pinot Noirs.

■ SIMILAR CHEESES: Durrus, Tomme de Savoie.

TOMME DE SAVOIE

This is more of a general type than a specific brand or precise appellation, although it does have an AOC pending.

■ TYPE: Raw cow's milk.

■ ORIGIN AND MAKERS: The mountainous Haute-Savoie region, on the Swiss border, south of Lake Geneva. There are many variations from many villages throughout the area, some even made with goat's milk. *Tommes* are made on farms, in dairies, and in factories. There are also many imitators produced outside of the region, some of which are subsequently imported for aging. Be sure to choose the ones with labels indicating they are both *fabriqués* (manufactured) and *affinés* (ripened) in Savoie.

■ PRODUCTION AND AGING: In general, Tomme de Savoie cheeses are pressed. Many traditional ones are made with skimmed milk and are therefore relatively low in fat (between 20 and 40 percent). They are generally aged for 2 months in cellars. An aged *tomme* has a darker paste with small holes and a crusty, cratered rind.

■ APPEARANCE: They generally come in somewhat irregularly shaped flattened cylinders, approximately 8 inches across and 2 to 5 inches tall, weighing 4 to 7 pounds. There are also some *tommes* that come in oversized 12-pound disks. They have hard, gray, crusty natural rinds, frequently with dustings of red and/or yellow mold, and their pâtes are ivory to straw yellow in color.

CLASSIC FRENCH GOAT CHEESES
(AKA CHÈVRES)

Cabécou de Rocamadour
Chabichou de Poitu
Crottin de Chavignol
Picodon
Pouligny-Saint-Pierre
Sainte-Maure de Touraine
Selles-sur-Cher
Valençay

- CONSISTENCY AND TASTE: Firm with mild nutty flavors.
- RECOMMENDED PAIRINGS: Gamay-based wines and lighter Pinot Noirs.
- SIMILAR CHEESES: Saint-Nectaire.

VACHERIN DU HAUT-DOUBS

Unfortunately, real Vacherin du Haut-Doubs is not legal for import into the United States. So we fall back on "Faux Vacherin," labeled *faux* ("fake" or "false") since it is a commercial pasteurized-milk version of its famous cousin. No worries: Faux Vacherin can be delicious.

- TYPE: Raw cow's milk.
- ORIGIN AND MAKERS: An AOC cheese from the Doubs *département* of the mountainous province of Franche-Comté, bordering on the province of Burgundy to the west and the country of Switzerland to the east. Look for the top "faux" brand, L'Edel de Cleron (factory-made). Vacherin Haut-Rive (dairy-made) is another excellent brand.
- PRODUCTION AND AGING: Brine-washed; aged less than 60 days. For Haut-Rive, the cheese-making season is mid-August to mid-March.
- APPEARANCE: Flattened cylinders 8 to 12 inches in diameter, 1 to 2 inches thick, weighing 3½ to 8 pounds, featuring a smooth rind that is yellowish to pinkish or reddish-gold with marks of the cheesecloth still visible on its surface. Vacherins are traditionally encircled in bands of spruce bark, which help hold the cheeses together and also give them a subtle woodsy flavor and aroma; they are also packed in wooden boxes.
- CONSISTENCY AND TASTE: In a word, unctuous. Vacherins have a characteristic satiny smooth texture, healthy shine, and subtle flavor. At peak, they melt to a gooey, runny consistency and are often eaten with a spoon. They feature very creamy, moist pâtes with small holes. The best ones have a bacon-like spicy flavor underlying the milkiness.
- SEASONAL NOTE: October through February (Haut-Rive only).
- RECOMMENDED PAIRING: Champagne.
- SIMILAR CHEESES: Vacherin d'Abondance, whose curds are cooked to a higher temperature, giving it a firmer, more dense pâte by comparison. It is also washed in white wine or *morge,* a mixture of wine, cheese scraps, and occasionally whey, that is rife with beneficial bacteria.

VACHERIN BY ANY OTHER NAME . . .

WHICH COUNTRY IS THE RIGHTFUL OWNER—FRANCE OR SWITZERLAND?

THE traditional French name for this superb unpasteurized mountain cheese was Vacherin Mont d'Or. The Mont d'Or Massif is a mountain range located very close to Switzerland within the borders of France. The French had always proceeded under the assumption that since Vacherin originated there, it should bear its place name. In 1973, however, the Swiss appropriated legal rights to the name, eventually granting it AOC status within their own borders in 1981. This meant the French had to resort to calling their cheeses simply Le Mont D'Or or Vacherin du Haut-Doubs, which became the AOC names. *Vacherin,* by the way, is the "cheese diminutive" of the word *vache* ("cow") just as *chevrotin* is the diminutive of "goat" and *pecorino* is the Italian diminutive of *pecora* ("sheep").

VALENÇAY

Napoleon was a big fan of this cheese; he used to visit Talleyrand at the Chateau de Valençay, which the statesman had bought in 1805, where they no doubt enjoyed plenty of this local delicacy. It was originally made in the shape of a four-sided pyramid. In deference to the emperor, who had a rough time of it in Egypt, the top of the pyramid was lopped off.

■ TYPE: Goat's milk.

■ ORIGIN AND MAKERS: From the village of Valençay in the Berry region of the Loire Valley. An AOC cheese, it comes in both fermier and laitier versions. Jacquin is one of the best affineurs.

■ PRODUCTION AND AGING: Ripened for a minimum of 8 days and usually up to 4 weeks.

■ APPEARANCE: Truncated pyramids about 3 inches square at their base, 3 inches high and weighing about 9 ounces. They have a dusting of charcoal ash on their surface, which attracts white and sometimes blue-gray molds.

■ CONSISTENCY AND TASTE: Smooth, creamy, rich texture and mild flavor.

■ SEASONAL NOTE: May through November.

■ RECOMMENDED PAIRINGS: Same as Sainte-Maure and Pouligny: Albariño, Sancerre Blanc, or other dry Sauvingon Blanc wines.

■ SIMILAR CHEESES: Sainte-Maure de Touraine, Selles-sur-Cher, Pouligny-Saint-Pierre.

A NOTE ON BRIE

BRIE DE MEAUX AND BRIE DE MELUN: The real AOC versions of these superb, world-famous soft-ripened raw cow's *(lait cru vache)* milk cheeses are illegal for import into the United States. Imitations abound; with so many other great cheeses available, I don't buy them.

Italy

FROM THE snow-covered Alps in the far north, across the sprawling Po Valley, and down its mountainous spine to the rugged, sparse lands of the south, Italy has excellent geographical diversity and produces a wide variety of cheeses. There are lush, high pastures throughout the land; cows are more prevalent in the north, and sheep in the center and south. The Romans loved cheese and tasted a variety of imports from the corners of their empire, including Roquefort from France and Cheshire from England. They also developed their own cheeses, many of which survive virtually unchanged.

Italy has a strong regional tradition; within the country, most cheeses are consumed locally. Their popularity—if not their reputations—don't travel as readily as, say, the French cheeses. Nevertheless, Italy can boast of arguably the world's greatest cheese, Parmigiano-Reggiano, along with several others that also find places on my boards. Italy exports a huge amount of cheese to the United States, considerably more than France, most of it in the form of Parmesan and Grana. It also has many types of Pecorino—sheep's milk cheese—from the famous Pecorino Toscano to Romano, Sardo, and Siciliano. You find the best raw-milk cheeses up north, in the mountains close to France and Switzerland. Real Fontina and Taleggio, for example, are superb, subtle, and sophisticated cheeses, both from northern alpine regions of the boot.

Like France and Spain, Italy has a system designed to protect and guarantee cheeses, similar to the one that governs its wines. It is called Denominazione di Origine Controllata (DOC). More than anything, it reflects the regional nature of Italian production. Some of the cheeses on the list are simple, reliable, and nutritious yet thoroughly unremarkable and uninteresting from the gourmet viewpoint. Others are giants among world cheeses. The most recent DOC lineup is as follows:

Asiago
Bitto
Bra
Caciocavallo Silano
Canestrato Pugliese
Casciotta d'Urbino
Castelmagno
Fiore Sardo
Fontina
Formai de Mut dell'Alta Valle Brembana
Gorgonzola
Grana Padano
Montasio
Monte Veronese
Mozzarella di Bufala Compana
Murazzano
Parmigiano-Reggiano
Pecorino Romano
Pecorino Sardo
Pecorino Siciliano
Pecorino Toscano
Provolone Valpadana
Quartirolo Lombardo
Ragusano
Raschera
Robiola di Roccaverano
Taleggio
Toma Piemontese
Valle d'Aosta Fromadzo
Valtellina Casera

BRA

Cheese as food, northern Italian style. A cheese you can't easily tire of, it is equally satisfying but not as challenging as Fontina.

■ TYPE: Cow's milk.

■ ORIGIN AND MAKERS: Bra is a market town in the region of Cuneo, Piedmont, the northwestern corner of Italy, near Barolo country, where mountain cheeses have been bought and sold since ancient times. (It is also the site of the Slow Food Convention, a modern biennial cheese-centered gathering.) The cheese is made in small coop dairies.

■ PRODUCTION AND AGING: A pressed, semihard, partially skimmed DOC cheese. There are two versions of Bra sold: a young, soft, fresh one that is ripened for 45 days; an aged one that is ripened for a minimum of 6 months. True Bra is made with cow's rennet and of milk from cows that feed only on natural grass.

■ APPEARANCE: Disks about 4 inches thick and about 15 inches in diameter, weighing about 15 pounds, with a grayish natural rind.

■ CONSISTENCY AND TASTE: The paste is medium-soft and riddled with very small holes. Its flavor is sour on the attack with a pleasant bitterness gradually building to the finish, altogether a fascinating impression. When young, Bra is fresh, grassy, and mild; it becomes stronger, drier, and more strawlike with age.

■ RECOMMENDED PAIRINGS: Barbaresco, Barolo, Dolcetto.

■ SIMILAR CHEESES: There are two other similar firm, pressed, brine-soaked Piedmontese DOC cheeses from the same area, Castelmagno and Raschera. Castelmagno, which is made in the Grana Valley around the Sanctuary of San Magno, comes in drums weighing 10 to 13 pounds and is aged a minimum of 3 months. It is a mildly blued cheese with a fine crumbly texture, a distant relative of Gorgonzola and believed to have been created around the same time, nearly 1,000 years ago. Raschera is made in either 15-pound squares or disks that are aged 3 to 4 months. (True Raschera is made only with kids' rennet.) Its paste is ivory colored, and its rind is thin and pinkish. Look for the DOC label on these cheeses as well as the specification "from alpine pastures" or *d'Alpeggio,* the Italian equivalent of the French alpage.

FONTINA D'AOSTA

Genuine Fontina, one of Italy's great cheeses, is not to be confused with the many imitation versions from Demark and other countries. This is an ancient cheese; historical references to the name date back more than 700 years, but it's likely much older.

■ TYPE: Raw cow's milk.

■ ORIGIN AND MAKERS: From the Val D'Aosta in the extreme northwest of the country, not far from Geneva, Switzerland. There are approximately 400 producers of genuine Fontina, including factories, cooperatives, and small independent dairies, which fall under the aegis of the Fontina Consortium. (Look for its distinctive circular stamp with a mountain silhouette and the word *Fontina* printed across the middle on the flat sides of a whole cheese.) The best Fontina I've ever tasted is made by Vallet Pietro (or Pietro Vallet, since according to Italian custom he reverses the order of his names in formal situations).

■ PRODUCTION AND AGING: A pressed, cooked cheese made from whole milk. Signor Vallet assures the purity of his milk by buying it only from his brother's farm. He makes cheeses for the 5 or 6 spring and summer months every year and ages them another seven. Vallet's curds are heated more gently than those in the cooperatives and factories.

■ APPEARANCE: Wheels weighing 19 to 40 pounds that are 12 to 18 inches across and 3 to 4 inches high. It has a thin, slightly concave natural rind that ranges in color from reddish-yellow to dark brown. The interior paste is pale yellow and has a few small holes.

■ CONSISTENCY AND TASTE: Semihard, of smooth consistency and fairly elastic with a nutty, buttery flavor and a characteristic sweetness includ-

ing hints of honey. Genuine Fontina is at once luscious and subtle, capturing the essence of milk from cows that feast on the succulent flowers and grasses of the Italian Alps.

■ SEASONAL NOTE: October through June peak.

■ RECOMMENDED PAIRINGS: Conventional wisdom says Barolos and Barbarescos, from around the town of Alba not far away, but I would also recommend it with a Burgundian Chardonnay, Barbera d'Alba, Dolcelto d'Alba, Minervois, Pinot Blanc, and Sangiovese in general.

■ SIMILAR CHEESES: Beaufort, Gruyère.

GORGONZOLA

According to legend, Gorgonzola was a stop on the summer and fall treks to and from the high mountain pastures. Local farmers made a similar nonblued cheese there for hundreds of years, aging it on wooden slats. One lucky producer accidentally discovered the properties of *Penicillium* mold and thereafter the cheeses were purposely allowed to go blue.

■ TYPE: Cow's milk.

■ ORIGIN AND MAKERS: Originally from around the town of Gorgonzola, Lombardy, in the center of northern Italy, the cheese is now aged, according to DOC regulations, in the environs of Novara, an industrial suburb of Milan. The Gorgonzola I buy through Rogers International is manufactured by Jean-Battista Arrigoni in his factory on the plains of Lombardy. Arrigoni begins maturing the cheeses in Novara and then sends them back up to the Taleggio Valley for final aging.

■ PRODUCTION AND AGING: Made with essentially the same type of milk as Taleggio. The cheeses arrive in the United States aged about 5 months. Inspectors rate Gorgonzolas according to the amount of mold in their interiors; the ones with the most green-blue striations are placed in the premium category. Regular aged Gorgonzola is now generally known as *Gorgonzola Piccante*; it was formerly known as *Gorgonzola Naturale* or *Stagionato* ("aged"). There is another variation called *Gorgonzola Dolce* ("sweet"), a creamy cheese with some mold in it, very spreadable, that tends to be more for casual consumption rather than serious tasting.

■ APPEARANCE: Arrigoni's Gorgonzola comes in 26- to 27-pound wheels that are 6 inches high and 12 inches across. Gorgonzolas for export start out as full drums that are cut in half either horizontally or vertically, then foil-wrapped. Its rind is rough and reddish; its paste is white or light yellow with blue-green flecks throughout.

■ CONSISTENCY AND TASTE: A firm, moist, buttery consistency and a flavor that is sharp and sweet.

■ RECOMMENDED PAIRINGS: Cabernet Sauvignon, Banyuls, Madeira, Muscat-based dessert wines, Vin Santo.

■ SIMILAR CHEESES: Cashel Blue, Fourme D'Ambert.

MONTASIO

Montasio as we know it is believed to have originated in an abbey called Moggio in the thirteenth century.

■ TYPE: Cow's milk.

■ ORIGIN AND MAKERS: From the Alpe Giulie (Giulian Alps) in the province of Friuli, near the city of Udine, the extreme northeast close to the border with Slovenia. Produced in factories and dairies throughout Friuli and the Veneto. DOC protected.

■ PRODUCTION AND AGING: There are three categories of this pressed, uncooked cheese: young (aged 2 months); partially aged (4 to 10 months); and aged (1 year plus). Like Asiago, it can be aged up to 4 years.

■ APPEARANCE: Medium-sized wheels that have a yellowish-gray natural brushed rind with cloth indentations and possibly some reddish-brown shading. The paste is a light straw color, which turns yellower with age, and it has small holes throughout.

■ CONSISTENCY AND TASTE: Young Montasio is pliable, aromatic, and mild with grassy, fruity flavors. When aged, it becomes hard and gratable and takes on deeper nutty flavors.

■ RECOMMENDED PAIRINGS: Red Bordeaux, Carignan, a big, fruity California Merlot, Pinot Grigio, Nebbiolo, Pinot Blanc, Txakolina.

■ SIMILAR CHEESES: Asiago.

PARMIGIANO-REGGIANO

Known in English simply as Parmesan, this is a straightforward, utilitarian, unpretentious cheese that many experts consider the greatest on the planet. There are many cheeses that casually usurp the name "Parmesan," but there is only one true Parmigiano-Reggiano.

■ TYPE: Raw cow's milk.

■ ORIGIN AND MAKERS: From the areas around the cities of Parma, Modena, and Mantua in the province of Emilia-Romagna, which is just to the north of Tuscany; DOC protected. Produced in dairies and small factories.

■ PRODUCTION AND AGING: The genuine article is made only from milk produced within the DOC zone according to strict regulations. Although the name-controlled version is only about 700 years old, the recipe dates back to the Roman Empire. Parmesan's stages of maturity are *giovane*, or young (1 year); *vecchio*, or old (2 years); *stravecchio*, or "extra-old" (3 years); and *stravecchione*, or "super extra-old" (4 years). There are between 700 and 800 active production sites for Parmesan. It is regulated by a consortium, the Consorzio del Formaggio Parmigiano-Reggiano, that upholds DOC standards, grades cheeses, and handles worldwide advertising and marketing. It defines three levels of producers: farmers, who make cheese from the milk of their own herds; *latterie* (dairies) and *caseifici* (cheese factories), which make cheese from sourced milk; and businessmen, or *negociants*, who do selection, aging, and export. The Consorzio has relatively high standards but not necessarily artisanal-quality ones.

■ APPEARANCE: A natural, brushed, oiled rind

that is yellowish-gold in color and has the words "Parmigiano-Reggiano" stamped on its sides in distinctive stenciled dot lettering. Comes in large drums that weigh 30 to 40 kilos (66 to 88 pounds; the legal minimum is approximately 53 pounds) and have convex sides. The paste is light ivory to straw yellow in color and contains small white crystals of denatured protein when properly aged. The cheese is at its peak when small drops of moisture are visible on a cut surface.

■ CONSISTENCY AND TASTE: A well-aged Parmesan has a hard, granular, crumbly, flaky paste that is ideal for grating yet melts in the mouth. Incredibly delicious and subtle, it offers a complex, mouth-tingling matrix of fragrant, vegetal, and savory flavors that linger luxuriously on the palate. Compared with its many imitators, real Parmesan is sweeter, more moist, and lower in salt.

■ RECOMMENDED PAIRINGS: Champagne, Nebbiolo-based wines (Barolo, Barbaresco), Pinot Grigio.

■ SIMILAR CHEESES: *Grana,* meaning "granular," is the generic term for similar hard cheeses from outside the DOC zone or not made according to as strict standards. Grana Padano, a DOC cheese aged around 6 months, is essentially a poor man's Parmesan with a wider zone of production.

PECORINO TOSCANO

Pecora means sheep in Italian, thus the diminutive becomes the name for the cheese itself. There are four major regional *pecorinos* in Italy: Toscano, Romano (from the countryside surrounding Rome; usually referred to as simply "Romano"), Sardo (from Sardinia), and Siciliano (from Sicily). Pecorino Toscano is the one at the top of my list.

■ TYPE: Ewe's milk.

■ ORIGIN AND MAKERS: A DOC cheese from Tuscany, where the cheese industry dates back to Etruscan times—long before the rise and fall of the Roman Empire. Made in small factories and dairies. Look for brands labeled *pura pecora* ("pure sheep") from the area around the town of Pienza in south-central Tuscany (Pecorino di Pienza). The mature version, which is aged at least 4 months, has a dark brown rind and a dry, hard, nearly brittle paste. I prefer a cheese that has been aged 6 months and has either tomato or olive oil rubbed into the rind to give it a special patina. I'm also partial to the "extra-aged" (*stravecchio*) that comes wrapped in walnut leaves.

■ PRODUCTION AND AGING: Made from pasteurized or nonpasteurized milk; pressed, with a natural rind.

■ APPEARANCE: Small drums about 3 inches thick and 7 inches across with convex sides, like a miniature Parmesan shape.

■ CONSISTENCY AND TASTE: Hard with an intense sheepy flavor and a mildly peppery finish.

■ RECOMMENDED PAIRINGS: Merlot, Sangiovese (e.g., Chianti, Brunello di Montalcino, or California), Cabernet Sauvignon, Barbera d'Alba.

■ SIMILAR CHEESES: Berkswell, Trade Lake Cedar, Tyning.

ROBIOLA DI LOMBARDIA

There is more than one cheese that bears the name Robiola; the one I like is Robiola di Lombardia, which is essentially a miniature Taleggio.

■ TYPE: Cow's milk.

■ ORIGIN AND MAKER: Lombardy. There are quite a few brands of Robiola di Lombardia with very different names; I've enjoyed one called Maurella, manufactured by Mauri.

■ PRODUCTION AND AGING: Aged 2 months.

■ APPEARANCE: Bricks weighing from 6 ounces to 1½ pounds.

■ CONSISTENCY AND TASTE: Buttery, supple, and pungent; reminiscent of clotted cream.

■ RECOMMENDED PAIRINGS: Alsatian Gewürztraminer, Muscat de Rivesaltes, Nebbiolo (Barolo, Barbaresco), northern Rhône Syrah, Alsatian Riesling, Savennières (dry Chenin Blanc).

■ SIMILAR CHEESES: Taleggio.

TALEGGIO

One of Italy's best if not most famous cheeses, Taleggio was popular in Roman times and mention of it is made in the works of Cicero, Cato, and Pliny. A good Taleggio virtually shouts "Sour milk!" It has so much going for it, all you need is a good hunk of it and a nice piece of crusty bread to make the perfect picnic lunch or snack.

■ TYPE: Cow's milk washed-rind.

■ ORIGIN AND MAKERS: Named after its place of origin, a small town northeast of Milan near Bergamo in Lombardy. A century ago, all Taleggio was made in the Val Taleggio, a remote area in the Alps north of Bergamo and east of Milan, about 20 miles north of the source of San Pellegrino water. Commercial producers subsequently moved down to the plains of Lombardy for economic reasons. The best cheeses are still made up in the valley, where cows feast on a rich natural diet and the cheeses benefit from ripening in the mountain air. My preferred brand is Appennino, which is made by Arrigoni Valtaleggio. Jean-Battista Arrigoni (see also Gorgonzola), a cousin of the producers of Valtaleggio Arrigoni, also makes an unusual and highly recommended Taleggio that is brine soaked (rather than dry salted) and aged 80 days. Other recommended brands: Defendi and Cisera.

■ PRODUCTION AND AGING: Uncooked, lightly pressed; ripens in about 40 days. Under ideal conditions, some Taleggio can mature for twice as long.

■ APPEARANCE: A square slab about 8 by 8 inches square and about 2½ inches high, weighing 3¾ to 4¾ pounds. It has a crust that is a warm brown color and often mottled with gray and/or red-brown mold. (The industrial cheeses don't have mold; their rinds are clean, evenly colored, and spotless.)

■ CONSISTENCY AND TASTE: The paste is semisoft, creamy, and supple when fresh, becoming softer as it ripens; it has a sweet, mild, fruity, salty, slightly tangy taste that intensifies, becoming more and more full-flavored—buttery, beefy, and pleasantly sour—with age.

■ RECOMMENDED PAIRINGS: A light white wine, tending toward neutral, such as a Pinot Grigio, Sauvignon Blanc, or Pinot Blanc. Also Alsatian Gewürztraminer, dry Chenin Blanc–based wines (e.g., Savennières), Chardonnay, Jurançon late-harvest Muscat-based wines, Nebbiolo (Barolo, Barbaresco), Barbera d'Alba, Sangiovese, Merlot, northern Rhône Syrah.

■ SIMILAR CHEESES: Durrus, Reblochon, Robiola.

TIRED COWS . . . THICK MILK . . .
GREAT CHEESES

ON THE BENEFITS OF ANIMAL EXERCISE

T ALEGGIO is just one prominent member of the Stracchino family of northern Italian "tired cow's milk" cheeses. By the time the cows were brought down from grazing in the high alpine pastures to their barns in the valleys for milking, they had walked a good distance, which means they were tired and their milk was richer, less watery, more acidic. Down through the years, the herds stopped at places like Taleggio and Gorgonzola, where these great cheeses were developed. The Stracchino family also includes certain types of Robiola and Crescenza (some of which are sold fresh or unripened) as well as Quartirolo, Taleggio's more acidic cousin, made with the same type of milk.

The Netherlands

H OLLAND is the biggest exporter of cheese in the world and it always has been. The problem is that almost all Dutch cheeses are factory made and undistinguished. Just a few of them make my select list. They are cooked, semihard, mild-flavored cheeses, which, with age, can become very interesting indeed.

GOUDA

The correct pronunciation is *"How-*duh," with a guttural sound in the *How,* which will raise a few eyebrows—most of us grew up pronouncing it *"Goo-*dah."

■ TYPE: Cow's milk.

■ ORIGIN AND MAKERS: The version of this cheese I offer is called Goudse Boerenkaas ("farmer cheese") and is the raw-milk farmhouse variety.

■ PRODUCTION AND AGING: Goudse Boerenkaas has a pressed, semihard paste, a natural brushed rind, and is sold after 4 months of aging but only becomes interesting when matured for about 3 years.

■ APPEARANCE: Wheels about 15 inches in diameter, up to 5 inches high, weighing 18 to 29 pounds, with bulging, convex sides.

■ CONSISTENCY AND TASTE: Properly aged, it is hard, grainy, salty, tangy, and sharp with a hint of butterscotch on the finish.

■ RECOMMENDED PAIRINGS: A big spicy red such as Côtes du Rhône, Châteauneuf-du-Pape, or Merlot; late-harvest Muscat, Jurançon, or Amarone.

■ SIMILAR CHEESES: Coolea, Mimolette, Roomano. Edam is another widely exported and extremely popular cooked cow's milk cheese from Holland that in well-aged versions can be delicious.

ROOMANO

While not widely recognized as among the world's finest, this one sure tastes great to me.

■ TYPE: Pasteurized cow's milk.

■ ORIGIN AND MAKERS: Dairy made in southern Holland.

■ PRODUCTION AND AGING: A cooked cheese made in the style of Parmigiano-Reggiano, some versions of Roomano are aged up to 6 years! To call it the Dutch version of Parmesan may not be entirely accurate, however, because it does deviate from its Italian cousin in several key aspects.

■ APPEARANCE: 10-pound wheels, 4 to 5 inches high and about 16 inches in diameter. Has a golden orange rind that is waxed, but not until after its long aging period. The paste is light caramel colored.

■ CONSISTENCY AND TASTE: Roomano, which was presumably given this name by its Dutch creators to suggest its "Italian character," has a hard paste that turns a dark, caramel color and can get pretty strong and spicy while still retaining its sweet, fruity flavors. Two of its more prominent notes are caramel and butterscotch, neither of which are associated with Parmesan.

■ RECOMMENDED PAIRINGS: Classified-growth red Bordeaux; a fruity, well-rounded Merlot-based wine; California Zinfandel, Carignan, Syrah.

■ SIMILAR CHEESES: Aged Gouda (Boeren Kaas), Parmigiano-Reggiano.

Portugal

T HIS beautiful country is a cradle of sheep's and goat's milk cheeses. Its cheesemakers follow ancient methods and traditions; they produce rustic cheeses, several of which are exquisite and rank high among my favorites. One of the country's best cheesemakers is Miguel Rolo, who is also president of Portugal's Association of DOP (Denominação de Origem Protegida) cheeses. I first experienced the pleasures of Serra at a tasting featuring Senhor Rolo, who is reviving some authentic artisanal cheeses that have been on the endangered list. He is based at his own farm, Quinta dos Vidais. Of the four cheeses listed below, he makes two (Azeitão and Évora) and selects the other two.

AZEITÃO

The word *Azeitão* is difficult to pronounce correctly, but it's something like "Ah-zhey-*tone*" with the accent on the last syllable, which sounds like a combination of "ow" and "on" with a bit of a muffled honk at the end. Whew!

■ TYPE: Raw ewe's milk.
■ ORIGIN AND MAKERS: Dairy, artisanal. A DOP cheese from the foot of the Arrabida Mountains in the region around Setubal, Palmela, and Sesimbra, just to the south of Lisbon. Named after the village of its origin.
■ PRODUCTION AND AGING: Coagulated with thistle rennet; aged a minimum of 90 days.
■ APPEARANCE: 9-ounce rounds.

■ CONSISTENCY AND TASTE: A thick, soft, smooth, shiny, creamy paste along the lines of a Reblochon that liquefies and oozes when ripe at room temperature. It has a strong, earthy, barnyardy aroma and it offers rich, creamy flavors with a flowery finish. It features a pronounced sour milk taste when ripe. As it continues to mature, its paste gets harder and drier and its flavors intensify to the point where it might be too "sheepy" for some palates.
■ SEASONAL NOTE: Winter through spring.
■ RECOMMENDED PAIRINGS: California Cabernet (Bordeaux-style blend); Carignan; assertive red Rhône wines (Syrah-Grenache-Mourvèdre blends—as in Châteauneuf-du-Pape and other southern French wines); Periquita (soft, low-tannin, light-bodied Portuguese red); California Pinot Noir; LBV Port; Rioja-style wines (Tempranillo-Garnacha blend), Bonnezeaux.
■ SIMILAR CHEESES: Queso de la Serena, Queijo Serra da Estrela; also reminiscent of Spanish Torta del Casar, although its physical dimensions are significantly smaller.

QUEIJO EVORA

An elemental, unabashed sheep cheese; the preservation of an older, sheepier type of milk flavor, one that I hope can survive.

■ TYPE: Raw ewe's milk.
■ ORIGIN AND MAKERS: A DOP farmhouse-made cheese from the town of the same name in the Alentejo region directly east of Lisbon.
■ PRODUCTION AND AGING: This excellent thistle-coagulated cheese is made beginning in November, with peak production in March and April, and is matured from 6 to 12 months.
■ APPEARANCE: Evora comes in 6-ounce disks that were once used as currency to pay workers.
■ CONSISTENCY AND TASTE: A semihard paste whose flavor is creamy and somewhat salty, with peachy, plummy overtones and a slightly acidic finish. It has a pungency that gets progressively stronger with age.

■ RECOMMENDED PAIRINGS: Rioja-type wines (Tempranillo-Garnacha blend), white Bordeaux, Malbec, Port.

■ SIMILAR CHEESES: Berkswell, Trade Lake Cedar.

QUEIJO SERRA DA ESTRELA

This is Portugal's most celebrated cheese, the one upon which the delectable Azeitão is based. I call Serra a "party cheese" because the best—some say the only—way to enjoy it is to buy a whole cheese, let it come to room temperature, carefully slice off the top of the rind, dip your serving spoon into the paste for a healthy dollop, and pass it around. (Spain's Torta del Casar, another of my absolute favorites, can be eaten the same way.) Serra really begs to be consumed in one sitting. It can be difficult to come by, so if you encounter a good specimen, snap it up! If possible, pick up the cheese and give it a gentle squeeze; it should have some "give," offering a hint of the luscious potential within.

■ TYPE: Raw ewe's milk.

■ ORIGIN AND MAKERS: A DOP cheese traditionally made by the shepherds' wives in stone cottages high on the Serra da Estrela plateau in east-central Portugal near the Spanish border. Made from the excellent milk of Bordaleira sheep that is coag-ulated with thistle extract, genuine Serra is strictly a handmade cheese, and it has been for at least the past 800 years.

■ PRODUCTION AND AGING: Each cheese takes an artisan about 3 hours to make; that's two, maybe three cheeses in a day. . . . Blessed are the cheesemakers!

■ APPEARANCE: Rounds about 10 inches in diameter and 3 inches high with a brown rind that can be tinged with a reddish hue.

■ CONSISTENCY AND TASTE: Soft with a full, round, oleaginous flavor. The term unctuous might have been invented for this cheese. When it is ripe and ready, it is deliciously intoxicating with salty, tangy, pleasantly musty, delightfully "sheepy" flavors—pronounced yet never sharp or biting—and a lingering aftertaste. (You'll find this is true of many sheep cheeses; they remain rounded and mellow, in part due to the richness and undercurrent of sweetness in the ewe's milk.) Don't forget to take a whiff: between its flavors and aromas, Serra delivers a phenomenal one-two punch. In Portugal, they also eat Serra at a more mature stage where it has become firm and pungent.

■ SEASONAL NOTE: December through April.

■ RECOMMENDED PAIRINGS: Red Bordeaux, full-bodied California Cabernet, Pinot Gris, Vintage Port, Trincadeira Ribatejana, Rioja-style reds (Tempranillo-Garnacha blend); Syrah-Grenache-Mourvèdre blend (as in Châteauneuf-du-Pape and other southern French wines), Barbera d'Alba.

■ SIMILAR CHEESES: Azeitão, Queso de la Serena, Torta del Casar.

Spain

Spain has a high average elevation and vast areas of pastureland, much of it rough and barren. It displays all the markers of superior cheesemaking: rustic local production; cheeses named after their places of origin; and ancient traditions upheld by many succeeding generations of farmers, herders, and cheesemakers. There are goats, sheep, and cows, and consequently a varied spectrum of cheeses.

Geographically, Spain has several distinct regions that determine a great deal about the character of its fine cheeses. The north of Spain, referred to as "Green Spain," is composed of a chain of mountainous, rainy microclimates that extends from Galicia in the west over to Catalonia in the east and includes the spectacular Picos de Europa range as well as the rugged Pyrénées, which form the natural border with France. This green belt has a much wetter, cooler climate than the rest of the country, and therefore features lush pastures, picturesque isolated valleys, and alpine conditions at higher altitudes. It is consequently home to more cows than anywhere else in Spain. Ancient traditions in these bucolic settings have produced a marvelous array of cheeses, particularly in Asturias. This is the heartland of Spanish cheese, home to a disproportionate number of the country's world-class artisanal cheeses (no less than six of the fifteen on the following roster).

Central Spain consists of a vast, rolling plateau called the *Meseta* that extends for about 250 miles in all directions around Madrid, which is both the capital and the geographical center of the country. Winters can be cold and damp; summers are very hot and dry. This extensive elevated plain is a great home for sheep. Originally exploited more for their meat and wool, they are now the source of rich milk ideally suited to cheesemaking.

A third significant geographical zone extends along the coasts of the Mediterranean Sea, beginning with Catalonia in the north. It has a more temperate climate but is nevertheless an arid, often sparse landscape. Goats, affectionately known in Spain as the "poor man's cow," thrive there, as they tend to do in the more rugged zones all over the Iberian peninsula.

There are over 100 cheeses in Spain, 14 of which are protected under the DO laws and labeled Denominacion de Origen *Protegida*. They are:

Cabrales

Idiazábal

Mahón

Majorero

Manchego

Picón Bejes

Queso de Cantabria

Queso Ibores (pending)

Queso de la Serena

Queso Tetilla

Quesucos de Liébana

Roncal

Valdeón (pending)

Zamorano

AFUEGA'L PITU

The name means "fire in the throat" in the Asturian dialect and this is a cheese that can certainly live up to its name; it is not for the faint of heart.

■ TYPE: Raw or pasteurized cow's milk.

■ ORIGIN AND MAKERS: Central Asturias, on the north coast of Spain. Small farmhouse and artisanal producers.

■ PRODUCTION AND AGING: Made year-round from uncut, unpressed curds. Some of the cheeses are shaped the old-fashioned way—that is, by hand inside a piece of cloth that clearly leaves its mark on the rind. Aged from 2 weeks to 50 days.

■ APPEARANCE: An irregular, somewhat amorphous bulb that weighs about a pound. The Picos de Europa brand weighs a bit less, at 300 grams or 10½ ounces. The interior is yellowish, with white "eyes" (small white-rimmed holes).

■ CONSISTENCY AND TASTE: Afuega's paste is semisoft, smooth, delicate, and quite dense with a stimulating granularity to its texture. Young Afuega has a milky and mildly acidic flavor. When fully aged, its flavor intensifies to the point where it is piquant and astringent on the palate with a hint of mustiness. Did I mention the smell? A ripe Afuega is a real eye-opener. Strong, funky, raunchy . . . This is one cheese whose aroma can measure up to its powerful taste. Its paste should always feel slightly firm; once it starts to go soft, it's probably overripe. Ditto if the rind starts to turn distinctly reddish.

■ RECOMMENDED PAIRINGS: A soft, light California Pinot Noir; a Côtes du Rhône or Languedoc red; a Rioja-style Tempranillo blend (Ribera del Duero); Nebbiolo; Riesling.

■ SIMILAR CHEESES: Queso de los Beyos is somewhat similar but really there's nothing like Afuega.

CABRALES

Along with Roquefort, Gorgonzola, and Stilton, a member of the quartet of the world's most famous blues. Spaniards claim it is actually the first blue, although I doubt the French would agree.

■ TYPE: Raw cow's milk blue. But traditional Cabrales is made from a mixture of milks—cow, sheep, and goat—particularly in the summer months. Most Cabrales is now made from 100 percent cow's milk. The old-style mixed-milk Cabrales, if you can find it, is a truly exceptional cheese. Its typically dryish texture is made smoother by the sheep's milk component and more piquant by the goat's milk.

■ ORIGIN AND MAKERS: Primarily from three villages—Cabrales included—in the Penamellera Alta township of the Picos de Europa mountains in eastern Asturias on the north coast of the country. DO protected.

■ PRODUCTION AND AGING: Made by traditional farmhouse methods and finished with a minimum of 3 months' aging in the natural caves under conditions very similar to those of Roquefort.

■ APPEARANCE: Flattened cylinders between 3 and 6 inches high and from 8 to 12 inches in diameter weighing 6 to 9 pounds. Cabrales was originally sold wrapped in sycamore leaves (known as *plageru* in Spanish), but now the DO laws don't permit it, so the real Cabrales we receive is wrapped in a light foil. It has a rutted, somewhat bumpy brownish natural rind, and its paste is heavily marbled with veins of dark purplish-blue mold that turns almost uniformly blue with age.

■ CONSISTENCY AND TASTE: When ripe, Cabrales is almost uniformly blue throughout, fine textured, dense, crumbly, and salty. The paste is semisoft, and, although it can become quite dry, I prefer my Cabrales more moist and sticky. It delivers strong aromas and delivers powerful, lingering flavors. I know of only one cheese that could follow this one in a sequence: a mature Roquefort . . . maybe.

■ SEASONAL NOTE: For the mixed-milk variety, late summer to midwinter.

■ RECOMMENDED PAIRINGS: Aged Madeira, Pedro Ximenez Sherry. Also commonly paired with hard apple cider in Asturias.

■ SIMILAR CHEESES: Gamonedo, Picón Beyes, Valdeón.

GAMONEDO

One of a vanishing breed—that is, one of the very few remaining naturally blueing blues.

■ TYPE: Cow's milk blue.

■ ORIGIN AND MAKERS: Artisanal, farmhouse production in the heart of the Picos de Europa range in Asturias, on the north coast of the country, around the famous peak known as El Cornion.

■ PRODUCTION AND AGING: Traditionally a transhumance cheese made with cow's, goat's, and sheep's milk; it is now made year-round principally with cow's milk. Gamonedo (aka "Gamoneu") is lightly applewood smoked and matured in natural caves for a minimum of 2 months. The smoking was originally accidental as the cheeses were set on shelves in mountain cabins kept warm by small fires.

■ APPEARANCE: Cylinders that weigh 3 to 5 kilos (up to 11 pounds); usually a larger cheese than its fellow Asturian blues, Cabrales, Valdeón, and Picón Bejes, although there is significant variation depending on which family makes it. The rind has a characteristic dusty gray appearance (with frequent patches of reddish or greenish fuzzy mold) and extra thickness due to the smoking.

■ CONSISTENCY AND TASTE: A fairly piquant blue with a semihard paste, a somewhat grainy texture, and complex flavors. Its paste is tighter, has fewer holes, and less veining than similar blues due to the lower humidity in its ripening caves. Compared with Cabrales, it is drier, not as sticky, less acidic, and less aromatic.

■ RECOMMENDED PAIRINGS: Periquita (soft, low-tannin, light-bodied Portuguese red), Rioja-style Tempranillo blend (Ribera del Duero), late-harvest Pinot Gris dessert wine, Muscatel; Sherry.

■ SIMILAR CHEESES: Cabrales, Picón Beyes, Valdeón.

IBORES (OR QUESO IBORES)

Offers delightful, sprightly flavors but is more gregarious and cooperative, and less egotistical, than almost every other goat cheese.

■ TYPE: Raw goat's milk.

■ ORIGIN AND MAKERS: Artisanal, from near Caceres in the high sierra of the Extremadura, in west-central Spain toward the border with Portugal; AOC pending.

■ PRODUCTION AND AGING: Molded, uncooked.

■ APPEARANCE: Irregular cylindrical shapes weighing 1 to 2 pounds. Can have several different types of rind: some are natural, some are oiled, and others have paprika rubbed in, giving its exterior an orangish-red tinge.

■ CONSISTENCY AND TASTE: Semisoft paste with a light airy consistency, compact but open-textured with some holes. Salty, zesty, and acidulous with earthy notes, hints of sour milk, and an agreeable slight bitterness. It has a balance of sweetness and never seems to become overly goaty or barnyardy.

■ SEASONAL NOTE: Late fall to summer.

■ RECOMMENDED PAIRINGS: A versatile cheese with wines; try it with Alsatian Riesling, Barbaresco (Nebbiolo-based), red Bordeaux, white Burgundy, California Merlot, Rosé Champagne, Grüner Veltliner, Rhône reds (Châteauneuf-du-Pape, St. Joseph), Ribera del Duero (Rioja-style Tempranillo blend), German Riesling Spätlese, Sauvignon Blanc.

■ SIMILAR CHEESES: Garrotxa, but the Ibores is stronger and zestier.

MAHÓN

A straightforward, no-nonsense taste with relatively high acid that is simply enchanting.

■ TYPE: Cow's milk.

■ ORIGIN AND MAKERS: A DO cheese from Menorca, the northernmost of the Balearic Islands, in the Mediterranean off the eastern coast of Spain. A small, flat island with salty soil and vegetation, Menorca is known mostly as a tourist destination; it is nevertheless dotted with farms and pastures. From fall through late spring, its climate is fairly moderate and wet, making it conducive to dairy farming, which has been practiced there for at least 700 years.

■ PRODUCTION AND AGING: Pressed and uncooked. Farmhouse or *artesano* versions are made with unpasteurized milk. After the curds are cut, they're bundled in a cloth that is gathered in at the corners for further drainage; the cheese's shape reflects this technique. Mahón is produced only from September to June, ripened by *affineurs* on the island, and sold according to its degree of aging: fresh, or *fresco* (within 10 days); *semi-curado*, or medium-ripe (at least 2 months old); *curado*, cured (5 months); and *viejo*, old (10 months old). I prefer the artisanal raw-milk *viejo*, or *anejo*, variety; the industrial pasteurized version is simply not the same cheese.

■ APPEARANCE: Approximately 8-inch squares that are about 2 inches thick with rounded edges and weigh 5 to 6 pounds.

■ CONSISTENCY AND TASTE: The light ivory-colored paste has many small holes and is dryish, somewhat crumbly, and Parmesan-like in texture, but it should not be rock hard. Its flavor is tangy, sharp, sourish, and salty, an indication of terroir. As the cheese ages, the rind darkens, the paste turns yellower and harder, and the flavor intensifies ultimately to the point where it can pack almost as much punch as a mature Cabrales.

■ RECOMMENDED PAIRINGS: Red Bordeaux, Ribera del Duero or similar Tempranillo-Garnacha blend, California Pinot Noir, Trincadeira Ribatejana (Portugal), German Riesling Spätlese, Barbera d'Alba, Grüner Veltliner, Chardonnay, Oloroso Sherry, Tawny Port.

■ SIMILAR CHEESES: Queso de los Beyos; a sharp Cheddar.

MAJORERO

Considered one of the finest Spanish goat cheeses.

■ TYPE: Goat's milk.

■ ORIGIN AND MAKERS: A DO cheese from the island of Fuerteventura in the Canaries, just 60 miles off the coast of Africa and 700 miles from the Spanish mainland. The genuine farmhouse raw-milk version is superior but can be difficult to obtain.

■ PRODUCTION AND AGING: Majorero is a pressed cheese made in winter and spring. The local breed of goats munch on all kinds of scrubby vegetation—including lichen attached to volcanic

rocks—and produce a relatively thick, high-fat milk.

■ APPEARANCE: Flattened cylinders weighing from 1 to 4½ kilos with a diamond pattern on the rind from the forming molds, which are made from plaited palm fronds.

■ CONSISTENCY AND TASTE: Features a distinct, mildly goaty, sweet, mouth-watering taste, with creamy, firm texture and a delicate aftertaste reminiscent of dried fruits and nuts. Raw-milk Majorero has an open texture and its flavor is a little more acidulous, piquant, and toasty.

■ RECOMMENDED PAIRINGS: Albariño, Vinho Verde (a DOC in northern Portugal known primarily for its white wines, but it also produces reds that are young, acidic, and lightly sparkling). In its native archipelago, Majorero is typically served with potatoes boiled in their skins or as a dessert with quince paste or guavas.

■ SIMILAR CHEESES: Ibores, Ticklemore.

MONTE ENEBRO

A delightfully unusual one-man cheese; designated one of the 100 best food products of Spain in a national judging. (Alternate spelling: Montenebro.)

■ TYPE: Pasteurized goat's milk.

■ ORIGIN AND MAKER: Produced by Rafael Baez, a Spanish cheese hero, in Avila, west of Madrid.

■ PRODUCTION AND AGING: Farmhouse; aged 21 days.

■ APPEARANCE: Loaves about the size and shape of a brick that have a mottled reddish-brown and white rind with a covering of bluish gray *Penicillium* mold.

■ CONSISTENCY AND TASTE: A semisoft, smooth, pure chalky-white, creamy pâte and a tangy, lingering, insistent, and complex goaty flavor. Can be a dense mouthful; a classic French chèvre from the Loire Valley might seem light and fluffy in comparison.

■ RECOMMENDED PAIRINGS: Alsatian Gewürztraminer, Ribera del Duero (Tempranillo-Garnacha blend), German Riesling Kabinett,

Alsatian Pinot Gris, Muscat de Rivesaltes.
- SIMILAR CHEESES: Harbourne Blue.

QUESO DE LOS BEYOS

A peasant-style cheese also sometimes referred to as Beyusco. One of the more unusual ones I serve.
- TYPE: Cow's or goat's milk.
- ORIGIN AND MAKERS: From the Los Beyos Gorge in the western foothills of the Picos de Europa on the edge of Asturias, the central-northern coast of the country. Farmhouse made; four producers only.
- PRODUCTION AND AGING: Cured for 40 days at high humidity.
- APPEARANCE: Comes in small cylinders weighing about 1 pound that have a slightly bloomy, straw-colored, orange-tinted rind, which turns mottled and bluish-gray with patches of white mold as it ages.
- CONSISTENCY AND TASTE: Its paste is semihard—firm but not rock hard—dense and compact, tending toward crumbly with a dryish texture and mouth feel that quickly turns deliciously buttery as the slice literally melts in your mouth. Its flavors should be lactic and creamy with a moderate acidity and delightful tang; it also has an unusual yeasty taste. When past its prime, it becomes overly chalky.
- RECOMMENDED PAIRINGS: Matches well with straightforward Chardonnays, Pinot Noirs, Merlots, Sauvignon Blancs, Pinot Blancs, Zinfandels, Nebbiolo, and Barbera d'Alba
- SIMILAR CHEESES: Afuega'l Pitu, but this is more lactic and claylike.

QUESO DE LA GARROTXA

A traditional, indigenous "rustic" cheese that had all but died out but was revived in the past 20 years by an influx of youngish city dwellers who moved back to the land and chose cheesemaking as their new vocation. (Pronounced "garrocha.")
- TYPE: Pasteurized goat's milk.
- ORIGIN AND MAKERS: Made throughout Catalunya, in northeastern Spain, but principally in Garrotxa in the north-central part of the province, close to the Pyrénées.
- PRODUCTION AND AGING: Aged for a minimum of 20 days in natural caves at high humidity.
- APPEARANCE: A cylinder with rounded edges weighing 2 to 3 pounds that has a bluish-gray moldy, velvety soft rind from the growth of *P. glaucum*.
- CONSISTENCY AND TASTE: The paste is bone white and semisoft with a mild herbal flavor and a wonderful tangy taste.
- RECOMMENDED PAIRINGS: Blanc de Blancs Champagne, Grüner Veltliner, Sauvignon Blanc, white Burgundy (Meursault, Corton-Charlemagne), Riesling Spätlese, Chardonnay, Periquita (soft, low-tannin, light-bodied Portuguese red), Ribera del Duero (Rioja-style Tempranillo blend).
- SIMILAR CHEESES: Ticklemore.

QUESO DE LA PERAL

One of my favorite blues, it has relatively high pH (low acidity).
- TYPE: Pasteurized cow's milk with blue veining.
- ORIGIN AND MAKERS: Originally from San Jorge de la Peral in the central coastal area of Asturias, near Oviedo, it was invented by a local dairyman at the end of the nineteenth century and is now made in the small town of Illas by descendents of Antonio Leon.
- PRODUCTION AND AGING: Inoculated with *Penicillium* mold and matured in natural caves. The secret ingredient that gives it its distinguishing characteristics is a small amount of sheep's milk cream.
- APPEARANCE: It comes in cylinders weighing 1 to 3 kilos (2.2 to 6.6 pounds). Its moist natural rind is golden in color; the interior is yellowish cream-colored with slashing veins of deep blue.
- CONSISTENCY AND TASTE: Firm paste with fairly sharp-tasting lactic flavors. Peral can get fairly intense, which is why one of my former

assistants, Morgan Forsey, used to call it "Queso de la *Peril*."

■ RECOMMENDED PAIRINGS: Jurançon, Ribera del Duero (Tempranillo blend), Riesling Kabinett, Viognier, Oloroso Sherry.

■ SIMILAR CHEESES: Valdeón.

QUESO DE LA SERENA

Truly a superb and highly desirable cheese, one of Spain's best.

■ TYPE: Ewe's milk.

■ ORIGIN AND MAKERS: Dairy-made in the Serena and Castuera communities in Badajoz Province of Extremadura, which is in the west-central part of Spain, bordering Portugal. It was awarded DO status in 1992.

■ PRODUCTION AND AGING: It is traditionally made with raw milk, but there is a pasteurized version available from larger commercial producers. Produced twice daily during the grazing season, from January through May, when the climate is moderate and quite rainy. The milk is coagulated with rennet from the *Cynara cardunculus* (cardoon thistle) plant, imparting subtle bitter and sour hints to the cheese.

■ APPEARANCE: Flattened cylinder or disk, weighing about 1 kilo, or just over 2 pounds.

■ CONSISTENCY AND TASTE: Its paste, which has air holes, is semifirm to soft and virtually spreadable when very ripe. Rich and buttery in consistency with emphatic, fairly pungent flavor, featuring concentrated grassy notes and a sweet fruitiness.

■ SEASONAL NOTE: Available year-round; best April to November.

■ RECOMMENDED PAIRINGS: Albariño, red Bordeaux, Rosé Champagne, Grüner Veltliner, California Merlot, Periquita, late-harvest Pinot Gris dessert wine, Sangiovese (e.g., Chianti, Brunello di Montalcino, or California), Syrah-Grenache-Mourvèdre blend (as in Châteauneuf-du-Pape and other southern French wines), Chenin Blanc, Riesling Kabinett, Malvasia delle Lipari, Temparanillo, Oloroso Sherry, Tawny Port.

■ SIMILAR CHEESES: Torta del Casar, which is more acidulous and saltier.

RONCAL

An ancient type of cheese and Spain's first to be awarded official DO status (1981).

■ TYPE: Raw ewe's milk.

MERINO SHEEP:
A NATIONAL TREASURE

THE ANCIENT AND VENERABLE BREED RESPONSIBLE FOR SOME OF SPAIN'S GREATEST CHEESES

THE milk for Queso de la Serena, Torta del Casar, and other fine cheeses comes from the celebrated Merino breed of sheep, which is practically Spain's national mascot. A rustic animal able to survive extremes of climate and provide excellent wool and delicious meat, it became the preferred breed for the Extremadurans beginning in the Middle Ages, when a successful agricultural economy was established after the reconquest of Spain from the Saracens. Merinos, now mostly milked for cheese, generally feast on grasses amid pastures dotted with old oak trees that provide delectable snacks in the form of acorns. They produce a relatively small amount of milk that's very high in solids (around 20 percent) and fats (around 10 percent), which yields exceptional cheeses.

■ ORIGIN AND MAKERS: The Roncal Valley in northwestern Navarra, in the northern part of Spain bordering on Basque country, where it is still made in farmhouses according to carefully guarded old recipes. The Larra family makes an excellent brand.

■ PRODUCTION AND AGING: Made from the milk of the free-ranging Latxa and/or Aragonese Rasa breed of sheep. Uncooked and pressed, it is aged a minimum 4 months.

■ APPEARANCE: Comes in cylinders that weigh 2 to 3 kilos (4 to 7 pounds). Its rind ranges from straw-colored to grayish-blue to reddish-brown; its paste is ivory colored with small holes. A good Roncal, like some of the hard French or Swiss mountain cheeses or a fine Pecorino Toscano, will often have fissures or splits in its interior and will ooze some butterfat.

■ CONSISTENCY AND TASTE: Hard and dense-textured with a pronounced nutty flavor that is fairly piquant and definitely mouth-watering.

■ SEASONAL NOTE: December to July.

■ RECOMMENDED PAIRINGS: Rioja and other Spanish Tempranillo blends; Sauvignon Blanc–based wines; big, fruity Zinfandels, Merlot; Albariño; Sangiovese.

■ SIMILAR CHEESES: Roncal is similar to the ubiquitous Manchego but much more interesting. After you've tried Roncal, it's difficult to go back to Manchego; instead, try a Zamorano.

TORTA DEL CASAR

A mind-bogglingly delicious cheese, certainly one of Spain's greatest alimentary artifacts and among the best cheeses in the world.

■ TYPE: Raw ewe's milk.

■ ORIGIN AND MAKERS: From the small town of Casar de Caceres in Extremadura Province in west-central Spain near the Portuguese border. One of the better makers is the Andrade family dairy.

■ PRODUCTION AND AGING: Made primarily from the end of winter into spring, its curds are coagulated with cardoon thistle extract, which adds a pleasantly bitter hint to the taste.

■ APPEARANCE: Comes in flattened cylinders with rounded edges 2 to 3 inches high and 8 inches in diameter that weigh 3 to 4 pounds. The natural rind is somewhat loose and undulating; it has a tendency to detach from the paste and even crack open when a mature cheese is at room temperature. A traditional way to eat it is to slice off the top of the rind and scoop the runny paste out with a crusty piece of bread.

■ CONSISTENCY AND TASTE: Has a thick, soft, creamy, oily paste, maturing to a gooey consistency and offering provocative, rich, sour, nutty flavors with floral notes.

■ SEASONAL NOTE: Spring to early winter.

■ RECOMMENDED PAIRINGS: Ribera del Duero (Tempranillo-Garnacha blend), Syrah, Sangiovese, Trincadeira, Ribatejana (Portugal), late-harvest Riesling, Chenin Blanc.

■ SIMILAR CHEESES: Queso de la Serena. The differences? The Torta's curds coagulate more slowly, and the milk used is less oily. The Tortas are also salted a bit more. The resulting cheese has more acid and less fat.

VALDEON

Valdeón is strong, saltier than Stilton, and a long-time favorite of mine.

■ TYPE: Cow's milk blue (may include goat's milk).

■ ORIGIN AND MAKERS: From the province of León, to the northwest of Madrid, specifically the remote Valdeón Valley. Dairy-made.

■ PRODUCTION AND AGING: Aged a minimum of 2 months in cavas. It is made according to virtually the same recipe as Cabrales, but with the added benefit of being wrapped in plageru (sycamore) leaves, which allow certain bacteria to penetrate the cheese and add complexity. I sometimes call Valdeón "illegal Cabrales" because this is how Cabrales used to be wrapped. In order for Spanish producers to conform to EEC regulations and sell the esteemed Cabrales throughout the rest of Europe, they weren't allowed to use the leaves anymore but instead had to wrap it in plastic and/or aluminum foil.

- APPEARANCE: Cylinders weighing roughly 4½ to 6½ pounds with a natural rind.
- CONSISTENCY AND TASTE: Semisoft with a powerful and complex ensemble of flavors.
- RECOMMENDED PAIRINGS: Muscat de Rivesaltes, German Riesling Kabinett, Cabernet Sauvignon.
- SIMILAR CHEESES: Cabrales, Gamonedo, Picón Beyes.

ZAMORANO

A good Zamorano has the same regal bearing as Beaufort or Parmesan; it often reminds tasters of a sheep's milk version of those noble cow cheeses.

- TYPE: Ewe's milk.
- ORIGIN AND MAKERS: From Zamora in the province of Castile-León, northwest of Madrid, near the northeast corner of the Portuguese frontier. Made from the end of winter to the end of summer by fourteen small- to medium-sized producers.
- PRODUCTION AND AGING: Pressed, uncooked, and aged a minimum of 100 days.
- APPEARANCE: Comes in drums weighing up to 4 kilos (nearly 9 pounds) with a hard, grayish-brownish natural rind that has a distinctive zigzag pattern on its sides, from the *esparto* grass band tied around it during pressing, and a wheat-ear pattern stamped on top and bottom.
- CONSISTENCY AND TASTE: The paste is very firm, yet creamy in taste and consistency with a full nutty, lingering flavor and a rich bite of tartness and saltiness.
- RECOMMENDED PAIRINGS: Red Burgundy (e.g., Côte de Nuits), Carignan, Oregon Pinot Noir, Syrah-Grenache-Mouvèdre blend (southern Rhône and other regions of southern France), California Zinfandel, Riesling Kabinett, Txakolina.
- SIMILAR CHEESES: Berkswell; also comparable, but in my estimation definitely superior, to its more famous cousin, Manchego (see also Roncal).

Switzerland

IT MAY be a small, divided country, but Switzerland has a rich and ancient tradition of cheesemaking that dates at least back to the Roman Empire and probably long before. Its high alpine grazing lands produce excellent cheeses, mostly of the hard mountain variety— dense, concentrated, and long-lasting. The Swiss have a knack for cooking with cheese; world-famous fondue is just the tip of the iceberg. In the German-speaking part of Switzerland, the cheeses are named after their places of origin; just take the village or town name and tack on the "er" suffix, which denotes somebody or something that comes from that particular place. Thus, the cheese from Appenzell becomes Appenzeller and so forth. Any cheese that bears a very specific place-name, especially if the place is small, is worth investigating. My pipeline for artisanal Swiss cheeses is Caroline Hostettler, a journalist-turned-cheese importer, who works with Rolf Beeler, the most exacting of the Swiss affineurs. (The local media have dubbed him "The Pope of Swiss Cheese.") Rolf operates out of a small village 20 miles from Zurich, selecting and purchasing cheeses directly from the farmhouse producers. He sells to the top Swiss restaurants, and he also has stands at the weekly Lucerne and Baar retail produce markets.

APPENZELLER
When our Swiss importer, Caroline Hostettler, said "There is no 'Swiss Cheese' but there are 'Swiss cheeses,'" it was this type of cheese to which she was referring. It is stalwart and arrestingly delicious.
- TYPE: Raw cow's milk
- ORIGIN AND MAKERS: The pride of Appenzell, a small town in the eastern part of the country between St. Gallen and Thurgau. There are only three dairies in the area that still make authentic raw-milk Appenzeller.
- PRODUCTION AND AGING: The rinds are formed with the aid of special marinades, which consist of brine, white wine, fresh herbs, and a dose of the local "herb liquor," also called Appenzeller. As they ripen, the cheeses receive regular washings of this Swiss moonshine. Each cheesemaker has his or her own variation of the marinade, assuring their cheeses of individuality. Appenzellers are aged a minimum of 7 months and reach their peak at 10 to 12 months.
- APPEARANCE: Small wheels 3 to 3½ inches tall and weighing about 15 pounds with a light brown rind. The sign of a genuine Appenzeller is a striation of grayish-blue just under the rind, the remnant of the marinade.
- CONSISTENCY AND TASTE: A traditional semihard mountain cheese that really explodes with a burst of flavor in your mouth. Yet it is also smooth, not too fatty or buttery and somewhat reminiscent of a sheep's milk cheese from the Pyrenées. It has a close-textured paste that is homogenous and fairly dense with a more rounded, finished flavor than its cousin, the Prattigauer (see below).
- RECOMMENDED PAIRINGS: Red Bordeaux or California Cabernet, Grüner Veltliner, Merlot, Gewürztraminer.
- SIMILAR CHEESE: Prattigauer.

CENTOVALLI TICINO
Grace with dignity. Unending finesse. An expertly crafted mountain cheese.
- TYPE: Raw cow's milk.
- ORIGIN AND MAKERS: A mountain-style cheese from the Valle Leventina in the Valais canton, which is the southwestern, Italian-speaking part of Switzerland. Farmhouse production.
- PRODUCTION AND AGING: Ticino is made strictly in summer with no salt added, a rarity. The cheeses are aged between 9 and 12 months in stone cellars where high humidity promotes the growth of furry, grayish-white cat's hair mold that is pressed down to help form the rind.
- APPEARANCE: 10-pound wheels, fairly cylindrical but with slightly rounded edges.
- CONSISTENCY AND TASTE: The paste is firm with a smooth, sweet, buttery flavor. The first big taste impression is smokiness.
- RECOMMENDED PAIRINGS: Nebbiolo (Barbaresco), Grüner Veltliner, Chenin Blanc, white Bordeaux, Sauternes, Minervois, Dolcelto d'Alba, Sherry (Oloroso).
- SIMILAR CHEESE: Prattigauer.

GRUYERE
One of the most prevalent and best cheeses in Switzerland.
- TYPE: Raw cow's milk.
- ORIGIN AND MAKERS: Dairy-made over a wide area of the country, but the unofficial capital of production is the Bulle region of the Canton of Fribourg in western French-speaking Switzerland. Some of the best genuine Gruyère comes from the Brevine Plateau around La Brevile, a small village close to the French border in the Jura mountain range. They call this area "the Siberia of Switzerland" due to its extreme climate, and it yields the most interesting cheeses.
- PRODUCTION AND AGING: Unlike most of the large mountain cheeses, genuine Gruyère is still hand-washed with brine. Many Swiss cheeses

are sold at 6 to 8 months, well before they've had a chance to achieve their potential. Farmhouse Gruyères take about 16 months to properly mature. At about 12 months they begin to emit gases and thereafter begin to develop a few evenly placed holes.

■ APPEARANCE: Very large wheels about 2 feet across and 4 inches high with convex sides, weighing up to 40 kilos (88 pounds). The color of a mature farmhouse Gruyère is pale, not yellow or creamy. In the old days, all Gruyères had pea- or small cherry-sized holes spread throughout their interiors; the cheesemaking has been cleaned up so much that now there are very few if any holes, particularly in the factory versions.

■ CONSISTENCY AND TASTE: A hard to semihard paste that melts in your mouth and a nutty, slightly sweet taste with complex musty, mushroomy flavor notes and a long, full aftertaste that hints of spoiled milk. One of the best things about Gruyère is that it's salty on the attack but not on the finish. The paste should be moist yet crumbly— of a consistency that can be balled up easily in between thumb and forefinger.

■ RECOMMENDED PAIRINGS: Champagne (Blanc de Blancs), Zinfandel, Sangiovese.

■ SIMILAR CHEESES: Beaufort, Fontina D'Aosta.

HOCH YBRIG

One of Switzerland's great hidden treasures.

■ TYPE: Raw cow's milk.

■ ORIGIN AND MAKERS: From the area known as Ybergeregg in north-central Switzerland about 50 miles east of Zurich. Made year-round in the village of Oberiberg and surroundings, an area probably better known for its skiing than for its cheese. Technically only a mountain cheese, but some versions do qualify for alpage status.

■ PRODUCTION AND AGING: The recipe is similar to that of Gruyère. Hoch Ybrig is usually aged 9 to 12 months, but the better ones go for 14 months. During maturation, they are washed at least three times a week with a white wine brine, which lends a sweet undercurrent to their flavor. Their rinds develop a reddish smear and a white dusting of mold, while the interiors transform themselves from white to gold and the flavors intensify.

■ APPEARANCE: Wheels weighing about 16 pounds.

■ CONSISTENCY AND TASTE: A mature Hoch Ybrig has a wonderfully smooth, sumptuous,

WHAT IS AN ALP?

A VERY SMALL PLACE IN THE MOUNTAINS WHERE SUPERIOR CHEESES CAN BE MADE

MOST of us learned in geography class that the Alps are a large chain of mountains stretching in an arc across south-central Europe. More specifically, I was under the impression that an alp—in French, Swiss, or German parlance— was any large mountain over 5,000 feet tall. Apparently, this is true, but there's more to it. As explained to me by Caroline Hostettler, our Swiss importer-distributor, an alp can also be something more specific: an isolated mountain locality, smaller than a hamlet, far from a village, possibly with a single shack or chalet, a stream, and a pasture. Often, you have to blaze your own trail to get to an alp; there may be no well-worn path. An alp is a place where they make alpage cheeses during spring and summer. In Switzerland, alpage cheeses are protected and guaranteed by a system of regulations equivalent to the French and Italian DOCs. "Mountain cheeses" are a less stringent category.

yet dense texture that is absolutely mouth-watering. At about 9 months, it has the consistency of butter, then it starts to concentrate and become more crystalline, like a good Gruyère. Its complex, harmonious, and long-lasting flavors include salty, nutty, sweet, and tangy with a hint of butterscotch. Overall, a superior rendition of what most people consider the classic "Swiss cheese" taste.

■ RECOMMENDED PAIRINGS: Rosé Champagne, Grüner Veltliner, a big fruity Merlot, late-harvest Alsatian Riesling, German Riesling Auslese.

■ SIMILAR CHEESES: Genuine Swiss Gruyère.

PRATTIGAUER

A classic alpage-style cheese.

■ TYPE: Raw cow's milk.

■ ORIGIN AND MAKERS: From the Prattigau zone of the Graubunden region in northeastern Switzerland, between the world-famous ski resorts of Davos and Klosters. Most of the Prattigauer I get comes from the high hills at the end of the valley in one little village called Fanas, where three independent farm producers make it from a very traditional recipe.

■ PRODUCTION AND AGING: The farmhouse artisans use wood fires and copper cauldrons, lending the cheese a hint of smokiness. Prattigauer is aged for at least 7 months in a cellar with regular brine washings.

■ APPEARANCE: Relatively small rounds, 10 to 12 pounds and 2½ to 3 inches high.

■ CONSISTENCY AND TASTE: It has a firm, dense paste; thick rind; and a stout, sharp, almost bitter flavor. An aged Prattigauer is not subtle. It can become quite intense, even obstreperous.

■ RECOMMENDED PAIRINGS: Jurançon Petit, Cabernet Sauvignon, Menseng late-harvest Muscat, Alsatian Riesling.

■ SIMILAR CHEESES: Appenzeller.

SBRINZ

This is Switzerland's *ur*-cheese. The Swiss are understandably very proud of it. Some claim that it predates Parmesan and that the Roman Legions actually took the recipe back to Italy with them. Sbrinz outdid Parmesan in a public tasting at the 1998 Slow Food Convention in northern Italy.

■ TYPE: Cow's milk.

■ ORIGIN AND MAKERS: From the foothills of the Berner Oberlander Alps near Lucerne in central Switzerland, it is named after the village of Brienz where, five centuries ago, there was a huge central produce market. While there are just three small dairies left that make genuine raw-milk Appenzeller (see earlier entry), there are thirty that make the real Sbrinz.

■ PRODUCTION AND AGING: Pressed and cooked with a washed, brushed, oiled rind. It is made with whole milk and aged a minimum of 2 and up to 4½ years.

■ APPEARANCE: Drums about 2 feet across and 5½ inches high, weighing around 90 pounds. The interior is more yellow or golden in color than Parmesan.

■ CONSISTENCY AND TASTE: An extra-hard paste and dense texture that is used for grating and shaving in various dishes. Although it is strong, spicy, and nutty, proponents claim it is creamier with less salt on the aftertaste than a Parmesan. An aged Sbrinz is so dense and hard that you can cook with it and it will never completely melt! In Switzerland, they put it in risotto and pieces of it survive the cooking process. For effect, the risotto is often served in the hollowed-out rind of a full drum of cheese.

■ RECOMMENDED PAIRINGS: Sbrinz is quite versatile with wines; try it with a light white, Champagne, a fruity full-bodied red (Nebbiolo-based Barolos or Barbarescos or a Merlot), even an old Port. Also Amarone, Malbec, Docello d'Alba, Sauvignon Blanc, Barbera d'Alba, Riesling, Pinot Blanc, St. Aubin.

■ SIMILAR CHEESES: Grana Padano, Parmigiano-Reggiano.

STANSER FLADÄ

The name of this cheese (Fladä) comes from the Swiss word for "cow patty" (as in dung) and was given due to its flat, round shape.

■ TYPE: Raw cow's milk.

■ ORIGIN AND MAKER: Joseph Barmettler makes this cheese in his small dairy in the small town of Stans, which is in central Switzerland, close to Lucerne.

■ PRODUCTION AND AGING: The milk comes from carefully selected small farms around and above Stans. It is an uncooked, unpressed cheese made to the same recipe as Vacherin Mont d'Or and aged 3 weeks.

■ APPEARANCE: Flat wheels weighing 12 ounces with a reddish-brown rind and bumpy surface that may harbor some white mold. The paste is cream colored to light yellow with small holes.

■ CONSISTENCY AND TASTE: Smooth, creamy, and collapsing. (The cheese needs to be spooned when ripe.) Its aroma is pronounced and barnyardy but not arresting; the flavor is big and sweet, with hints of mountain grasses, but no excessive saltiness or sharpness.

■ RECOMMENDED PAIRINGS: Champagne, Sauvignon Blanc, Viognier.

■ SIMILAR CHEESES: Vacherin Fribourgeois.

STANSER SCHAFCHÄS

Up front, no-holds-barred, it will grab you and won't let go until it's had its full say, telling you what milk can really do.

■ TYPE: Ewe's milk.

■ ORIGIN AND MAKER: From Canton Schwitz, the same area where they produce Hoch Ybrig, made by Joseph Barmettler (see also Stanser Fladä).

■ PRODUCTION AND AGING: Uncooked, unpressed, washed-rind, aged a minimum of 2 months with regular washings and turnings. A mountain cheese, not an alpage one, but nevertheless superb. The milk comes from farms in the hills around the small town of Stans, and the sheep breed is the same as that which produces Roquefort.

■ APPEARANCE: Small cylinders or wheels, weighing 4 to 5 pounds, about 3 inches tall and about 6 inches across. The rind is thin, moist, and light brown.

■ CONSISTENCY AND TASTE: A smooth, compact paste with the consistency of butter but firmer. The flavor is sheepy, grassy, and herbal and gets progressively stronger from 2 months on. By 5 to 6 months, Stanser has obtained provocative and persistent flavors—full, spicy, and pungent—and a daunting aroma. The flavor can be challenging at first; its finish comes as somewhat of a relief.

■ RECOMMENDED PAIRINGS: Jurançon Petit Menseng, Muscatel, Malmsey Madeira, Pinot Blanc, Sauvignon Blanc (from fairly dry to dessert-style), Sauternes.

■ SIMILAR CHEESES: Munster, Vacherin Fribourgeois.

VACHERIN FRIBOURGEOIS

This is the cheese that gives Swiss fondue its smooth, creamy consistency and keeps it from getting gummy.

■ TYPE: Cow's milk.

■ ORIGIN AND MAKERS: Produced in small, old-fashioned dairies in a zone that includes the Canton of Fribourg and other parts of western Switzerland, right up to the Jura Mountains on the border with France.

■ PRODUCTION AND AGING: Not to be confused with Vacherin du Haut Doubs or Mont d'Or (see above under France), Vacherin Fribourgeois is a pressed, uncooked, washed-rind cheese that is cured 3 to 4 months. It is relatively soft compared with the typical Swiss cheese, for example, Gruyère.

■ APPEARANCE: Comes in comparatively small wheels, about 16 inches in diameter and 3 inches thick, weighing approximately 15 pounds. Its rind is gray with tinges of yellow, brown, or pink; its paste has many small holes and some slits.

■ CONSISTENCY AND TASTE: Firm with a sourish flavor.

■ RECOMMENDED PAIRINGS: Classified-growth red Bordeaux, Grüner Veltliner, Alsatian Riesling, California Syrah, Muscat, Barbera d'Alba.

■ SIMILAR CHEESES: Morbier, which is better known but has far less character.

VAL BAGNER

The quintessential *raclette*-type cheese; personally, I don't see why you'd want to melt it down. Just eat it and enjoy.

■ TYPE: Raw cow's milk.

■ ORIGIN AND MAKERS: From the famous ski town of Verbier in the Valais region of southwestern Switzerland. The best cheeses in the region are acknowledged to come from the Bagner Valley (Val Bagner) around Verbier where this cheese is produced in a small co op dairy.

■ PRODUCTION AND AGING: Apart from its terroir, the other key to this cheese's excellence is that it's made from the milk of two breeds: the Fribourgeois (which also produce the milk for Vacherin) and the Ehringer, an old German breed of large, sparse milk producers. Val Bagner is an uncooked, unpressed, washed-rind mountain cheese that is aged for 5 to 6 months and can be eaten up to a year.

■ APPEARANCE: Flat wheels about 12 inches in diameter and 2 to 3 inches high, weighing about 12 pounds. They have hard, dry, light brown rinds with a possible dusting of white mold. The paste is yellowish with some small holes.

■ CONSISTENCY AND TASTE. A firm cheese that will get harder with age, it has a stout, lactic, authentic mountain pasture flavor.

■ RECOMMENDED PAIRING: Barbaresco (Nebbiolo-based), Merlot, Syrah, white Bordeau.

■ SIMILAR CHEESES: Appenzeller.

United States and Canada

IN AMERICA, a "real cheese" culture is blossoming. We've come a long way in the past 10 to 15 years. Gourmets of several generations are joining the ranks of caseophiles. This is good news.

In addition to providing a huge potential market for fine cheeses, America is also fertile ground for cheesemaking. The United States produces more milk by far than any other country. Now a handful of American artisans is making real cheese, which is an encouraging sign. Some U.S. cheesemakers are building caves and acting as affineurs for their own and other local farms.

Sometimes I worry that American cheeses may be nothing more than good—or merely passable—imitations of the European originals. I want to encourage our artisans and also issue them a challenge: America's potential for superior production is mostly unfulfilled. We have a long way to go in terms of variety and originality. This said, I'm fully aware of and sympathetic to their plight. Many U.S. artisanal cheeses are pricier than their foreign counterparts, for example, because they don't receive the price supports available in Europe. Rather, they encounter institutional *resistance* to their mission. In proportion to our overall population, the demand for their cheeses is small. We all need to contribute to its growth.

CLASSIC BLUE

This is designated a "surface-ripened blue goat's milk cheese," an unusual if not unique category.

■ TYPE: Pasteurized goat's milk.

■ ORIGIN AND MAKER: Westfield Farm, Hubbardston, north-central Massachusetts. Proprietor-cheesemakers Bob and Letitia Kilmoyer retired in 1996 and handed the reins to Bob and Debby Stetson.

■ PRODUCTION AND AGING: A fascinating cheese that begins its life as fresh white chèvre-type curds that are inoculated with the Roquefort mold (*P. roquefortii*). The cheeses dry over a period of about 2 weeks, evaporating from 10 ounces to about 7 and developing an exterior covering of blue mold. Then they are wrapped in permeable cellophane and shipped after about 1 week; they are best sold and consumed after an additional 2 to 4 weeks' curing.

■ APPEARANCE: Logs about 5½ inches long and 2 inches in diameter.

■ CONSISTENCY AND TASTE: Semisoft, fluffy. Gentle, mellow goat milk flavor with a bit of zip from the blue.

■ RECOMMENDED PAIRINGS: Champagnes.

■ SIMILAR CHEESE: Monte Enebro.

DOELING CAMEMBERT

Donna Doel, once a soil scientist, followed her true calling to become a farmer and cheesemaker.

■ TYPE: Goat's milk.

■ ORIGIN AND MAKERS: Doeling Dairy, Fayetteville, Ozark Mountains, northwestern Arkansas.

■ PRODUCTION AND AGING: Made from the milk of the farm's herd of about fifty goats. Aged 6 to 8 weeks. Production methods similar to cow's milk Camemberts, allowing for heavy rind formation.

■ APPEARANCE: Approximately 5-ounce disk, 4½ inches in diameter and 1 inch thick, with a white rind.

■ CONSISTENCY AND TASTE: Deep, mushroomy, almost blue flavor with a rind that is deliciously edible. Interior is creamy to firm depending on season and ripeness.

■ SEASONAL NOTE: Generally available March through early January. Late fall and early spring cheeses are best.

■ RECOMMENDED PAIRINGS: Blanc de Blancs Champagne, Sauvignon Blanc, California Syrah, California Viognier, Zinfandel

■ SIMILAR CHEESES: Cow's milk Camemberts.

■ ADDITIONAL CHEESES: Donna also makes an aged Gouda, which comes in 2½- and 7-pound wheels and peaks at about 5 months. It has a moist, smooth texture, nutty flavor and a sweet, pleasantly milky finish. Goudas aged more than 1 year offer more intense flavors, similar to butterscotch. Donna also makes a Crottin, plain and herbed Chèvre, and Feta-style cheeses.

GREAT HILL BLUE

The farm has been in the Stone family since the early twentieth century; Tim Stone is currently the head cheesemaker.

■ TYPE: Raw cow's milk blue.

■ ORIGIN AND MAKER: Great Hill Dairy, Marion, Massachusetts, on the shores of Buzzard's Bay, about 50 miles south of Boston.

■ PRODUCTION AND AGING: The only non-homogenized raw-milk blue in the United States, made from the milk of local Jersey and Holstein cows by traditional manufacturing methods. Aged at least 6 months.

■ APPEARANCE: 6-pound wheels.

■ CONSISTENCY AND TASTE: Firm and robust with a balanced finish. Has a more dense, yellower curd and a richer, creamier-tasting paste than is possible in a factory milieu.

■ RECOMMENDED PAIRINGS: Late-harvest Muscatel or Chenin Blanc.

■ SIMILAR CHEESES: Bleu D'Auvergne, Bleu de Causses, Fourme D'Ambert.

HUMBOLDT FOG

A fine American chèvre, evocative of its *terroir*, particularly the prevailing climactic conditions.

- **TYPE**: Goat's milk.
- **ORIGIN AND MAKERS**: Cypress Grove Chèvre, Inc., McKinleyville, Humboldt County, Northern California. Humboldt Fog is the work of Mary Keehn, who began making goat cheeses at her farm in 1984 and was later joined by her daughter, Malorie McCurdy.
- **PRODUCTION AND AGING**: A traditionally made mold-ripened *tomme*. The milk is sourced from small family-owned farms in the area, which is second only to certain parts of England in terms of its amount of fog per annum. Its shelf life is generally anywhere from 3 to 15 weeks, but it has been enjoyed at ages up to 6 months.
- **APPEARANCE**: Rounds about 2 inches tall and 3½ inches across that weigh 11 to 14 ounces. (There are also larger rounds, 7 inches in diameter and weighing around 4½ pounds.) They have a center layer of vegetable ash and rinds dusted with ash and white mold that are reminiscent of the morning fog, hence the cheese's name.
- **CONSISTENCY AND TASTE**: Has a light, creamy, yet earthy flavor when young that turns stronger and more complex with age.
- **RECOMMENDED PAIRINGS**: Sauvignon Blanc.
- **SIMILAR CHEESES**: Wabash Cannonball, Valençay.
- **ADDITIONAL CHEESES**: At Cypress Grove, they also make a goat's milk cheddar as well as fresh chèvre-type cheeses in logs, bricks, rounds, and small Valençay-style pyramids.

JERSEY BLUE

Karen Galayda and Tom Gilbert are American pioneers of farmstead mold-ripened cheese. They started their own farm in 1992, and they've made the best American versions of Camembert and Brie as well as this superb blue, among others.

- **TYPE**: Raw cow's milk blue.
- **ORIGIN AND MAKER**: Blythedale Farm, Corinth, northeastern Vermont.
- **PRODUCTION AND AGING**: Made to a Stilton recipe. Tom and Karen manage their own herd of about thirty Jersey cows and make their cheeses by hand, the old-fashioned way.
- **APPEARANCE**: 5-pound drums or wheels 8 inches in diameter and 4 inches high. A brown, bumpy rind with grayish-white mold growth. Ivory to light yellow paste with heavy, at times hollow, striations of grayish blue-green mold.
- **CONSISTENCY AND TASTE**: Has a firm, dense, creamy curd that marries perfectly with the flavors of the *Penicillium* mold to produce well-balanced flavors.
- **RECOMMENDED PAIRINGS**: Madeira, Tawny Port, Vintage Port.
- **SIMILAR CHEESE**: Stilton.

LE CHÈVRE NOIR

One of the best hard goat's milk cheeses made anywhere.

- **TYPE**: Goat's milk.
- **ORIGIN AND MAKER**: Fromagerie Tournevent, Chesterville, Quebec, Canada.
- **PRODUCTION AND AGING**: A Cheddar-type recipe. Aged a minimum of 12 months.
- **APPEARANCE**: 2.4-pound blocks encased in black wax
- **CONSISTENCY AND TASTE**: Has a hard ivory-white paste with an underlying crystalline texture, which provides one of the more remarkable taste sensations of any cheese. Imagine a medium-to full-flavored Cheddar-style cheese with a touch of sweetness on the attack, a pleasantly goaty finish, and a dense texture that is actually crunchy when you bite into it—and there you have Le Chèvre Noir.
- **RECOMMENDED PAIRINGS**: California Sauvignon Blanc, California Syrah, California Zinfandel.

- SIMILAR CHEESE: Doeling Dairy Goat's Milk Gouda.

NANCY'S HUDSON VALLEY CAMEMBERT

Possesses a good balance of two milk types. It gives the continental double and triple crèmes a run for their money.

- TYPE: Ewe's and cow's milk.
- ORIGIN AND MAKER: Old Chatham Sheepherding Company, Old Chatham, New York, in Shaker Country, southeast of Albany. Cheesemaker Benoit Maillol learned traditional methods on his family farm in France.
- PRODUCTION AND AGING: A Camembert-style cheese. Old Chatham is believed to have the largest herd of dairy sheep in the country; the cow's milk component comes from a nearby farm.
- APPEARANCE: 2-pound wheels. White, natural, edible rind.
- CONSISTENCY AND TASTE: Semisoft with a mild buttery flavor.
- RECOMMENDED PAIRINGS: Great with Champagne; white Burgundy and Bordeaux; German Riesling Kabinett; also late-harvest ice wines.
- SIMILAR CHEESE: Roucoulons.

ORB WEAVER VERMONT FARMHOUSE CHEESE

Marjorie Susman and Marian Pollack settled in Vermont's Champlain Valley two decades ago and have been making a fine farmhouse cheese ever since. They named their farm after the type of spider that weaves its web in an orb shape embodying, for them, their ideal of diligent artistry. Orb Weaver won first place in the farmhouse category at the 2000 ACS meeting. Shortly thereafter, they built their own ripening cave.

- TYPE: Raw cow's milk.
- ORIGIN AND MAKER: Orb Weaver Farm, New Haven, Vermont.
- PRODUCTION AND AGING: Most of the cheeses are waxed and aged 7 months or more; since the midnineties, Marjorie and Marian have also been making a nonwaxed version that is aged for a minimum of 8 months. The cheeses are made seasonally from November to May entirely by hand. Their outstanding component is the farm's award-winning milk, which comes from its small herd of magnificent pure-bred Jersey cows.
- APPEARANCE: 2- and 7-pound wheels.
- CONSISTENCY AND TASTE: A butter-colored, rich, creamy, Colby-style cheese more moist than Cheddar, with a slightly tangy, full-bodied flavor.
- RECOMMENDED PAIRINGS: Fruity reds with some backbone: try it with Merlots, Pinot Noirs, Languedoc reds, Cabernet Franc, or Barbera d'Alba. Also Chardonnay.
- SIMILAR CHEESE: Single Gloucester.

ROTH KÄSE GRAND CRU GRUYÈRE

This is one of the best Alpine-type cheeses made in the United States, by Bruce Workman.

- TYPE: Cow's milk.
- ORIGIN AND MAKER: Roth Käse U.S.A., Monroe, Wisconsin.
- PRODUCTION AND AGING: Cooked in copper cauldrons and aged on wooden boards (as they do in Switzerland) anywhere from 6 months to 2 years.
- APPEARANCE: Amber paste, washed rind, in a medium-sized wheel.
- CONSISTENCY AND TASTE: Hard, sweet, nutty.
- RECOMMENDED PAIRINGS: Chardonnay, Riesling, Pinot Blanc.
- SIMILAR CHEESES: Beaufort, Fontina d'Aosta, and Swiss Gruyère.
- ADDITIONAL CHEESES: Workman makes a variety of other cow's-milk cheeses, but this Gruyère is the star.

SALLY JACKSON CHEESES

Sally and Roger Jackson make raw sheep's and goat's milk cheeses on their farm in the Okanogan Highlands of eastern Washington.

■ TYPE: Raw sheep's and goat's milk.

■ ORIGIN AND MAKER: Jackson Farm, Oroville, Washington.

■ PRODUCTION AND AGING: Artisanal. Mold-ripened under leaf covers for 2 to 3 months. To help distinguish between the sheep and goat, Sally uses a hexagonal ceramic mold for the goat cheese and a round ceramic one for the sheep.

■ APPEARANCE: White paste, no rinds. The sheep cheese is wrapped in chestnut leaves, the goat cheese in grape leaves.

■ CONSISTENCY AND TASTE: Semisoft.

■ RECOMMENDED PAIRINGS: Like their European counterpart, Brin d'Amour, these cheeses can pair well with Albariño, red Bordeaux, Carignan, Grüner Veltliner, Alsatian Riesling or German Riesling Auslese, Sancerre Blanc, and Sherry (Oloroso).

■ SIMILAR CHEESES: Banon, Brin d'Amour.

TRADE LAKE CEDAR

LoveTree Farmstead is located in the woodsy wilds of northern Wisconsin surrounded by eight small lakes, after which its cheeses, including Trade Lake Cedar, are named.

■ TYPE: Raw sheep's milk.

■ ORIGIN AND MAKER: LoveTree Farmstead in Grantsburg, Wisconsin, where cheesemaker Mary Falk and her husband, David, have been farming and raising livestock organically since 1986.

■ PRODUCTION AND AGING: A natural-rind cheese aged on cedar boughs in the farm's fresh-air aging caves that overlook the shores of one of its 5-acre ponds. The Falks emphasize living in harmony with nature, and their cheeses aim to capture the indigenous flavors and aromas of their environment. Trade Lake Cedar is aged a minimum of 2 months.

■ APPEARANCE: The average wheel of Trade Lake Cedar is approximately 8 pounds. Its rind is a deep buff color with a nubby texture; the paste is dense and a light ivory color when young (60 days), deepening to a light caramel cover as it ages up to 4 months.

■ CONSISTENCY AND TASTE: Firm, robust, and aromatic with a silky smooth texture, it offers grassy, fruity, spicy, and nutty flavors with a light woodsy undertone.

■ RECOMMENDED PAIRINGS: Champagne (Blanc de Noirs), Chardonnay, Syrah, Zinfandel, Pinot Noir.

■ SIMILAR CHEESE: Berkswell.

■ ADDITIONAL CHEESES: At LoveTree, they also make a series of Young Artisan Sheepmilk cheeses, bearing the name Holmes. These are soft-ripened cheeses made in the style of Brin d'Amour and aged 4 to 6 weeks. One of these, Big Holmes, is among my favorite U.S. cheeses; it is beautiful, rustic, herb-encrusted and not unlike Monte Enebro or Garrotxa in appearance and texture but altogether different in flavor. Gabrielson Lake, made from 100 percent Jersey cow's milk, is another excellent LoveTree cheese. It is aged a minimum of 3 months, has a melt-in-your-mouth consistency, and buttery, nutty, and zesty flavors with hints of apple. As it ages, it takes on a more meaty, intense woodsy flavors without turning sharp or bitter.

VERMONT SHEPHERD

This cheese makes me proud to be an American. It is hands down the best made in the United States—rustic, uncomplicated, elegantly simple, hearty, and incredibly delicious.

■ TYPE: Raw ewe's milk.

■ ORIGIN AND MAKERS: Cynthia and David Major, Major Farm, Putney, southern Vermont.

■ PRODUCTION AND AGING: Made in the style of the French Pyrénées. Aged 4 to 8 months. The Majors operate their own cave—one of the first, if not the first in the United States. They do not use artificial insemination, so the cheese is only available 7 to 8 months a year, September until April or May.

■ APPEARANCE: Drums weighing 5½ to 10 pounds with bulging sides—a kind of flying-saucer shape—that have golden brown brushed rinds.

■ CONSISTENCY AND TASTE: Has a smooth, creamy paste that is simultaneously soft and dense. The cheeses are aromatic and herbaceous, pleasingly full-flavored, elegant, and profound, but not overwhelming, revealing subtle layers of complexity with sweet, rich, earthy, nutty tones and hints of clover, wild mint, and thyme as they melt in your mouth.

■ RECOMMENDED PAIRINGS: Vermont Shepherd is among the most wine-friendly cheeses I've encountered. Try it with red Burgundy, white Burgundy, Chardonnay, Pinot Noir, Sauvignon Blanc, Syrah, Viognier, Zinfandel, Albariño, Blanc de Noirs, Viognier, Languedoc reds, Kabinett, Sangiovese, and Port. It's best with Pinot Noir wines.

■ SIMILAR CHEESES: Berkswell, Ossau-Iraty Brebis AOC, Spenwood.

■ ADDITIONAL CHEESES: The Majors also make some other superior cheeses. Their Shepherd's Tomme is simply the lower grade—or "lesser selection"—of Vermont Shepherd. Another, Timson, is a slightly stinky washed-rind cheese that comes in wheels weighing around 5 pounds and is made from the raw milk of a neighbor's herd of Jersey cows. Aged 5 to 6 months, it has an orangish-yellow rind, a pale yellow paste, and a delightful smokiness to its flavor. Putney Tomme, which is aged 4 months, is also made from the same raw Jersey cow's milk. It is made in the style of a Tomme de Savoie and has a gray rind, yellow paste, and wonderful earthy flavors. The Majors act as ripeners for other farms, many of whom make their cheeses to Cindy and David's recipes; the best of the farm's output, however, always seems to come from its own herds.

WABASH CANNONBALL

Master cheesemaker Judy Schad, a shining light of the cheese world, named this one after the famous train and eponymous song of southern Indiana. She also recalled a visit to France where similar small ball-shaped cheeses are called *boulets*, which translates to "cannonball."

■ TYPE: Pasteurized goat's milk.

■ ORIGIN AND MAKER: Capriole, Inc., Greenville, Indiana.

■ PRODUCTION AND AGING: Made from the milk of the farm's own goat herd in the style of chèvre. Aged 10 days to 3 weeks.

■ APPEARANCE: 3-ounce balls with a light external dusting of ash and *P. candidum* mold.

■ CONSISTENCY AND TASTE: A semisoft paste with a gentle, creamy, slightly acidic flavor. The Cannonball might be better dubbed the Wabash Snowball, because when it's right, it's very white and fluffy—definitely denser, creamier, and mellower than your average fresh goat cheese. With age it will turn harder and darker and start looking more like a rock or a cannonball than a snowball. Wabash Cannonballs should be served when full, plump and not at all shriveled.

■ RECOMMENDED PAIRINGS: Champagne (Blanc de Noirs), California Sauvignon Blanc, California Zinfandel, Grüner Veltliner.

■ SIMILAR CHEESES: Crottin de Chavignol, Humboldt Fog.

■ ADDITIONAL CHEESES: At Capriole, they also make a raw goat's milk washed-rind cheese called Mont St. Francis after a nearby Franciscan monastery. Aged 5 to 8 months, it comes in an 8-inch wheel with a pale orange rind and creamy white paste. It offers the earthy pungent aromas typical of washed-rind cheeses and a hearty, beefy flavor. I liken it to a goat's milk version of Taleggio; it is made in the style of and not unlike Chevrotin des Aravis, but it gets smellier. Judy makes other fresh goat's milk cheeses, including one that comes in an elongated pyramid shape and is called Crocodile Tear.

Glossary

ABOMASUM: The fourth, or digesting, chamber of a ruminant animal's stomach. Also known as the vell.

AFFINAGE: French word for ripening of cheeses.

AFFINEUR: In French, a ripener, that is, someone who is expert in the care and aging of fine cheese. Traditionally, cheesemakers would often sell their product at an unripe or "new" stage to affineurs who would do the subsequent ripening, packaging, marketing, and distribution.

ANNATTO: A reddish-yellow dye made from the crushed outer seed coating of the South American Annatto or Orlean plant.

À POINT: French expression for when a cheese is at its absolute peak of ripeness.

AROMATIC ESTERS: Fatty acids and glycerides contained in milk that give cheese its flavors and aromas; the animal's milk-making apparatus transmits them from the oils in the pasture plants.

AU LAIT CRU: French for "made with raw milk."

BASKET: A cheese shape equivalent to a cylinder with rounded edges or a flattened sphere; many of the world's best sheep cheeses, notably Pecorino Toscano or Pyrénées-style Brebis, come in this shape.

BREBIS: Ewe or ewe's milk cheese in French; la brebis (feminine article) is the ewe while le brebis (masculine article) is the cheese itself.

BUTTON: A cheese shape—small, round, and most often a goat's milk cheese.

CASEOPHILE: A cheeselover; the term is not found in dictionaries but neither is "oenophile" for winelover. So why not "caseophile"?

CASEIN: The principal protein in cheese, it is precipitated out of the milk by curdling.

CENDRÉ: French adjective for a cheese that is coated with the ashes of roots and vines.

CHYMOSIN: A more up-to-date or scientific term for the enzyme rennin; avoids confusion with renin, another enzyme produced by the kidneys.

CLOSTRIDIUM: A genus of bacteria that thrives in wet grass or silage whose spores can find their way into milk and later ruin a cheese by "gas-blowing."

COLOSTRUM: The milk produced immediately after a calf is born; also known as "beestings."

CREAMERY: In English parlance, a small factory or dairy.

CRUST: Another word for "rind"; the French equivalent is croûte.

DOUBLE CRÈME: French term for a cheese that has at least 60 percent matières grasses (see also triple crème).

ELEVEUR: In French, someone who raises animals.

ENZYMES: Organic proteinlike compounds that are catalysts in the breakdown of many organic substances, including fats and proteins. Specific enzymes target specific types of compounds. Enzymes are responsible for the human body's ability to digest food. In cheese, enzymes break down fats and proteins to create flavor-giving volatile compounds.

FERMIER: In French, the noun farmer or an adjective describing a farmhouse cheese.

FRUTIÈRE: A small dairy in French.

HALOIR: The room where cheeses are set to dry out and, in traditional cheesemaking, acquire ambient molds; sometimes also known as the sechoir ("drying room").

JUNKET: A cheesemaking term for the set milk after renneting.

LACTOSE: The type of sugar contained in milk.

LAIT CRU: Raw (unpasteurized) milk in French.

LAITIER: In French, dairyman or adjective describing a cheese made in a dairy.

LISTERIA MONOCYTOGENES: Strain of the common *Listeria* bacteria that can be carried in cheese and can cause serious health problems.

LIPOLYSIS: The breakdown of fats. In maturing cheese, enzymes produced by bacteria and/or molds break a portion of the fats down into free fatty acids and other flavor-giving compounds.

MASTITIS: An infection and inflammation of the udder of a milk-giving animal that ruins the milk.

MATIÈRES GRASSES: French term for fat in dry matter, expressed as a percentage; this stays the same as a cheese ages and dries out (its water evaporates).

MILLSTONE: According to Randolph Hodgson of Neal's Yard Dairy, this is a term, coined by Patrick Rance, to describe a cheese shape that is a flat cylinder several inches high with a diameter about three to four times its height.

MORGE: A solution of wine, cheese scraps, and (sometimes) whey used for washing cheeses and promoting development of a moldy protective rind.

MOULÉ À LA MAIN: In French, ladled by hand (as in the curds for making cheese); *moulé à la louche* means the same thing.

OXIDATION: A chemical reaction that is part of the aging process of a cheese that, in excess, creates a "cardboardy" flavor.

PASTE: The interior portion of the cheese as opposed to the rind or crust, which is the exterior. The French equivalent for "paste" is *pâte*.

PEPSIN: A digestive enzyme present in rennet.

PERSILLÉ: "Parsleyed" or green-tinged in French; a term used to refer to some blue cheeses, including Roqueforts, which have greenish veins of mold running through them.

PROTEOLYSIS: The breaking down of proteins into simpler compounds, which in an animal's or human's stomach makes those proteins more easily digestible.

In cheese, enzymes break long chainlike protein molecules up into a number of flavor-giving compounds.

PYRAMID: A cheese shape, most often for French-style goat cheeses.

RANCIDITY: A chemical reaction called hydrolysis transforms milk fats into fatty acids and glycerols, creating an accumulation of free fatty acids and giving a cheese a stale, spoiled flavor. A small amount of rancidity is desirable in some cheeses.

RENNET: An extract of the stomach lining of young mammals containing digestive enzymes designed to coagulate milk; used to promote and advance the coagulation of milk in cheesemaking.

RENNIN: The principal digestive enzyme in rennet.

SCALD: A quick heating of the curd; involves less heat than "cooking" the curd.

SECHOIR: French term for drying room, which is used in the ripening and aging of cheeses. (See also *haloir*.)

SERUM: the liquid portion of milk or whey is often referred to in technical or scientific terms as "milk serum."

SILAGE: Animal fodder consisting of a mixture of plants and grasses that is fermented in a silo.

THERMISATION: French term for a gentler form of pasteurization or heat treatment that sanitizes milk while allowing it to retain many of its typical enzymes and bacteria, which are important to cheesemaking.

TRANSHUMANCE: French term for the migration of herds from valleys to higher mountain pastures as spring gives way to summer, then their return to lower elevations in the fall.

TRIPLE CRÈME: In France, a cheese made with the addition of extra cream that has more than 75 percent *matières grasses* (fat in dry material).

VELL: calf stomach

Resources

UNITED STATES ARTISANAL
CHEESEMAKERS

Blythedale Farm
HCR 82, Box 100
Corinth, VT 05039
Phone: 802-439-6575
Karen Galayda and Tom Gilbert, cheesemakers

Capriole, Inc.
P.O. Box 117
Greenville, IN 47124
Phone: 812-923-9408
Judy Schad, cheesemaker

Cypress Grove Chevre, Inc.
4600 Dows Prairie Road
McKinleyville, CA 95521
Phone: 707-839-3168
Fax: 707-839-2322
Mary Keehn, cheesemaker

Doeling Dairy
2877 South Leo Ammons Road
Fayetteville, AR 72720
E-mail: dairy @doelingdairy.com
Website: www.doelingdairy.com
Phone: 501-582-4571
Fax: 501-582-1213
Contact: Donna Doel

Fromagerie Tournevant
7004 IIince Road
Chesterville, Quebec GOP 1J0
Canada
E-mail: j.eggena@chevre-tournevent.qc.ca
Website: www.chevre-tournevent.qc.ca
Phone: 819-382-2208
Fax: 819-382-2072
Contact: John Eggena

Grafton Village Cheese Co.
P.O. Box 87
Grafton, VT 05146
Phone: 802-843-2221
E-mail: peter@graftonvillagecheese.com
Peter Mohn, vice president

Great Hill Dairy, Inc.
160 Delano Road
Marion, MA 02738
Phone: 508-748-2208
Contact: Tim or Nancy Stone

LoveTree Farmstead
12413 County Road "Z"
Grantsburg, WI 54840
Phone: 715-488-2966
Fax: 715-488-3957
E-mail: lovetree@win.bright.net
Website: www.lovetreefarmstead.com
Contact: Dave or Mary Falk
If you'd like to visit, please call ahead to schedule
    an appointment.

Major Farm
875 Patch Road
Putney, VT 05346
Phone: 802-387-4473
Fax: 802-387-2041
E-mail: vtsheprd@sover.net
Website: www.vermontshepherd.com
Contact: Cindy Major

Orb Weaver Farm
3406 Lime Kiln Road
New Haven, VT 05472
Phone: 802-877-3755
E-mail: orbweavr@together.net
Contact: Marjorie Susman or Marian Pollack
Cheeses are sold from the farm.

Old Chatham Shepherding Co.
155 Shaker Museum Road
Old Chatham, NY 12136
Phone: 888-SHEEP60 (743-3760)
Fax: 518-794-7641
E-mail: cheese@blacksheepcheese.com
Website: www.blacksheepcheese.com
Contact: Jodie Wische
Visitors welcome. Last Saturday in April is "Farm
    Day," like a country fair with flock-shearing and
    other activities.

Westfield Farm
28 Worcester Road
Hubbardston, MA 01452
Phone: 978-928-5110
Fax: 978-928-5745
E-mail: stetson@tiac.net
Website: www.chevre.com
Contact: Bob or Debby Stetson
Visitors welcome, cheeses sold on site.

Resources *(continued)*

THE AMERICAN CHEESE SOCIETY

Administrative Offices
304 West Liberty Street, Suite 201
Louisville, KY 40202
Phone: 502-583-3783
Fax: 502-589-3602
E-mail: ACS@hqtrs.com
Website: www.cheesesociety.org
To join, contact the ACS at their headquarters, at the information above. The society has a directory of members, which is a valuable resource, as well as an annual conference and special events.

RECOMMENDED CHEESE RETAILERS

Stores where you may be able to find well-tended selections of the world's finest cheeses:

Alaska
Sagaya, Anchorage

Arizona
Whole Foods, Tempe

California
Artisan Cheese, San Francisco
24th Street Cheese Company, San Francisco
Bocatto's, Larchmont
Cheeseboard, Berkeley
Corti Brothers, Sacramento
Dean & DeLuca, St. Helena
Food for Thought, Santa Rosa
Full of Life, Clairmont
La Brea Bakery, Los Angeles
Lazy Acres, Santa Barbara
Oakville Grocery: Oakville, Palo Alto, Walnut Creek
Pasta Shop: Berkeley, Oakland
Palasades Market, Calistoga
Tomales Bay Foods: Point Reyes, San Francisco
Wally's, Los Angeles
Whole Foods: Various stores including Berkeley, Beverly Hills, Brentwood, Campbell, Costa Mesa, Glendale, Hillcrest, LaJolla, Los Gatos, Mill Valley, Monterey, Palo Also, Pasadena, San Francisco, San Rafael, Sherman Oaks, Sherman Oaks East, Tustin, West L.A., Woodlands Market, Woodlands

Colorado
Alfalfa's: Boulder, Fort Collins
Whole Foods, Boulder

Connecticut
The British Shop, Madison
Culinary Capers, Mystic
Sutton Place Gourmet, Riverside

Florida
Epicure Market, Miami
Gordon's Wine, Boca Raton
Whole Foods, Winter Park
Uppercrust Products, Gainesville

Georgia
Whole Foods, Atlanta

Illinois
Con Vito Italiano, Chicago
Whole Foods; Riverforest, Chicago

Louisiana
Martin's Wine Cellar, New Orleans

Maine
The Market Basket, Rockport
Portland Green Grocer, Portland
Treats, Wiscasset

Maryland
Sutton Place Gourmet, Bethesda

Massachusetts
Formaggio Kitchen, Cambridge
Fahey and Fromagerie, Nantucket

Michigan
Whole Foods, Ann Arbor
Zingerman's, Ann Arbor

Minnesota
Broviaks, Minnetonka
Surdyk's, Minneapolis
Whole Foods, St. Paul

Missouri
The Cheese Place, Rockland

New Hampshire
Hanover Coop, Hanover

New Jersey
Madison Shoppers, Madison
Summit Cheese Shop, Summit
Market Basket, Franklin Lakes

New Mexico
Cookworks, Santa Fe

New York
ABC Warehouse, NYC
Artisanal, NYC
Balducci's, NYC
Citarella, NYC
Dean & DeLuca, NYC
Eli's Manhattan, NYC
Fairway: 125th Street, 74th and Broadway (both NYC)
Grace's, NYC
Ideal Cheese Shop, NYC
Loaves and Fishes, Sagaponack
Murray's Cheese Shop, NYC
Sutton Place Gourmet, Woodbury
Village Market, Southampton
The Vinegar Factory, NYC
Wegman's: Ithaca, Rochester
Zabar's, NYC

North Carolina
Dean & DeLuca, Charlotte
Fowlers, Durham
Wellspring Grocery: Chapel Hill, Durham, Raleigh

Ohio
Dorothy Lane, Dayton
Katzinger's, Columbus
West Point Market, Akron

Oregon
Nature's Fresh, Portland
Pastaworks, Portland

Pennsylvania
Ardmore Cheese Shop, Ardmore
DiBruno, Philadelphia
Downtown Cheese, Philadelphia

Rhode Island
Wickford Gourmet, Wickford

Tennessee
The Corner Market, Nashville

Texas
Whole Foods: Various stores including Arlington, Austin (6th and Lamar), Gateway Austin, Preston Dallas, Plano
Sigels, Dallas
Central Market, Austin North, Gateway Austin, San Antonio
Lomart, El Paso

Utah
Liberty Heights Fresh, Salt Lake City

Vermont
Brattleboro Food Co-op, Brattleboro
The Cheese Outlet, Burlington
F.H. Gillingham, Woodstock
Harlow Farm Stand, Westminster
Hunger Mountain Coop, Montepelier
Provisions International, White River Junction
Putney Food Co-op, Putney
Shelburne Market, Shelburne
Tasftville General Store, Taftsville

Virginia
Sutton Place Gourmet, Alexandria
WF/Fresh Fields: Annandale, Arlington, Vienna
Wine Cellars, Williamsburg

Washington
Brie and Bordeaux, Seattle
James Cook Cheese Co., Seattle
DeLaurenti's: Seattle, Bellevue
Larry's Market: Seattle, Bellevue
Queen Anne Thriftway, Seattle

Washington, DC
Dean & DeLuca, Georgetown
Sutton Place Gourmet
WF/Fresh Fields: Georgetown, Tenley

Britain
Neal's Yard Dairy has two London locations: the original one in Neal's Yard, Covent Garden. There is also a small retail shop in Borough Market near London Bridge. So if you're ever in London, I highly recommend a pilgrimage to either location. When the shops aren't too busy, they'll take you on a tour of their ripening caves.
Paxton & Whitfield, Jermyn Street, London
Ticklemore Cheese Shop, Totnes, Devon (Robin Congdon and Sarie Cooper's shop)
Wells Stores, Streatley, Berkshire (founded by Patrick Rance)

France
If you're in Paris, be sure to visit one of the Androuët cheese shops. The original shop at 41 Rue d'Amsterdam is defunct but there are three new locations throughout the city. The main branch, with restaurant, is located at le rue Arsenel Houssail (8th arrondisement).

Acknowledgments

FIRST, I would like to thank the cheesemakers and, of course, Terrance Brennan, who conceived and nurtured the Picholine cheese program; then Angela Miller, who recognized a need for this book and who introduced me to David Gibbons, whose energy and enthusiasm for this project seemed limitless. Thanks go to Roy Finamore and Chris Pavone, the consummate professionals, whose insights gave this book its form, to Susan Salinger, whose respect for the subject gave it the lively perspective it deserves, to Marysarah Quinn and Jane Treuhaft for unparalleled art direction, and to Jill Armus for the design. Also Corky Tyler and Pata Tropp at Takashimaya, and everybody at Ostefin Designs.

Hundreds of people have contributed to my life in cheese and to this project in one way or another. I am indebted to each and every one of them. Thanks to the staffs of Picholine and Artisanal and particularly the *fromagers* and *sommeliers*: Teresa Labarga, Nancy DaVita, Andrew Gray, George Riffle, Barry Fleischmann, Morgan Forsey, Fred Price, Ken Pratt, Alex Marie-Anne, David Pinkard, Morgan Rich, T. J. Siegel, Peter Kindel, William Kinser, Amy Sisti, Richard Shipman, Gillian Balance, Mark Sutherland. Thanks also to Steve Jenkins, Rob Kaufelt, Gerd Stern, Chung Park, Sarah Stern, Laura Jacobs-Welch, Judy Shad, Lisa McGee, Michael Kapon, David Merves, Scott Carney, Jason Hinds, Caroline Hostettler, Dick Rogers, David and Cynthia Major and family, Donna Doel, Sister Noella Marcellino, Peter Dixon, Caroline Smialek, Arlene Feltman-Sailhac, Jon Kapon, Peggy Tagliarino, Tom and Nancy Clark, Dr. George Haenlein, Avice Wilson, Bob and Letticia Kilmoyer, Bob Stetson, Harry Kaplan, Ric Bing, Bob Giambalvo, Charles Leary, Betty Graf, Dominic Coyte, Regina McDuffy, Corrine Levenson, Jeanne O'Brien, Joan Ward, Bill Ryan, Karen Galayda, Tom Gilbert, Job Baas, Anna Schwitzer, Robin Weisswasser, Dana Ostrowski, the Shore family, Debra Dickerson, the Cabrero family, the Placencias, Hope Wilson, the Penas, the Garcias, Lonnie Allen, Suzanne Wade, David and Mary Falk, Marjorie Susman, Marian Pollack, Sarah Power, Sean McIlhenny, Mark Shay, Miles Cahn, John Greeley, Ruth Flore, Mary Keehn, Paula Lambert, David Grotenstein, Liz Parnell, Chantal Plasse, Diana Solari, Tim Stone, Jonathan White, Jodie Wische, Daphne Zepos, Heather Cook, Alex Carvajal, Barbara Kafka, Florence Fabricant, Randolph Hodgson, Ruth Kirkham, Nargis Poinda, Daniel Castillo, Peter Meltzer, Rich Santillo, Carol Goodrich, Amy Sultan, Ed Sturmer, Peter Daledda, David Pasternak, the Kams, Sarah Stewart, Glynn and Claudia McCalman. And finally, many thanks to the legions of diners at Picholine and Artisanal who have given me their critiques on the cheeses.
— MAX McCALMAN

THANKS to Max and Angela for inviting me to work on this book and thereby opening my eyes to the big world of cheese; to all the people who generously shared their knowledge with us; to our editors, Roy and Chris, for making it happen; to my wife, Samantha, and my children, Marley and Willy, for putting up with me; and to my mother, Mary, for raising and supporting me.
— DAVID . GIBBONS

Credits

Unless otherwise indicated, tableware shown in the photographs is privately owned.

Page iv (copyright page), top, and **page 71:** both plates and sake server from Takashimaya.

Page iv (copyright page), bottom, and page 23: plate and knife from Takashimaya.

Page 16: bowl, fork, and tray fro Ostefin Designs.

Page 24: plate from Williams-Sonoma.

Page 56: tray and bowls from Takashimaya.

Page 78: both plates from Takashimaya.

Page 96: both plates from Takashimaya.

Page 103: tray, plate, and pedestal plate from Takashimaya.

Page 111: plate, fork, and spoon from Ostefin Designs.

Page 120: plates and glasses from Ostefin Designs.

Page 134: plate, fork, and tray from Ostefin Designs.

Page 137: three plates from Takashimaya.

Page 157: plate and tray from Ostefin Designs.

Index